CAMBRIDGE TEXTS AND STUDIES IN THE HISTORY OF EDUCATION

General Editors

A. C. F. BEALES, A. V. JUDGES, J. P. C. ROACH

THE RISE OF A CENTRAL AUTHORITY FOR ENGLISH EDUCATION

IN THIS SERIES

Texts

Fénelon on Education, edited by H. C. Barnard
Friedrich Froebel, a selection edited by Irene Lilley
Matthew Arnold and the Education of the New Order,
edited by Peter Smith and Geoffrey Summerfield
Robert Owen on Education, edited by Harold Silver
James Mill on Education, edited by W. H. Burston
Samuel Hartlib and the Advancement of Learning,
edited by Charles Webster
Thomas Arnold on Education, edited by T. W. Bamford
English for the English, by George Sampson, edited by
Denys Thompson
Public Examinations in England, 1850–1900, by John Roach

Studies

Education and the French Revolution, by H. C. Barnard

OTHER VOLUMES IN PREPARATION

THE RISE OF A CENTRAL AUTHORITY FOR ENGLISH EDUCATION

A. S. BISHOP

Deputy Principal
Philippa Fawcett College

CAMBRIDGE

AT THE UNIVERSITY PRESS

1971

CAMBRIDGE UNIVERSITY PRESS
Cambridge, New York, Melbourne, Madrid, Cape Town, Singapore, São Paulo, Delhi

Cambridge University Press
The Edinburgh Building, Cambridge CB2 8RU, UK

Published in the United States of America by Cambridge University Press, New York

www.cambridge.org
Information on this title: www.cambridge.org/9780521080231

First published 1971
This digitally printed version 2008

A catalogue record for this publication is available from the British Library

Library of Congress Catalogue Card Number: 70–128634

ISBN 978-0-521-08023-1 hardback
ISBN 978-0-521-08615-8 paperback

CONTENTS

He who administers, governs, because he infixes his own mark and stamps his own character on all public affairs as they pass through his hands.

Matthew Arnold

PREFACE

The late Professor Tawney in his book on Equality drew attention to the singular fact that English educational policy has been made, except at brief intervals, 'by men few, if any, of whom have themselves attended the schools principally affected by it, or would dream of allowing their children to attend them'. It was this reference to one of the more curious features of the English educational system, that led the present writer to explore the origins of the paradox, and to try to assess its effects on educational policy and practice over a specified period.

Such an inquiry necessarily began with an examination of the three principal components in the 'national system' during its formative years – the Education Department, the Science and Art Department, and the Charity Commission so far as its educational work was concerned – prior to their amalgamation into one government department under a single responsible minister. Subsequently, the initial, somewhat narrow, field of study was widened into an investigation of the genesis of the Board of Education.

This book, then, traces the nineteenth century formation, growth and structure of the central authority for education in England, the present Department of Education and Science. It describes the influences – religious, social, political, economic and other – that moulded that authority, or more correctly those authorities, and considers the way in which the form they took affected educational provision and progress throughout the Victorian era. In particular, it discusses the impact of the machinery of government upon the developing educational system.

It also considers, and attempts to answer, a number of questions arising from such a survey. To what extent, for example, was the provision and content of institutionalized education determined by essentially administrative considerations? How far was the professional educator, that is the teacher and inspector, permitted or encouraged to contribute to the formulation of educational policy? What factors caused the unhappy fragmentation of such educational services as were provided in England, and was the absence of unity of control or superintendence at the centre the product of chance or design? What difference did the phenomenon that Tawney observed make to the quality and structure of English education?

For much of the material upon which this book is based, I have drawn extensively upon numerous British official publications, including the Public General Acts, the official reports of debates in Parliament (commonly referred to as Hansard), and the Parliamentary Papers. This last category comprises a wide variety of documents, viz., accounts and estimates; official returns and communications; annual reports; reports of royal commissions, and of parliamentary, departmental and advisory committees, and frequently the evidence upon which the reports were based. In addition, considerable use has been made of unpublished material – confidential memoranda, correspondence, minutes, inquiries, reports, etc. – deposited for the most part in the Public Record Office, the British Museum and the Reference Library of the Department of Education and Science. Newspapers and periodicals, and the collection of pamphlets, articles and tracts to be found in the archives of that same Department, have also yielded much valuable information as well as providing an indication of contemporary opinion. Equally, I owe much to the specialized work of others in this field, a debt which is acknowledged in the footnotes and bibliography.

More particularly, I wish to place on record my gratitude to the late Dr S. Weitzman, formerly of the Institute of Education, University of London, whose teaching inspired in me an interest for educational history; to Professor N. R. Tempest and Dr D.G. Pritchard, both of the University of Liverpool, for their guidance and advice concerning the doctoral thesis out of which this study developed; to my colleague Mr Geoffrey Leyland, who gave generously of his time in reading the manuscript, and of his scholarship in suggesting improvements; to the Editor of this series, Professor A. V. Judges, for his wise and helpful criticism of the book in typescript; and to my wife, without whose patience and encouragement it could not have been written. Needless to say, for any imperfections that remain, I am solely responsible.

For their assistance during my research I should, in addition, like to thank Mr John Vaughan and the staff of the Library of the School of Education, University of Liverpool; Mr John Williams and Mrs M. Wallace, Librarian and Assistant Librarian respectively of St. Katharine's College of Education, Liverpool; Miss

P. M. Downie, formerly Librarian of the Department of Education and Science, and her colleagues; and the staffs of the Public Record Office, and of the British Museum State Paper Room and Newspaper Library.

Acknowledgement is also due to the following: Professor A. C. F. Beales, the Editor, and Messrs. Faber and Faber, the Publishers, of the *British Journal of Educational Studies*, for permission to use material from an article on Ralph Lingen which I contributed to that Journal; Constable and Co. Ltd, for permission to include extracts from *The Educational Department and After* by Sir George Kekewich; and the London School of Economics for permission to quote from *Our Partnership* by Beatrice Webb.

A. S. B.

1

THE YEARS OF INCIPIENT
STATE INTERVENTION

There are other enemies of liberty than the State and it is in fact by the
State that we have fought them.

– L. T. Hobhouse

In 1899, just as the Victorian Age was drawing to its close, a
relatively minor but potentially valuable piece of legislation
received the royal assent. This statute – the Board of Education
Act – marks for the social historian both the beginning of a new
era in the development of state intervention in English education
and the ending of an old. On the one hand it laid the foundation
upon which a national system could be built, on the other it can
be regarded as the coping-stone of a structure that had taken
almost a hundred years to erect. The nineteenth century, which
closed with a growing acceptance of education as being a legitimate
function of government requiring central co-ordination and unified
control, had opened with the firm belief that the state constituted
no fit instrument for the task of educating the people. So strongly
held and so powerfully supported was this belief that three generations were needed to change it, based as it was upon theories of
human nature which, in sum, encompassed virtually every aspect
of life. Although these concepts were interrelated, they may, for
convenience, be grouped under four main headings.

First there were the political doctrines. One of the more
unfortunate legacies of the eighteenth century was the conviction
that government interference tended to be incompetent and government expenditure tended to be corrupt. This feeling, to which
was added a general dislike of 'centralization', was shared by
men of very different political persuasions. To Tories and conservative Whigs the institutions of local government were sac-
rosanct: hence any encroachment on local autonomy was to be
fiercely resisted; to liberal Whigs and moderate reformers the
function of government was not to lead but to follow public
opinion; to Radicals a strong central government was thought likely

to be oppressive; and common to all these groups was a natural antipathy to the higher taxation that would be an inevitable consequence of increased activity by the central authority. All these arguments were reinforced by events on the Continent. Paradoxically, the fact that a number of European countries already possessed national systems of education operated rather as a deterrent than as an inducement to following their lead. The French and Prussian models, particularly, seemed to serve as a warning of the dangers in allowing the state to use education as an instrument of policy. Moreover, the fate of minority groups in those same countries confirmed the fears of any such in England who were similarly placed, and who in the past had been penalized by an autocratic government.

In circumstances such as these, *any* government would have found difficulty in extending the range of its activities. As it happened, the problem did not arise. Britain for the first three decades of the nineteenth century was under Tory rule, and if every Tory did not subscribe to the view that all change was to be deprecated, the majority felt that innovation and reform were unnecessary. This was, in Dicey's phrase, a period of 'legislative quiescence', attributable as much to the prevailing mood of complacency, if not optimism, as to a dread of revolution.

Related to these political attitudes were the tenets of the various religious denominations. The Established Church claimed the exclusive, not to say divine, right to educate the nation's young, and regarded state interference as an invasion of her legitimate preserves. The dissenters quite understandably resisted this claim; furthermore, having previously suffered from authoritarian intolerance, they had no wish to see government control of education. Thus both clerical pretensions and sectarian rivalry effectively blocked the path leading towards any national system financed and guided by the state.

These religious and political arguments were in turn supported by the prevalent economic theories concerning the function of government. The doctrine of *laissez-faire* largely determined the course of legislation throughout the first half of the nineteenth century. It was based upon the conviction that general happiness would be promoted more surely by self-help than by regulation. Private enterprise was the talisman that would lead inevitably to progress and prosperity. This belief, first applied to commerce, gradually invaded other spheres of human activity, including that of education. It produced a distrust of what was termed 'grand-motherly' legislation; and it generated the idea that any restrictions imposed by law or custom which interfered with the liberty of the subject were not only ineffectual in promoting industrial advance and social well-being but positively injurious. In fact, many influential economic thinkers contended that the state was actively malignant in addition to being incompetent.

Complementing this somewhat negative view was that of the statesmen who presided over the nation's financial affairs. Part of the reluctance of successive administrations to assume wider responsibilities lay in the firmly-held creed that government must be conducted as cheaply as possible. The less it did and spent, the better. Any extension of state action must necessarily involve increased public expenditure, and, in an age when 'Economize' was an abiding watchword, such a prospect could only be regarded as undesirable.

These views found ready endorsement from the rising middle-class entrepreneurs. They argued that state interference would stifle individual initiative and weaken character by reducing incentives to personal effort. Besides, education cost money and produced no immediate return on capital; its value in commercial terms was difficult to measure. Most manufacturers, who in other respects showed much astuteness, stubbornly believed that an educated labour force would result in greater industrial unrest, not more efficient operatives.

Echoing such sentiments were those who saw in both education and its promotion by the state twin threats to social stability and cohesion. Upon the eighteenth-century notion that the poor should never be trained for anything but honest toil was super-imposed the early nineteenth-century concept that popular education would prove a fertile source of social unrest. Out of an instinctive need for self-preservation, the ruling classes resisted the educating of the 'lower orders', seeing in it, if not the seeds of revolution, then at least the erosion of their own privileged position.

Even those who did not subscribe to such conservative views, and who felt that education was a beneficial rather than a pernicious influence, found themselves in a genuine dilemma; that of deciding what agency should be employed for its transmission. There was among them no general agreement as to whether the individual parent, or a religious body, or the state, should be held primarily responsible for a child's education.

Finally, there was during this period a strong faith in the many voluntary institutions that provided such social services as then existed. These organizations were held in high esteem, both in themselves for the principle they enshrined, and in their capacity as bulwarks against state compulsion and control. Moreover, while voluntary effort, unaided by the state, had achieved much in the field of education, it created, at the same time, vested interests which constituted a formidable obstacle to the development of a national system.

Powerful and numerous these forces opposing state intervention may have been; they were nevertheless being challenged by a whole battery of arguments which grew more compelling as the century advanced. Providing the evidence upon which this counter-movement rested was the impact of rapid industrial change; supplying the energy with which it was pursued were the efforts of a few determined reformers.

By the introduction of factory methods the Industrial Revolution had disrupted the old social order. Formerly, the nation's young had been exposed to the educative influences – albeit limited in their compass – of a peasant culture. Now, the creation of an urban proletariat, lacking roots and ill-equipped to deal with the problems of adapting to a totally different and less healthy environment, made the need for the civilizing effect of education – other than that provided at the mother's knee – a matter of vital and immediate concern.

Moreover, the very concentration of large numbers of workers in towns had led to their combining to press for an improvement in the conditions of their employment. In consequence it was surmised that the dangers of a little learning might well prove less alarming than the hazards of total ignorance. And among the wealthy there grew an uncomfortable feeling that it was unwise, if not unjust, to permit the steadily increasing majority of the population to remain uninformed and socially depressed.

Some manufacturers, too, began to acknowledge the need for their labour force to be equipped with at least a rudimentary education. Also, with the coming of machinery, apprenticeship, which had previously afforded some sort of technical training, became less and less important, and a new system of general and technical education had to be devised to supplant it.

In any event, the coincidence of a rapidly rising birth-rate and of the gradual growth of factory legislation meant that the streets in the overcrowded towns were swarming with children. Schools would, at the very least, keep them out of mischief and away from corrupting influences for most of the day. The fact that the first effective Factory Act and the first state grant for schools occurred in the same year was no mere accident.

Meanwhile, a small number of men of very different political leanings were endeavouring, both in print and in Parliament, to change the climate of opinion in favour of state intervention. As early as 1776, Adam Smith had warned that the state must take positive steps to reverse the process of degeneration observable among the poor. That warning took on a new and urgent significance as the side-effects of the Industrial Revolution became so alarming that they could no longer be ignored. Subsequently, and at about the time when that other revolution which had convulsed a continent was becoming less of an obsession and more of a challenge, a handful of missionaries took up Smith's lead. There were the progressive Whig leaders, Whitbread and Brougham; the Radical philosophers led by Bentham; and the articulate champions of the working classes, Robert Owen and Francis Place.[1] By their constant efforts these men, and a few others similarly inspired by humanitarian motives, paved the way for state intervention.

While the grant of 1833 is generally regarded as the first deliberate governmental action in the field of education, it should not be thought of as an isolated occurrence; it was, in fact, a logical outcome of a whole series of preceding events as well as the point of departure for succeeding ones.

If we ignore the Commonwealth period, when Treasury grants-in-aid of education were originally introduced, the earliest, albeit abortive, attempt to persuade Parliament to intervene in educational matters was made by Pitt in 1796. His Bill to provide a

---

[1] Bentham's remedy for curing social problems – inquiry, report, legislation, administration, inspection – was to be enthusiastically adopted by educational, as well as other reformers.

universal system of schools of industry within the framework of the Poor Law was not even put to the vote.

Partial progress came in 1802 when for the first time the state accepted a modicum of responsibility for the education of apprenticed children in the northern textile mills; but this intervention did not come about as a directly educational issue. It arose as a reaction against the exploitation of child labour in factories and mines, and it is in fact in the earlier factory legislation that the genesis of state action in education is to be found. The pioneering statute, Peel's Health and Morals of Apprentices Act, was designed to regulate children's employment in certain trades, and required that elementary instruction should be given during part of the day. As events turned out, the Act was easily evaded and imperfectly enforced. Yet it proved of value, for it demonstrated that the state was prepared to intercede on behalf of some children in certain circumstances. The precedent had been created and a principle established; the needs now were to build upon the precedent and to extend the principle.

But the time for such an assumption of further obligations had not been reached by 1807, when Whitbread introduced his Bill to provide parochial schools throughout the country. This measure passed the Commons but was rejected by the Upper House. Nevertheless here too something was achieved, for the representative (if unreformed) chamber had placed on record its support of the idea that the state should exercise some responsibility, admittedly indirect, for popular education. Cracks in the apparently solid edifice of parliamentary apathy or antagonism were beginning to show.

On Whitbread's death in 1815 the leadership of what was derisively labelled the 'education-mad' party passed to Henry Brougham. The following year he began his crusade in the cause of education by persuading the government to appoint a select committee whose brief was to 'inquire into the Education of the Lower Orders of the Metropolis and to report their observations thereon'. Seemingly, the money granted for meeting the expenses of this committee was the first to be voted on education since the Commonwealth.

Having completed their investigation, the committee 'found reason to conclude, that a very large number of poor Children are wholly without the means of Instruction, although their parents appear to be generally desirous of obtaining that advantage for them'.[1] In consequence of this finding the committee made a vague and tentative recommendation for government action. They felt 'persuaded that the greatest advantages would result to this Country from Parliament taking proper measures, in concurrence with the prevailing disposition of the Community, for supplying the deficiency of the means of Instruction which exists at present, and for extending this blessing to the Poor of all descriptions'.[2]

The 'prevailing disposition' in Parliament was to take note of the information gathered and then to ignore it. Yet the labour had not been wasted. In the first place Brougham had begun to arm himself with the statistics he needed to stir the government into action; in the second he secured the renewal of the committee's powers and the extension of the inquiry to the remainder of the country; finally, he had in the course of his investigations discovered numerous disquieting facts concerning educational endowments, discoveries which prompted him to demand a full-scale inquiry into their administration and disposal.[3]

The select committee, reappointed in successive years, issued its final Report in 1818. Although its recommendations brought no immediate response, they are important in that they foreshadowed the line of least resistance adopted by the government of the day fifteen years later. Thus, having 'clearly ascertained, that in many places private subscriptions could be raised to meet the yearly expenses of a School, while the original cost of the undertaking, occasioned chiefly by the erection and purchase of the schoolhouse, prevents it from being attempted', the committee conceived 'that a sum of money might well be employed in supplying this first want, leaving the charity of individuals to furnish the annual provision requisite for continuing the school'.[4]

They then offered alternative proposals as to the method by which this public expenditure might be disbursed. 'Whether the money should be vested in Commissioners, empowered to make the fit terms with the private parties desirous of establishing the schools, or whether a certain sum should be intrusted to the two great Institutions in London for promoting Education, your

---

[1] *Parliamentary Papers* [*PP*] 1816, IV, 3. [2] *Ibid.*
[3] See chapter 10. [4] *PP* 1818, IV, 59.

Committee must leave to be determined by the wisdom of Parliament.'[1] When the time came, Parliament, in its wisdom, chose the latter course; in this decision lay the roots of the dual system.

Brougham did, indeed, make one vain attempt to secure the implementation of the committee's suggestions. In 1820 he introduced a Bill for the promotion of education. The project was not even debated; but even if the Queen's trial had not distracted the legislature's, and in particular Brougham's attention, its fate was entirely predictable, for it incurred the disapproval of churchmen and dissenters alike.

For the next dozen years the education question was allowed to rest, partly because Brougham was now as much distrusted by his friends as disliked by his opponents, partly because hopes raised by the spread of the monitorial system remained high, and partly because the explosive nature of the subject had made members cautious of tackling it. An indication of this wariness is shown in the Home Secretary's reply to the call made by the British and Foreign School Society in 1823 for public funds to assist its educational work. Peel declared the impossibility of his advising a parliamentary grant since it might establish a precedent 'extremely inconvenient to Government'.

On the other hand, the problem had been given a public airing, and there gradually emerged an active movement favouring a national system of education. Certainly such a system was needed. By 1830 it was clear to many unprejudiced observers that voluntary effort alone was not, and could never expect to be, sufficient. If, for example, the ability to write one's name provides a crude index of literacy, then some of the marriage registers of the period suggest that the National and British schools were achieving only a very limited success. Government intervention was rapidly becoming a pre-requisite of educational progress, especially as the societies' subscription appeals appeared to be subject to the law of diminishing returns.[2]

It was the passing of the Reform Bill in 1832 that created a situation in which positive action by the state became possible and, in one sense, necessary. The Whigs were dependent for their parliamentary majority upon Radical support, so that expediency,

---

[1] *Ibid.*

[2] See, for example, G. C. T. Bartley, *Schools for the People*, 1871, pp. 53–4; and the *Final Report of the Cross Commission*, 1888, pp. 3–4.

as well as principle, induced them to embark upon a programme of reform over a wide field. In no quarter was the need more pressing than in education, and in none were the Radicals more determined to secure action. The era of state opposition and indifference was drawing to a close; the era of state intervention and support about to begin.

2

THE PERIOD OF
TREASURY GRANTS-IN-AID

This growth of a large administrative department with rules and principles of its own creation, without any assistance from the legislature, is the most remarkable instance of the experimental and empirical fashion in which some of the great English institutions have developed.[1]

In 1833 the Grey Administration was at last prodded into activity. The main credit for this achievement goes in roughly equal shares to two men, Henry (now Lord) Brougham, and a young Radical M.P., John Roebuck. The latter, despairing of any government initiative, took matters into his own hands. On 30 July he introduced into the Commons a resolution calling for the establishment of a national system of education to be controlled by a minister of cabinet rank.

Although so ambitious a scheme could command little support, Roebuck's gesture was by no means a futile one. He succeeded in drawing an expression of interest from the government, with the implication that some action might be forthcoming. Yet Parliament's rejection of the proposal, together with its replacement by the measure soon afterwards adopted, was to have most unfortunate consequences, for it meant that each branch of education was allowed to evolve independently, thus contributing to the administrative confusion that bedevilled English education throughout the second half of the nineteenth century.

That Roebuck's initiative was not entirely fruitless was due to Brougham, who had long believed that voluntary effort could make the necessary educational provision if only it were assisted in meeting the initial costs involved. He therefore pressed the Cabinet to sanction a grant of public money for this purpose.

At two o'clock in the morning of 16 August, in a sparsely attended House, Lord Althorp, the Chancellor of the Exchequer, moved 'that a sum of money not exceeding £20,000 be granted by

---

[1] J. Redlich and F. Hurst, *The History of Local Government in England*, 1958, pp. 190–1.

His Majesty in aid of private subscriptions for the erection of school houses for the education of the poorer classes in Great Britain'. He justified the vote, which was duly passed,[1] on the grounds that it was in accordance with the recommendation of the select committee of 1818.

The proposal had, from the government's point of view, several merits. It committed them to no policy and entailed no increase in their responsibilities; it avoided the pitfalls of religious controversy; and, because it was embodied in a financial measure, it escaped the Lords' veto. It also left the government free to distribute the money in any way they thought fit, since Parliament had laid down no rules concerning its application. Because the subsidy was designed to furnish immediate, rather than long-term relief, no separate department was created to administer it. Responsibility for its distribution resided in the Treasury which had proposed the vote.

And so, 'this money, for want of any thought-out scheme based on any intelligible principle, was spent on a sort of subscription to two societies which ... did what they could in the way of affording to the English poor elementary education, combined with religious conviction'.[2] Dicey's criticism is, in the light of subsequent events, understandable, yet it hardly takes account of the contemporary situation. For, in the absence of any suitable local authorities, there was no practical alternative to the parochial system, and in that respect the granting of public funds to the organizations already engaged in the work of providing schools was unavoidable.

Nevertheless, Dicey's further condemnation of the subscriptions as 'niggardly and haphazard' is fully justified. It was niggardly in that the current education vote in Prussia amounted to £600,000, and that during the same session £20 million were voted for compensation to the West Indian planters on the emancipation of their slaves. It was haphazard in that the policy adopted by the government had already been tried and found wanting in Ireland, and was in fact abandoned the year before. For many years voluntary societies there had been in receipt of parliamentary grants in aid of education. It is perhaps no more than a remarkable coincidence that in 1831 a member of Grey's cabinet, Edward

[1] Appropriation Act, 1933. 3 & 4 Will. IV, c. 96.
[2] A. V. Dicey, *Law and Opinion in England*, 1914, p. 46.

Stanley, should have written to the Duke of Leinster condemning the system. The letter stated that the government were of the opinion that 'no private society, deriving a part, however small, of their annual income from private sources, and only made the channel of the munificence of the Legislature without being subject to any direct responsibility could adequately and satisfactorily accomplish the end proposed' (i.e. a national system of education). The precedent, then, was hardly encouraging.

As events showed, the scheme as it applied to England proved equally ill-conceived, for it recognized religious distinctions in the distribution of public money, and it gave the impression that education was considered to be a charity rather than a social service to which everyone was entitled.

A Treasury Minute of 30 August 1833, supplemented by further Minutes in 1834 and 1835, laid down the regulations under which the grants were to be made. The main conditions were that the money was to be spent on school-houses only, that at least half the cost of the building was to be raised by private subscription, that building accounts should be liable to audit, and that preference should be shown to large towns and cities. The fact that no rules were laid down as to the suitability of the premises or of the curriculum, or as to inspection for ensuring that the schools were properly maintained, strongly suggests that the grant was intended to be a merely temporary expedient. More positively, one can argue that it would surely have been a mistake, and might have been disastrous, had the applications for, and the spending of, grants been subjected to rigorous scrutiny, since the whole purpose of the exercise was to facilitate school construction, and this called for the minimum of restraint.

But because the regulations that were framed afforded barely adequate security against the misapplication of public funds, and as the officials concerned possessed no real knowledge or qualifications for their work, it was hardly surprising that doubts should soon be expressed as to the efficacy of the arrangement, or that Roebuck should be the member who led the demand for an investigation into it. In June 1834 he moved for a committee to inquire into 'the means of establishing a system of National Education'. The government, while not prepared to go to this extreme, agreed to the appointment of a select committee 'to inquire into the present state of the education of the people in

England and Wales and into the application and effects of the grant made in the last Session of Parliament for the erection of school houses, and to consider of the expediency of further grants in aid of education'.

This committee sat for just two months before issuing a Report which had no right to the name since it consisted merely of the evidence that had been collected. Of considerable significance, however, in view of subsequent developments, was the interest shown in the matter of inspection. One distinguished witness, Professor Pillans, declared that he could not conceive 'how any extensive system of schools, whether organised by Government or by societies, can ever be brought to its full efficiency without a regular inspection'.[1] A year later a second committee was appointed, and with equally slender results. Like its predecessor it felt unable or unwilling to make any recommendations as to the administration or extension of the grant system.

Ministers might mark time, but to Brougham the whole problem of educational provision and control required urgent attention. Free now from the burdens and restrictions of office and acquainted with the revelations of the Charitable Trusts Commissioners,[2] he submitted to the Lords in May 1835 a long series of resolutions on education. The eighth of these merits quotation, for to a large degree it anticipated by some sixty years the measure Parliament ultimately adopted for the establishment of a single and unified central authority.

That in order to superintend the due and just application of the funds, from time to time, voted by Parliament for the promotion of Education, ... to encourage the trustees of Charities connected with Education, in using beneficially the powers now possessed by them, to watch over the abuses of trust committed by such trustees, and to control the exercise of such new powers as Parliament may grant them, it is expedient that a Board of Commissioners be appointed, with powers and duties to be regulated by Act of Parliament.

On the advice of Lord Melbourne, Brougham withdrew his resolutions, but he returned to the attack later in the year by introducing a Bill based upon them. This, too, found little support and was not proceeded with. Another opportunity to advance the cause of education had been missed.

[1] *Report from the Select Committee on the State of Education*, 1834, q. 518.
[2] See below, p. 207ff.

The session of 1836 passed without further progress being made,[1] although outside Westminster the question of appointing some central body exercising control over education was being widely canvassed. Evidence was rapidly accumulating that the existing arrangement was defective, and many saw little reason why the Irish System, with its Board of Commissioners possessing wide powers of supervision, should not be introduced into this country. During the following two years the government was urged from different directions to make some move towards creating a central authority. Addressing the Lords in June 1837, Brougham argued that 'the supervision of a general system of education ought to be placed under one of his Majesty's Ministers'; and later that year, when re-introducing his Bill in a modified form, he averred that 'it seemed to be on all hands admitted that whether they were to go further in the way of making grants of money or not, at any rate a public department' (he would have called it the Education Board) 'was essentially necessary', if only to ensure the judicious application of public funds.

But before Brougham could secure discussion of his Bill, the matter was raised in the Commons. Several bodies advocating the establishment of a national system of education, complete with a central office, had arisen in various parts of the country. The most important of these, the Central Society of Education, had as its chairman Thomas Wyse, a politician who had earlier been instrumental in the creation of the recently formed Irish Board of Education. When Roebuck lost his seat in 1837, it was Wyse who took his place as the leader of the education movement in the Lower House, to such good effect that he became affectionately dubbed 'the Member for Education'.

In June 1838 Wyse moved an Address for the appointment of

a board of Commissioners of Education in England, with the view, especially, of providing for the wise, equitable, and efficient application of sums granted, or to be granted, for the advancement of education by Parliament, and for the immediate establishment of schools for the education of teachers in accord with the intention already expressed by the Legislature.[2]

[1] The establishment of a Normal School of Design – the embryonic Science and Art Department – is discussed in chapter 7.

[2] *Hansard*, 3rd ser., XLIII, cols. 710–11. The government had, in 1835, set aside a further £10,000 for teacher training.

After painting a sombre picture of widespread educational destitu-
tion in the country, he criticized the existing mode of administering
the grant. It was obvious to everyone, he asserted:

that with so many and pressing public duties to perform, it was impossible that the Treasury ... could discharge the necessary duties of
superintendence, direction, control, and correction, relative to the
schools, to which the grant was applied, in a satisfactory and complete
manner; they could not have time to inquire fully into a number of
points on which it was essential a directing body should be informed – as
for instance, the numbers of the scholars, the subjects of education, the
wants of different districts in respect of education, and a variety of other
particulars.[1]

Replying to the debate, the Home Secretary, Lord John Russell,
declined to take any immediate action, on the grounds that the
administration could not attempt to establish a commission or
board until 'there was more likelihood of agreement among the
leading persons who were in favour of general education in this
country ...'. Without government backing and opposed by the
Church, the motion was lost, but by only four votes. The closeness
of this division indicated the growing support for more positive
state intervention, and demonstrated to ministers that parliamentary action, if not legislation, might soon be feasible.

But caution, not to say artifice, would have to be employed.
This was made apparent in the following month when a third
select committee on education produced its Report. Appointed
the previous November, its members had been required 'to
consider the best means of providing useful education for the
children of the poorer classes in large towns throughout England
and Wales'.

In contrast to its predecessors of 1834 and 1835, this committee
arrived at definite conclusions and made recommendations. Its
findings were couched in unequivocal terms. The unanimous
view was

first, that the kind of education given to the children of the working
classes is lamentably deficient; second, that it extends (bad as it is) to
but a small proportion of those who ought to receive it; third, that
without some strenuous and persevering efforts be made on the part
of Government, the greatest evils to all classes may follow from this
neglect.[2]

---

[1] *Ibid.* col. 715.   [2] *PP* 1837-8, VII, 163.

However, the remedial treatment suggested fell far short of that demanded by the diagnosis. The committee felt that 'under existing circumstances, and under the difficulties which beset the question', it was 'not prepared to propose any means for meeting the deficiency beyond the continuance and extension of the grants which are at present made by the Treasury for the promotion of Education, through the medium of the National and the British and Foreign School Societies'.[1] In other words vested interests and doubts as to the benefits of further state action were strong enough to persuade a majority of the committee that a radical departure from the course already embarked upon was neither desirable nor practicable.

The government was caught on the horns of a dilemma. On the one hand the mounting evidence supplied by parliamentary inquiry, by statistical societies, by the reports of factory and poor law inspectors, coupled with the rising demand from numerous pressure groups, made palpable the necessity for such increased intervention; on the other, the Established Church energetically opposed any additional encroachment by the state: revived, and reinvigorated by the Oxford Movement, it abandoned its defensive attitude and moved into the attack.[2] Ministers might well have complained that it was a case of those behind crying 'Forward!' and those before crying 'Back!' Wavering uncertainly between were the Nonconformists. Forced through lack of money to accept state aid, they were at the same time alarmed at the disproportionate advantage accruing to the Church of England. By 1838 their suspicion of government interference had been sufficiently overcome and their fears of Anglican domination sufficiently aroused for the Committee of the British and Foreign School Society to address a Memorial to Russell recommending that a Board of Education should be established which should

[1] *Ibid.* 167. A resolution 'that it is desirable a Board or Office of Education should be established under the control of Parliament' was negatived by five votes to four.

[2] Paradoxically, this more belligerent policy may have supplied one of the reasons which prompted government action. In 1843 Kay-Shuttleworth wrote to Russell: 'When your Lordship and Lord Lansdowne in 1839 appointed me Secretary of the Committee of Council on Education, I understood the design of your Government to be to prevent the successful assertion on the part of the Church of the claim then put forth for a purely ecclesiastical system of education.' Quoted in H. J. Burgess, *Enterprise in education*, 1958, p. 70.

enjoy 'the confidence of the various religious denominations'.[1]

At all events the situation could not remain as it was. Wyse in 1837 had bluntly condemned the failure of this first attempt to create a satisfactory relationship between private enterprise and the public interest. 'The voluntary system of public instruction, with no central power to guide, aid or control, has not only not worked well, but worked nearly as ill as any system well could.'[2] Within a year the government was being driven to a similar conclusion, though ministers would doubtless have couched the criticism in Kay-Shuttleworth's more diplomatic language:

After the experience of six years had been obtained of the administration of these grants, it was felt that their application might be open to public question, because they were administered through two irresponsible bodies, who merely presented certificates to the Treasury. It seemed expedient that some considerable change should take place in those arrangements.[3]

In fairness it must be added that the Treasury was not unaware of the shortcomings of the system; in particular, officials were worried because they could not ensure that the subventions were both legitimately required and wisely spent. The obvious solution was to create an inspectorate. But to this there were difficulties, some financial, some due to the fact that the ground was already partially occupied, the two societies themselves having instituted local inspection on a small scale. In an effort to resolve the quandary the Chancellor of the Exchequer proposed in 1838 that the societies 'should be invited to direct an inspection to be made of the several Schools . . . for the erection of which Grants have been appropriated out of the Parliamentary Votes', so that he might procure and lay before Parliament 'more specific and detailed information than has been as yet obtained' concerning them. The results of such inspection were to be communicated to the Treasury from time to time.[4]

[1] Quoted in J. Murphy, *The Religious Problem in English Education*, 1959, p. 150.
[2] Quoted in F. Smith, *A History of English Elementary Education*, 1931, p. 161.
[3] *Report of the Newcastle Commission*, 1861, vol. 6, q. 2308.
[4] *PP* 1837-8, XXXVIII, 365 (Treasury Minute). Apparently, the Treasury at first intended to appoint its own inspectors, but this idea was soon abandoned.

This *ad hoc* proposal, however, could be regarded as a temporary expedient only. The Treasury dispensation of grants-in-aid had outlived its usefulness. What was urgently needed was a system educationally more appropriate, administratively more convenient.

During the autumn of 1838 Lord John Russell pondered over the problem of how to steer between the Scylla of a militant Church and the Charybdis of an obstructive Lords. By November he had devised a possible solution. One of the weirdest pieces of government machinery that England has ever known was about to begin its sixty years of eccentric and improbable existence.

3

THE EDUCATION DEPARTMENT:
THE FORMATIVE DECADE, 1839–49

From the very beginning ... the policy of the British government in education has been one of indirect rule ... [It] may be said to have administered popular education with the benevolence due to a reasonably well-behaved colony, which, though not worthy of more than a modest financial investment, can be relied upon to cause no embarrassment, and, with a little encouragement, will progress steadily towards self-government.[1]

Russell's original hope was that it might prove feasible to set up a central authority along the lines of that working successfully in Ireland. There, in 1831, an independent and responsible Board of Commissioners representing the various denominations was appointed possessing considerable powers, and exercising absolute control over the funds voted by Parliament for Irish education. Lord John therefore took soundings among leading Anglicans, only to come to the conclusion that a united inter-denominational approach was out of the question. In consequence, the idea of recommending the adoption of the Irish System had to be abandoned.

The only viable alternative was the creation of a department of state with a political head responsible to the legislature. Towards the end of 1838 the scheme was discussed by the Cabinet. Prime Minister Melbourne voiced his disapproval, at which Viscount Howick remarked, 'Thank God there are some things which even you cannot stop and that is one of them'.[2] And so it proved, for in February the following year Russell set the parliamentary wheels in motion by addressing a letter to the Lord President, the Marquess of Lansdowne. It expressed the Queen's 'very deep concern at the want of instruction which is still observable among the poorer classes of Her subjects'. (The concern was probably genuine, but, in any case, the death of William and the accession of

[1] G. S. Osborne, *Scottish and English Schools*, 1966, p. 34.
[2] Quoted in D. Cecil, *Lord M.*, 1954, p. 279.

the young Victoria made educational reform a little less difficult for the tottering ministry.) The letter went on to list some of the main faults in the prevailing system, and concluded:

Some of the defects appear to admit of an immediate remedy, and I am directed by Her Majesty to desire, in the first place, that your Lordship, with four others of the Queen's servants, should form a Board or Committee, *for the consideration of all matters affecting the Education of the People*.[1] For the present it is thought advisable that this Board should consist of The Lord President of the Council, The Lord Privy Seal, The Chancellor of the Exchequer, The Secretary of State for the Home Department and the Master of the Mint.[2] It is proposed that the Board should be entrusted with the application of any sums which may be voted by Parliament for the purpose of Education in England and Wales. Among the first objects to which any grant may be applied will be the establishment of a Normal School.

Such was the initial plan; but when Russell came to make his statement outlining the government's intentions, the italicized phrase had been removed from the duties to be discharged by the Committee. Explaining the alteration later, Lansdowne commented: 'When the propriety of appointing the Committee of her Majesty's Ministers came to be considered, it struck me that the words were of too vague a character, liable to be misunderstood, and involving the committee in a scope of action too wide for such a body.'[3] And many years afterwards Russell revealed that Lansdowne had refused to head the Committee unless its functions were limited to the superintendence of the application of parliamentary grants for the education of the poor. The powers of the new body were thus confined to a narrow field, and, although they proved capable of liberal interpretation, they remained so restricted until 1870 when certain additional responsibilities were specifically assigned to it. By reducing the Committee's functions to those exercised by the Treasury during the previous six years, Lansdowne doubtless hoped to make the plan more palatable to those most likely to oppose it.

The Home Secretary's proposals encountered an immediate reception which was, if hardly enthusiastic, certainly not hostile.

---

[1] Author's italics.
[2] By 10 April 1839, when the Order in Council appointing the Committee was promulgated, the Master of the Mint, a sinecure office, had been omitted.
[3] *Hansard*, 3rd ser., XLVIII, col. 1266.

And, indeed, there appeared to be very little about them that warranted either enthusiasm or hostility. The constitutional propriety of the intended board was not challenged, presumably because it was based on reasonably well-established precedent. For over two centuries the Privy Council had been the begetter of executive departments, the most recently formed being the Committee of Council for Trade which was created by an Order in Council in 1786. The analogy was sufficiently close for the new committee to be accepted initially without demur. Moreover, the government had been careful not to repeat the recent (1834) administrative experiment of the Poor Law Commission, an agency that had generated much antagonism largely because its members, all of whom received payment, were debarred from sitting in the Commons. But the calm was deceptive; it proved to be the harbinger, not of a smooth passage, but of a storm.

The government, aware that the measure had no hope of passing the Lords which it was in no condition to fight, adopted the stratagem of an Order in Council. Use of the royal prerogative rendered the formal approval of the legislature unnecessary; in this way a central authority for education was created virtually without parliamentary sanction.

The Committee of Council lost no time in formulating and declaring its policy. In the first instance it proposed to found a Normal School for the training of teachers 'under the direction of the State and not placed under the management of a voluntary Society'; next it recommended that 'no further Grant be made, now or hereafter, for the establishment or support of . . . Schools, unless the right of inspection be retained, in order to secure a conformity to the regulations and discipline established in the several schools, with such improvements as may from time to time be suggested by the Committee';[1] thirdly it intimated that the grants would not necessarily always be confined to the two societies which had hitherto been the sole recipients.

An outburst of criticism greeted these Minutes. The Anglicans, particularly, were incensed by the plan to establish a non-denominational training college which they felt would lead to a weakening of Church control over the elementary schools. From attacking the projects to attacking the body that devised them was but a

[1] For the formation and growth of the early inspectorate see below, pp. 33–6.

short step. Suddenly the government, discredited by the Bed-chamber Incident and on the point of collapse, saw the very existence of the Committee of Council threatened. It capitulated by cancelling the offending proposal, but, as Russell wrote later: 'The throwing out of one of our children to the wolf did little to appease his fury.'

All the Church's latent hostility to state intervention rose to the surface when the Commons came to consider the renewal of the annual grant. Leading for the opposition, Lord Stanley launched a formidable assault on the government's educational policy, especially its decision to create a central board, (though by a strange coincidence this same politician had himself set up eight years previously a Board of Commissioners of National Education in Ireland): 'So long as the Committee was irresponsible, so long as its object was undefined and uncertain, so long as its powers were unlimited, and while the exercise of those powers was not checked, not fettered, not restrained, not limited by Parliament, so long would it remain a fertile source of new plans.' Seldom has a prophecy been more amply fulfilled. The chorus of protest swelled as other members rose to attack what Lord Ashley described as 'this hideous chimera of an Educational Committee of the Privy Council'. Some denounced it for its purely political character which, the argument went, would render it incapable of pursuing a consistent policy; some protested that its entirely lay member-ship meant the exclusion of any official religious element; some objected to state interference in whatever guise it might appear.

The debate, which extended over three days, ended with what amounted to a vote of censure on the government, the House dividing on the question of whether the Crown should be asked to rescind the Order in Council appointing the Committee. By merely five votes the motion was rejected. The annual grant, now increased to £30,000, was approved by the even narrower margin of two.

A fortnight later the battle was renewed in the Upper House, where their Lordships passed a series of resolutions condemning the government's actions as unconstitutional. In vain Lord Lansdowne tendered a plea of 'Plus ça change ...', by asking what difference there was between the apportionment of three or four of her Majesty's responsible servants, including the Chan-cellor of the Exchequer, to superintend the distribution of money, and the leaving of that distribution to the Chancellor alone. But the Lords were unimpressed by this and other arguments. In being by-passed their dignity had been affronted, and they showed their displeasure by carrying an Address to the Queen praying that no steps be taken towards the establishment of an educational plan without the peers being given the opportunity of considering it. But the Queen, and the government, stood firm; the Committee of Council survived.

The significance of that survival was not immediately apparent to some educational reformers who regarded it more as a feeble compromise than as a major advance. Henry Brougham, who knew better than most the magnitude of the task and the need for suitable machinery to deal with it, could be pardoned for minimizing the achievement. 'I am ashamed...' he declared, 'that after all that has been confessed... of the utter inadequacy of our present means of education, that all we have been able to screw our courage to, has been the asking Parliament for a paltry £30,000, and appointing a committee of noblemen to distribute it.' And by way of demonstrating the degree to which Parliament had misplaced its priorities he pointed out that in that same year £70,000 was voted for building royal stables.

Yet, small as the advance was in financial and administrative terms, the government had succeeded in laying down a principle of cardinal importance. For the creation of a state department, which proclaimed its right of inspection as a prerequisite of future aid, meant the assertion of civil, as opposed to ecclesiastical, jurisdiction over education. This was an immediate gain. Ultimately, as Lord Stanley foresaw, the Department extended the range of its operations far beyond the mere allocation and control of grants until it was actively engaged in promoting and improving the education it financed.

Needless to say, the Committee of Council was never designed to perform these latter functions. It was not even expected to become a lasting feature of the educational landscape. Indeed, Lansdowne regarded its supposedly ephemeral character as a virtue. 'If there be anything more than another to recommend the present arrangement,' he informed the Lords, 'it is this, that it is of a temporary nature...' And he warned Dr Kay that his position as secretary might prove 'precarious'. Long afterwards the Newcastle Commissioners, in their review of past developments, described the Committee of Council as 'neither plot nor policy. The arrangement was never intended to be ultimate or permanent. It was a compromise between the necessity of education, and the difficulty of devising a general system acceptable to the country'. While Robert Lowe likened it to 'a man who went to call on a friend, and who stayed with him thirty years'.

From such a vague contrivance, political and administrative difficulties inevitably arose, and in the course of time the Committee of Council became first an irrelevance, then an anachronism and finally a laughing-stock. The main cause of this decline in esteem lay in the fact that from the beginning it was provided with neither agreed principles of action nor settled rules of procedure. Its composition fluctuated from one administration to another, often for no discernible reason. It met with increasing irregularity. The result was a lack of continuity and a loss of control.[1]

At first, however, the casual, or at any rate informal, operations of the Committee worked to the benefit of educational advance. Neither of the Lord Presidents in the formative years was an able administrator, and in addition Lansdowne was too indolent and Wharncliffe too indifferent to become concerned with the complexities of the educational problem. In consequence the management of the new department came to reside in the capable hands of Kay-Shuttleworth, its first Secretary, and, in the words of his biographer, 'there was probably no man in England better equipped in all ways to guide the Committee of Council in its first steps'.[2]

That Kay-Shuttleworth was able to achieve as much as he did was nevertheless remarkable considering the curiously ambivalent and tentative nature of his appointment, and the anomalous position he held throughout his period of office. Lansdowne, when approaching him in 1839, did so with some diffidence in view of the lack of security of tenure involved, and asked if there were any way in which the risk could be diminished. Dr Kay, as he then was, replied that he thought he should retain the superintendence of the pauper school at Norwood so that if the attempt to found an Education Department proved abortive he could then return to his former position in the Poor Law Commission. In effect, then, the secretaryship was to be conducted on a part-time basis, and this

---

[1] See note pp. 277–8.
[2] F. Smith, *The Life and Work of Sir James Kay-Shuttleworth*, 1923, p. 81.

arrangement was formalized subsequently when the Treasury agreed that responsibility for the payment of Kay's salary should be equally divided between the Commission and the Committee as these two bodies were sharing his services.

Such were the inauspicious circumstances in which the first permanent head of the Education Department embarked upon his new career. In fact, even after the initial difficulties had been overcome, Kay-Shuttleworth, as he became in 1842, continued to labour under unnecessary handicaps; for his title was that of *Assistant* Secretary only, since the nominal Secretary was the Clerk of the Council who was *ex officio* Secretary of all the Privy Council Committees. This meant that Kay-Shuttleworth's status was far inferior to the importance of his work and that he could not even appoint his own staff.

Gradually the Department, which was housed in the Council Offices in Whitehall, took shape. A small number of Privy Council clerks were seconded to it, one of them, Harry Chester, becoming Dr Kay's deputy. In August 1840 the first of the specialist personnel, in the form of a legal adviser, was recruited, and it was soon found necessary, in view of the primary duties of the Department in connexion with the building of schools, to add an architectural clerk to the establishment. However, there was at this early stage no attempt to develop the Office in any ambitious or systematic way, whatever schemes may have been forming in the Secretary's fertile mind, for, quite apart from Treasury parsimony, the future was completely uncertain. The crucial question was, in fact, whether there would be a reversal of policy when the government changed hands. Kay-Shuttleworth was certainly alive to the possibility when, in 1841, the Tories returned to power, for he advised their leaders on taking office that the membership of the Committee of Council should remain exclusively lay. In the event, the transition went smoothly, for the Church could now assume that its interests would receive more sympathetic consideration.

Reassured and emboldened by the new ministry's welcome, and perhaps unexpected, acceptance of the *status quo*, Kay-Shuttleworth proposed, a little optimistically, that the many schools for which other departments of state were responsible[1] should be brought under the surveillance of a single central authority, that

---

[1] E.g. regimental and dockyard, workhouse and industrial, hospital, asylum and prison schools.

is, the Committee of Council. This suggestion, which if adopted might well have brought some cohesion to the administration of educational provision, (a cohesion which in some measure it still lacks), was turned down.

But, while the leading official of the Committee of Council was disturbed over the fragmentation of educational services, other interested individuals were expressing equal concern about a more basic issue: the very suitability of that Committee itself as a satisfactory central authority for elementary education. When, in April 1841, William Ewart, the member for Liverpool who devoted much of his life to educational causes, moved that 'some responsible Minister of the Crown shall yearly make to the House of Commons a statement of the condition and prospects of the Education of the people', he was voicing a dissatisfaction that numerous MPs were to echo for many years to come. His motion expressed a two-fold objection to the plan adopted in 1839. In the first place, it implied that the collective responsibility of the Committee of Council was all too likely to mean divided responsibility or no responsibility whatever; hence the request for its concentration in the hands of a single minister. In the second place, it plainly indicated that that minister ought to be accountable to the Commons, not the Lords. There was no constitutional reason why the Lord President of the Council – the putative Minister of Education – should not be a member of the Commons, but the chances of this happening seemed, on the basis of past experience, exceedingly slim. As it turned out, there was during the lifetime of the Committee of Council only one real instance of such an occurrence. Another member, W. S. O'Brien, argued that the Committee 'was not nearly so competent a body for the administration of the parliamentary grant as a Minister of Instruction, aided by a board of education, would be'. This observation is noteworthy in that it seems to be the earliest reference to the kind of advisory body that ultimately materialized in 1899 as the Consultative Committee.

Though nothing came of these proposals, the year 1843 did witness two events that were to have far-reaching consequences for the course of educational development. The early 1840s, it should be recalled, marked a period of rising discontent culminating in the Chartist agitation, and the ruling classes conjectured that an ignorant populace made a dangerous populace. It was in this atmosphere of alarm that the government, prompted by Lord Ashley, brought in a Factory Bill which, among other things, provided for what would nowadays be called 'half-time schooling' for children in certain industries. These educational clauses, because they appeared to entrench the power of the Church, aroused the bitterest opposition among Dissenters, and had to be withdrawn. The repercussions of this turbulent episode were doubly unfortunate. Not only did it rekindle Non-conformist suspicions of state intervention and engender feelings of hostility towards the government department concerned with education, but it also convinced successive administrations that, until there was a reasonable measure of agreement on fundamental issues, large-scale educational reforms did not enter the realm of practical politics.

But, if a frontal assault on the bastions of religious intransigence was out of the question, they might yet be made less harmful by a process of infiltration through the back-door. The mauling Graham's Bill had received served as a traumatic experience for Kay-Shuttleworth. At this point he became a realist. Abandoning his hopes for a national system, he applied his energies to improving and expanding educational provision within the existing framework. What could not be accomplished through legislation might still be achieved by administrative regulation, rendered acceptable by virtue of the financial inducement associated with it. This view was shared by the Prime Minister. Believing that government action at that time was inopportune, Peel felt that the cause of education would best be served 'by the cautious and gradual extension of the power and pecuniary means of the Committee of the Privy Council'.

In pursuance of this policy, the Committee in November 1843 extended its grants to the building of teachers' houses and training colleges and to the provision of school furniture and apparatus. This was to prove the fairly thick end of a very substantial wedge, for there were few limitations, outside purely fiscal ones, to what a government could do in the way of financing and hence promoting (and, incidentally, controlling) educational services of all kinds.

For the next few years, then, the work of the Committee mainly consisted, to use Kay-Shuttleworth's own words, in 'encouraging all voluntary effort, in making itself a central influence in order to guide and develop that effort, and in completing its own method of administration as its experience increased'.

But already there were signs that the administrative machinery was creaking under the strain that these fresh commitments imposed upon it. Early in 1845, 'Their Lordships', (by which was meant either the Lord President or more frequently the Secretary), were expressing concern at 'the very great augmentation of business which had been occasioned in the Education Department of this office since its establishment in 1839 by the increased and increasing number of applications for aid from the Parliamentary Grant for Education'; as a result, 'the efficient performance of the duties of the Department has been rendered extremely arduous [and] the health of some of the gentlemen seriously affected'. The ill-health, which a few years later forced Kay-Shuttleworth into premature semi-retirement, was even then casting its shadow, for doubtless the Secretary himself was one of the officials referred to.

That Kay-Shuttleworth was well aware of the need to adapt the administrative apparatus to changing conditions is shown in a letter he wrote to Russell in December 1845, when the latter, on Peel's resignation, was endeavouring to form a government. 'I am now able to restore into your hand the Education Department not only I trust uninjured, but, though not advanced by legislation, developed from being a mere limb of the Privy Council Office into a public department requiring reorganisation.'

However, when the Whigs actually did return to power the following year, the recommendation was ignored; on the contrary, the load was increased without any compensatory structural alterations being made. In December the Committee, apprised through its inspectors' reports of the inefficiency of the schools, took steps to improve the qualifications of teachers. The scheme constitutes a landmark in English educational history. Till then the state had confined its grants to buildings and equipment; now it was offering public money for the training, remuneration and pensioning of teachers. Such a development had revolutionary implications, yet parliamentary sanction was not sought, and indeed was not required; an administrative minute sufficed. The decision would not be discussed until the Commons were asked to approve the additional expenditure involved.

Hardly surprisingly, the ensuing debate on the estimates pro-

duced a lively attack on the Committee of Council, for the significance of the Pupil-teacher Minutes was not lost on those members
to whom state control of education was anathema. One opposition
speaker called for the appointment of a select committee to inquire
into the 'justice and expediency' of the scheme and to investigate
'whether the regulations attached thereto do not unduly increase
the influence of the Crown, invade the constitutional functions of
Parliament, and interfere with the religious convictions of Her
Majesty's subjects'. From the government benches a spirited
defence of the Committee was presented by Thomas (later Lord)
Macaulay, one of its members, who contended that its actions
were under adequate parliamentary control since the government
had, in conformity with strict constitutional procedure, to come to
the House of Commons for all moneys it proposed to spend. After
a debate extending over three days the credits were voted by a
large majority.

The government's triumph proved to be the Department's
tragedy, for the task involved in implementing the controversial
Minutes threatened to overwhelm an already fully extended staff.
Grant procedures were growing ever more complex. For example,
no fewer than twenty-three forms were issued in connexion with
examinations, and maintenance payments for schools. Again,
each pupil and certificated teacher was paid directly from Whitehall. Circumstantial evidence of the mounting pressure is provided
by the Minutes of the Committee of Council themselves. Their
annual publication in book form became increasingly delayed, and
the absence of consistency in the arrangement of their contents
suggests hurried compilation and lack of time for revision. Admittedly, the establishment of the Office since its inception had
grown from one to forty, yet its organization remained primitive.
There was little division of labour, no clear lines of demarcation
between those who were concerned with policy-making and those
engaged in routine clerical duties. The most glaring defect was a
deficiency of well-educated administrators who could take some
weight from the Secretary's shoulders, for Kay-Shuttleworth
virtually did the work of ten men. He was responsible not only
for advising the Committee and carrying out its instructions, but
also for the discipline and efficiency of the Office. In addition he
conducted a voluminous correspondence, received numerous

deputations, consulted with school trustees and negotiated with various religious bodies.

Small wonder, then, that in May 1847 he felt constrained to appeal for some improvement in his official status to the Lord President. He pointed out that his situation had no parallel in any other department of the public service. The duties he was required to superintend were of critical importance and he had been placed in a position comparable to that of an Under Secretary of State. Despite this, all the members of his Department regarded not himself but the Clerk of the Council as their official head. In these circumstances he could not 'contemplate, without apprehension, an attempt to carry into execution the recent Minutes with official relations so ill defined, under the direction of an officer placed in a position which has neither dignity nor authority'. He went on to say that only his great respect for, and gratitude to, Lords Lansdowne and Russell persuaded him to remain at his post, but that he must 'unless an alteration be made, resign it with the first change of administration'.[1]

The government felt unable to accede to Kay-Shuttleworth's request, whereupon he asked that, since the work of the Department was too much for one man to administer, he might be afforded the assistance of certain officers who could act in a supervisory capacity. This second petition was granted, albeit in a half-hearted manner. In July 'My Lords'[2] approved the 'provisional' appointment of two officials who were each given the appellation 'Examiner'.[3] They were engaged, in effect, to scrutinize inspectors' reports. For some time the Department had been disturbed by the considerable measure of independence enjoyed by Her Majesty's Inspectors and was seeking for some means of exercising greater control over them. The need for supervision became more urgent when, as a result of the 1846 Minutes, the power of inspectors to advise the payment or with-

---

[1] Letter to Lord Lansdowne dated 3 May 1847. Quoted in Smith, *Kay-Shuttleworth*, p. 214.

[2] All official communications emanating from the Education Department were ostensibly from 'My Lords the Committee of the Privy Council on Education'.

[3] This title, which became a civil service curiosity and which survived until the 1920s, was borrowed from the Board of Control, the predecessor of the India Office, where Examiners were employed to study despatches received from the headquarters of the East India Company.

holding of grants increased considerably. In the words of the first chief examiner:

Up to the year 1846, as long as no money was distributed on reports, there were no examiners, and the reports were merely received in the office and printed from year to year, but as soon as ever annual grants began to be made to schools on the Inspectors' reports, I and a gentleman from Cambridge were made the first examiners, and our duties were to see that, within certain limits, uniformity of administration was observed in issuing public money on the reports of Inspectors.[1]

And, since the examiners were to read the latter documents and upon them recommend the action that the Committee of Council ought to take, it was thought expedient they they should be 'gentlemen of the same rank and character and class as the Inspectors'.[2] For its part, the Treasury decided that, as the duties of the new officials were to be strictly confined to the inspection of schools, their salaries would be paid from the education grant, not out of the Privy Council establishment. Furthermore, after a year had elapsed the continuance of their appointment would be open to consideration and would depend on the degree of effectiveness of the new system.

The first examiners were two men who subsequently reached the summits of their respective professions, one to become Archbishop of Canterbury, the other Permanent Secretary to the Treasury. The Rev. Frederick Temple had been selected as Principal of Kneller Hall, the proposed training college for workhouse schoolmasters, but as the premises were not ready he was brought into the Education Office. Ralph Lingen, a young barrister who had just completed his investigations as a Commissioner of Inquiry into the state of education in Wales, was retained also on a temporary basis.

Within a few months both these intellectually gifted men were complaining about the unsatisfactory terms of their employment. Temple expressed disappointment over his salary, while Lingen threatened to resign unless his appointment was made permanent. But these individual anxieties paled in comparison with the crisis that confronted the Department at the end of 1848, though perhaps it would be more appropriate to say that they were brought into

[1] *Report from the Select Committee on Education* (*Inspectors' Reports*), 1864, q. 636.
[2] *Ibid.* q. 156.

sharper relief by it. For, after nine years of unremitting endeavour in the face of intimidating difficulties, Kay-Shuttleworth collapsed from nervous exhaustion and was obliged to take a complete rest. He was, naturally, unwilling to relinquish control without first making provision for a competent deputy to assume responsibility during his absence. He conferred with the two examiners, suggesting that while he was convalescing one of them be appointed temporary secretary. Temple, aware that a clergyman might not be regarded as impartial, considered Lingen to be the more suitable choice. The latter accepted, on the understanding that he would not be bound by this decision should the position prove permanent.

It soon became clear that Kay-Shuttleworth's illness would not allow him to resume his work. Having once more urged the government to reorganize the Department, particularly with regard to drawing a distinction between administrative duties and those of a purely clerical nature, and having again received no tangible encouragement, he offered his resignation. At first it was refused, for the very good reasons that the government was unwilling to lose his services and was also unable to find an obvious successor. Ultimately, the decision was made to promote Lingen, though some misgivings were expressed over his rather brusque manner, and Kay-Shuttleworth retired in December 1849.

And so the man to whom in W. E. Forster's words, 'probably more than any other we owe national education in England', regretfully surrendered the reins of office, conscious that his mission was but partially completed. Yet, though there was still much to do, great things had been accomplished. Not the least of his achievements concerned the development of the infant Department itself. What was generally recognized as having been a merely provisional arrangement, devised without clear objectives, he had elevated into a function of state pursuing a dynamic and intelligible policy. The chorus of approbation with which historians in general have greeted his work is marred by only one discordant note. R. L. Archer, misled perhaps by his prejudice against state control, asserts that 'though a State official who was also a creative genius in educational matters is conceivable, no example can be produced from English history during the nineteenth century'.[1] Assuming this to be a proven rule, then Kay-

[1] R. L. Archer, *Secondary Education in the Nineteenth Century*, 1921, p. 4.

Shuttleworth is surely the exception to it; for, as one authority has written in tribute: 'If history judged men less by the noise than by the difference they make, it is hard to think of any name in the Victorian age which deserves to stand above or even beside Kay-Shuttleworth's.'[1]

At this point in the narrative, where a natural watershed occurs, a brief sketch of what was called 'the Education Department Establishment of the Council Office' is not inappropriate. In the ten years of its existence its staff had grown to some thirty strong. It consisted, apart from the (Assistant) Secretary, of two examiners, an advising counsel (shared with the Poor Law Board), and a statist-cum-librarian; the remainder were clerks of various grades headed by Chester, who was chief clerk and assistant to the Secretary, class-conscious Victorian officialdom drawing a nice distinction between those accredited with the courtesy title 'Esq.' and those referred to merely as 'Mr'. Because of the great volume of correspondence that poured from the Office, it had been found necessary to supplement the permanent clerical staff with a number of copying clerks engaged from a law stationer's establishment. The costs of administering the grant at this time were heavy, both in relation to the total grant and in comparison with succeeding years. In 1849 the aggregate outlay on education amounted to £109,949 of which no less than £18,333 (17·1 per cent) went on the Office in London and on inspection. The percentage was actually more than this, since part of the expenditure of the Department was borne on the grant for the establishment of the Council Office.

HM INSPECTORATE

If one may say that the Committee of Council was blazing a trail when it stipulated that inspection by its officers was to be a condition of aid, one may equally argue that it was also travelling along a well-trodden path. It had numerous precedents to follow and much experience to guide it. On the one hand, state inspection – firmly established in several continental countries – had already been introduced into England through the 1833 Factory Act and the New Poor Law of 1834; on the other, both the National and British Societies had conducted experiments in school

[1] G. M. Young (ed.), *Early Victorian England*, 1934, vol. 2, p. 490.

inspection. From the latter of these early forays into unknown territory the Committee could hardly fail to draw certain conclusions. Among these were that voluntary acceptance of inspection could not be relied on, that inspection on a parochial basis tended to be largely ineffectual and that, in order to secure the agreement of the sects on both the principle and practice of state inspection, denominational disputes must be avoided and a conciliatory approach adopted.

When, therefore, the government decided to impose inspection, it acted with both firmness and caution. It was determined to establish the doctrine that if the state spent public funds it had the right and the duty to ensure that they were put to purposes of which it approved and that full value was obtained for them. At the same time it was anxious not to give offence to the religious bodies whose co-operation was essential. Hence the Committee of Council was careful, when elaborating on the inspector's duties, to eschew controversial issues. As the relevant Minute decreed:

The right of inspection will be required by the Committee in all cases; inspectors, authorised by HM in Council, will be appointed from time to time to visit schools to be henceforth aided by public money; the inspectors will not interfere with religious instruction, or discipline, or management of the school, it being their object to collect facts and information and to report the results of the inspections to the Committee of Council.

The word 'henceforth' epitomized a wise concession to the societies' susceptibilities. Diplomatically, the government did not at first assert the claim to inspect 'Treasury grant' schools, though in 1844 these schools, too, were compelled to allow inspection or forfeit their grant.

But, however much the Committee might sugar the pill, the implications of this tentative step in the direction of state, and therefore secular, control of education were not lost upon the religious bodies, whose unfavourable reaction to the pronouncement may be ascribed to a mixture of narrow self-interest and genuine apprehension. Yet the government was guiltless of any sinister designs. Its motives sprang from an awareness that, in being the trustee of public monies, it was ultimately responsible for their proper expenditure. The inspectorate was, in short, to be a safeguard, not a straitjacket. Moreover, to make quite explicit the limited nature of the inspectors' functions, the Committee instructed the first HMIs to bear in mind that inspection was 'not intended as a means of exercising control, but of affording assistance'. Even this assurance failed in its primary purpose of placating the Church. The fear remained lest unsuitable men be appointed.

At this juncture, the bishops, conducting their campaign with impressive skill, delivered their *coup de main*. They could not refuse inspection if they accepted aid, so they refused the aid, and for a while they rejected some two-thirds of the total grants offered rather than admit 'Russell's Bashaws', over whose selection they exercised no control, into their schools. Clearly, if the children were not to suffer, one side would have to make concessions; which side was virtually determined when, after a Commons debate, the government barely escaped defeat. Following this, Russell arranged a meeting at which he, Lansdowne and three of the episcopate discussed the problem and arrived at a compromise. A Concordat was drawn up, to be issued subsequently as an Order in Council, the terms of which were almost wholly favourable to the Church. The two archbishops were given not only the right to veto the appointment of inspectors of Anglican schools, but also the power to dismiss them at any time. In addition they were to be consulted about the instructions given to inspectors, and copies of all reports on Church schools were to be sent to the archbishop of the province and to the bishop of the diocese in which the school concerned was situated. Within a few years similar agreements were made with other denominations.

These Concordats were to have far-reaching effects on the development and character of the inspectorate. On the debit side lay the disadvantage that for a whole generation it would be organized on a denominational, not a territorial, basis. This led to administrative waste on the one hand and to some disunity among inspectors on the other. Against these drawbacks may be weighed the consideration that, owing to the circumstances surrounding their appointment, the inspectors enjoyed a certain measure of independence of the government department by which they were employed and to which they were ultimately responsible.

The growth of the inspectorate, once it was established, followed to some extent a similar pattern to that of the office at headquarters. As the scope of the Committee of Council's operations widened so the need for more officers to supervise those operations arose. Thus, in 1843, when the grants were extended, it became necessary to appoint additional inspectors, the more so since the Department considered it desirable to conduct a periodical inspection in the most heavily populated areas. At the same time, Kay-Shuttleworth proposed that the country should be divided into five districts and that an inspector be responsible for Church of England schools in each of them. Again, after the 1846 Minutes, when the duties of inspectors increased appreciably, the staff was further augmented.

As the inspectorate grew larger, the benefits of holding regular meetings of its members became apparent. In January 1846, all of them were summoned to the Council Office, and subsequently the custom developed of arranging conferences in London each year. Seemingly, they were designed to secure greater standardization of procedure as well as to enable inspectors to exchange ideas. Following the Minutes of 1846, this innovation proved insufficient. Now that so much depended upon the inspectors' reports, some continuous check on them was rendered imperative. Hence the appearance at head office in the following year of examiners who, after studying the reports, would be required to recommend the appropriate action to be taken on them.

At the time of Kay-Shuttleworth's retirement, the inspectorate for England and Wales was sixteen strong, composed of twelve inspectors for Anglican, two for British and Wesleyan, and one for Roman Catholic schools. Training schools had one inspector separately assigned to them. In addition to this main body, there were four inspectors of Poor Law schools. The inclusion, and subsequent exclusion, of this contingent will be described in the next chapter.

4

THE EDUCATION DEPARTMENT:
THE LINGEN ERA, 1849–70

A more honourable or indefatigable public servant than Mr Lingen does
not exist; but the most indefatigable man sees difficulties in a course
for which he has no love. Mr Lingen's difficulties show the presence in
the heart of the Education Department of this want of love for the very
course which such a department is created to follow.

> – Matthew Arnold (published anonymously)

The years immediately following Kay-Shuttleworth's departure
were undramatic ones as far as the Education Department was
concerned. They were characterized by steady progress rather than
by spectacular advance.[1] The spotlight of interest shifts from the
central character, as it were, to the supporting cast. The early
1850s witnessed a resurgence of activity on the part of those who
were dissatisfied with the existing provision of education. Their
interests ranged over the whole educational spectrum, from the
universities at one extreme to elementary schools at the other, and
they embraced not only the public and endowed schools but also
technical and scientific instruction. Reformers, for the most part,
concentrated their energies on securing two essential requisites for
educational progress: the nationwide supply of schools resting on
a sound financial and administrative basis, and the appointment of
a minister, with a seat in the Commons, having undivided responsibility for a wide variety of educational institutions.

As to the first, there was growing approval for the idea of supplementing state grants with regular and compulsory local contribu-
tions. Several Bills incorporating this principle were introduced,
but none could command the necessary parliamentary support.
The times were not propitious for such measures, with an unsympathetic Gladstone at the Exchequer and public attention fixed on
the Crimea. But even without these obstacles, the perennial

---

[1] One notable event, occurring in 1851, was the extension of the grant to
evening classes. Lingen, who was already finding the work of the Department
extremely taxing, regarded the venture with misgivings, and opposed it.

stumbling-block remained. Advising the Prince Consort as to the slim prospects of Russell's projected Borough Bill which would have made provision for rate aid for education in corporate towns, the Lord President wrote:

I believe it will be difficult in the present state of religious feeling to adopt any great national plan. It is possible to extend the grants made by the Privy Council to elementary schools; to bribe Poor Law guardians to establish pauper district schools . . .; to provide for a better distribution of the funds of educational endowments. Beyond this it is difficult to go.[1]

Anticipating frustration in its parliamentary endeavour, the Committee of Council proceeded by departmental circular. The government came to the conclusion that, having created a large amount of educational machinery at considerable cost, it had now the duty, as well as the right, to keep that machinery in good running order. By a Minute of 2 April 1853 an annual grant was offered, on the fulfilment of certain conditions, to the managers of schools in rural districts. These 'capitation grants', as they were called, were extended three years later to urban districts also. According to the Newcastle Commissioners, when they came to survey the growth of popular education, this subsidy supplied 'the most remarkable illustration of the strong tendency . . . of the Committee of Council to branch out into fresh expenditure in compliance with local demand'.

The tactics of 1843 and 1846 were once more successfully employed. Educational expansion financed by the state – with its virtually inevitable corollary: increased powers of control by the government – had again proved possible despite the absence of any prior statutory authority to sanction it. Indeed, notwithstanding Russell's assurance that the Minute would be laid on the table, and that the House would have ample opportunity for duly considering it before making a decision, the matter was never debated. The education vote was hurried through unexpectedly amidst a host of miscellaneous estimates and the capitation grant was not discussed at all.

The new dispensation entailed an increase in the Office establishment. With Lingen enjoying at last the rank of full Secretary,

[1] Quoted in Lord E. Fitzmaurice, *The Life of Lord Granville*, 1905, vol. 1, p. 417.

Chester was promoted to one of the two newly-created posts of assistant secretary. At the same time three more examiners and six more clerks were appointed. As one contemporary official commentator observed: 'The Committee of the Privy Council has been gradually developed from a rather humble origin to its present large dimensions, mainly by fortuitous events, and principally by the legislative failure which demonstrated the inability of Government to carry out any large and comprehensive measure . . .'[1]

But these changes were not exclusively the outcome of the capitation grants. They were also, in part, aspects of a widespread reorganization of the entire civil service which was then in progress. Towards the close of the 1840s pressure from two directions had been exerted for an investigation into the structure and composition of the service. From outside there were attacks upon the method of recruitment by aristocratic nomination. As public opinion became more informed the patronage system appeared increasingly insupportable. Moreover, politicians themselves were growing tired of the constant importuning of place seekers, and of the sordid business involved in the distribution of favours which often led to general dissatisfaction. Within the service there was mounting awareness of the many structural faults that impaired efficiency. Specifically, there was 'no uniform system or standard of examination at admission, of probation, of division of labor according to intellectual or mechanical requirements, of promotion, of office routine, of salaries'.[2] What was required was a wholesale reform of methods of recruitment and a restructuring of each department in compliance with its particular functions. Accordingly, in 1848, when insurrections on the Continent created a disposition to reform English institutions of government, an investigation into the Treasury, the most important department, was begun; shortly afterwards it was extended to other offices.

The Committee of Inquiry into the Privy Council Office published its Report in August 1853. Needless to say, the central point at issue was the relationship between the Council Office and the Education Department. The Committee found that, while in certain circumstances the union of several departments in one

---

[1] *Census of Great Britain*, 1851. Horace Mann's *Education (England and Wales) Report*, 1854, p. lxxxiv.
[2] R. Moses, *The Civil Service of Great Britain*, 1914, p. 45.

office could be beneficial, 'to bring together under the charge of a single Establishment business of a wholly incongruous character, tends not to efficiency but to confusion'. Such being the case in the present instance, it therefore recommended that the two departments be 'altogether separated' and that 'no connexion should exist between them, except their common subordination to the Lord President'.

The Committee went on to consider the internal organization of the Education Office, proposing that the establishment should consist of a Secretary, two assistant secretaries, and such numbers of examiners and clerks as would be required for carrying out the work of the Department. In addition, the professional services of an architect for the inspection of school plans, and of a barrister for dealing with trust deeds and conveyances, would continue to be required.

Finally, having pointed out that there was no government department 'into which more elaborate mechanism is introduced' than the Education Office, the Committee stressed the need for the utmost care to be exercised in its administration. The Report continued:

A central Department can only carry on the direction of so complicated a system by the aid of very perfect machinery; and when it is borne in mind that the amount of the grant to be administered is now no less than £260,000; that there are . . . 5,509 schools subject to inspection . . .; 2,875 certificated Masters and Mistresses, of whom 2,200 are receiving annual additions to their salaries; and 6,180 Pupil Teachers in receipt of salaries from the Government, and consequently subject to annual examinations; . . . and that aid is given towards the building of nearly 300 schools a year; it will readily be perceived that great care and constant attention are necessary to prevent confusion and to carry on the business in a proper manner.[1]

Contained in the Report was an illustration of the almost unbelievable complexity of the office routine.

A great number of small payments are now made by the Education Committee to masters, mistresses, pupil-teachers, and others, in various parts of the country. Most of these are transmitted through the Post Office by means of money orders. They commonly vary from £5 to £30; and as no money order can be issued for more than £5, it is often necessary to obtain four or five orders payable to the same person. As the

[1] *PP* 1854, XXVII, 267.

particulars of every order which is sent out must be registered, the labour attending the book-keeping is greatly increased by this necessity.[1]

Small wonder that the concluding paragraph emphasized that the 'great and increasing pressure of work upon this Department renders it peculiarly important that every exertion should be made to reduce its modes of action to the greatest simplicity of which they are capable, and to curtail all unnecessary business . . .'[2] It was as if the authors had some premonition of impending misfortune, for these observations were to have a dramatic sequel.

Both the Lord President and the Treasury accepted the Report's recommendations, with the result that the Education Department severed its umbilical attachment to the Privy Council Office; both, however, remained under the ultimate, if remote, control of the Lord President, an arrangement destined to produce unhappy repercussions.

The series of investigations into public offices undertaken between 1848 and 1853 led not only to the carrying out of purely departmental reforms but also to the discovery that many departments were faced with common problems and suffering from similar defects. A general survey seemed to be called for, and the two chief Commissioners, Sir Stafford Northcote and Sir Charles Trevelyan, were asked to submit a report on the organization of the home civil service as a whole, and to make recommendations.

As is well known, the resultant Northcote–Trevelyan Report (1854) marked a turning-point in the history of the service. The main recommendations contained in this revolutionary document were: the abolition of patronage, recruitment by open competitive examination, the adoption of the principle of division of labour, and the introduction of promotion by merit. To sound out informed opinion on these proposals the Report was circulated to a number of officials, educationists and others for their observations. Most respondents expressed hostility or scepticism. Lingen, from the Education Department, affirmed that since rank and wealth held the keys to advancement socially, politically and commercially, he saw no reason for the abolition of patronage.[3] He also felt obliged to object to the argument propounded by some educationists

---

[1] *Ibid.* 271.   [2] *Ibid.* 273.
[3] Of those consulted, one of the very few to approve the method of open competitive examinations was Henry Cole, Joint-Secretary to the Department of Science and Art.

that the implementation of the Report would raise educational standards, pointing out that it was irrelevant to discuss the organization of the civil service as if it existed for the sake of the general education of the country. 'It exists,' he declared, 'at least it ought to exist, for the sake of the work to be done, just as much as ship-building exists for the sake of ships, or shoe-making for the sake of shoes.' Valid as this comment may have been, it came sadly from the pen of the man who was to be primarily responsible for the nation's education over a period of more than twenty years. Taken in conjunction with what is known of his predecessor, it also serves to illustrate the difference in attitude between Kay-Shuttleworth, the educationist, and Lingen, the bureaucrat.

As it happened, the proposed reforms were too sweeping and radical to be immediately acceptable; nevertheless, the Report set in motion the train of events that led, in the space of a generation, to the transformation of the civil service. A first step in this direction was taken in 1855 with the establishment, by Order in Council, of the Civil Service Commission whose members were charged with the duty of satisfying themselves as to the suitability of 'such young men as may be proposed to be appointed, to any junior situation in any department of the Civil Service'. From that date the principle, if not always the practice, of competitive examination began to operate, as did also the assertion of systematic Treasury control over all other departments.

Yet however necessary for the efficient conduct of the Education Department were its composition and structure, of considerably greater importance to Members of Parliament was its relationship to the House of Commons. No fewer than three Bills concerned in one way or another with this issue were introduced into the Lower House during the session of 1855. Two are of particular interest. Anticipating the Board of Education Act, the Free Schools Bill provided for the establishment of a 'Board of Public Instruction for England and Wales' as a central education authority, with a President, who would be a Member of Parliament, at its head. Its responsibilities would include the periodical gathering of fresh information about 'the nature and amount of instruction of the people in this country and in other countries'. This part of the scheme, which proved at once too ambitious and controversial to command much support, was finally realized just forty years afterwards when, within the Education Department, the Office of

Special Inquiries and Reports was formed.[1] The other proposed measure, titled the Education (No. 2) Bill, was sponsored by Sir John Pakington, a member who made education one of his special interests. He suggested that, considering the large grants of money currently being made for the purpose of promoting education, it was desirable for some Minister to be appointed who would be responsible to the House of Commons for the proper distribution of these grants and who could answer any question that might be put upon the subject.[2]

Pakington's speech drew the following statement from Lord John Russell:

When that Committee [of Council] was appointed I did not think that any better means could be adopted for managing the Educational Votes than by intrusting the control of them to a council of several Ministers, but circumstances [have] since changed, and I think that it would be for the benefit of the public service if the President of the Committee of Council were to be acknowledged as the Minister of Education, and that the department of education should be represented in [this] House by a person who might, perhaps, hold the rank of Privy Councillor, and who might be able to defend any measure that might be adopted, and who would be prepared at all times to explain the views of the Government with regard to the general question of education.[3]

He could assure the House that the whole subject was being earnestly considered and he hoped that in the near future a plan for the 'regulation' of the department would be laid before Parliament.

Since no agreement could be reached on the thorny question of rate-aid, all three Bills were abandoned; but Russell was as good as his word. The government, in the person of Earl Granville, the Lord President, had in fact already directed Lingen to draw up a memorandum on the subject of the 'Representation of the Education Department in the House of Commons'. Listing the difficulties arising from the existing situation, the Secretary pointed out that members complained that they were not effectively informed of the proceedings of a department by which large and annually increasing funds were administered, and that the Home

[1] See below, pp. 127–130.
[2] Hitherto, the duty of replying to the handful of inquiries made on educational matters during the course of a session had devolved upon the Home Secretary.
[3] *Hansard*, 3rd ser., cxxxix, cols. 386–7.

Secretary was too much occupied to be able to answer, except at second-hand, for more than the general outline and principles of the Department. For these and other reasons, Lingen concluded that there ought to be a direct and special representation of the Department in the Commons. His suggestion for solving the problem was to make the Secretary's office a parliamentary one, and to leave the two assistant secretaries as the highest of the permanent officers. The proposed Secretary would, he supposed, rank in about the same degree, and would be filled by politicians of about the same status, as the Under Secretaryships of the Colonies, War Office and Foreign Office.[1]

Whatever its demerits, Lingen's plan at least possessed the virtues of clarity and simplicity; it could not, however, satisfy the legitimate aspirations of the Commons. The government decided to adopt a different arrangement, at once politically more acceptable but administratively less workable.

The year 1856 undeniably constitutes a milestone in English educational history, but, unlike 1833, 1839 or 1870, it was no landmark. In other words, the events of that date, though important, were not decisive. In that they were steps in the right direction, the actions taken were to be welcomed; that they were not more substantial and that their potentialities were not realized are matters for regret.

The measures in question were designed to remedy two obvious defects in educational administration: the absence of any responsible Minister of Education in the House of Commons, and the lack of co-ordination among the various state agencies concerned with different forms of educational provision. As regards the latter, disquiet had for some time been expressed at the fact that there were no fewer than three major central authorities – the Education Department, the Science and Art Department, and the Charity Commission – at work in the field of education, and that these authorities were distinct entities having virtually no contact one with another.

In an attempt to make good both these deficiencies, the government, on 25 February 1856, issued an Order in Council which recommended that the educational establishments then attached to

[1] Public Record Office [PRO] Ed. 24/53. Memorandum dated 6 June 1855.

separate departments be united under one direction, and be represented in both Houses of Parliament. It went on to propose:

1. That, for the future, the establishment to be called the Education Department, be placed under the Lord President of the Council, assisted by a Member of the Privy Council, who shall be the Vice-President of the Committee of the said Privy Council on Education, and shall act under the direction of the Lord President, and shall act for him in his absence.

2. That the Education Department include the following establishments, viz:— a. The Educational Establishment of the Privy Council Office. b. The Establishment for the encouragement of Science and Art, now under the direction of the Board of Trade, and called the Department of Science and Art.

This presaged a substantial move towards a more unified central administration. Unfortunately, the possibilities opened up by the merger were considerably reduced by the sentence immediately following: 'That, until your Majesty's pleasure be further signified, the said establishments continue to conduct their several duties according to existing regulations, but that both establishments be under the orders of the Lord President.'

Since, in the event, successive governments made little or no effort to dovetail the work of the departments, they remained 'joined, like Siamese twins, but separate in their operations'.[1] Even the ministerial overlordship proved, for reasons that will become apparent, largely ineffective.

Other promising lines of development were sketched out in the Order's concluding paragraphs which envisaged that the combined Department might be charged with certain duties additional to those already being performed by its constituent elements. The proposed responsibilities would be to report on such questions as might be referred to the Department by the Charity Commissioners and to inspect both the naval and military schools on behalf of the Admiralty and War Department respectively. This section of the Order suggests that an over-all and co-ordinated supervision by one department of much, if not most, of the education that came under the purview of the state was contemplated at this time. When, however, the moment came to translate the laudable

---

[1] W. H. G. Armytage, *Four Hundred Years of English Education*, 1964, p. 119.

intention into an acknowledged fact, little real effort was exerted. In particular, the links between the Education Department and the Charity Commission remained tenuous and unsatisfactory, and the opportunity of drawing all three departments together into a coherent whole was missed.

Another interesting feature of the Order was the almost complete omission of any reference to the Committee of Council, which appeared to have become superfluous in official eyes. Indeed, but for the Vice-President's title, the document might be held to have abolished the Committee, especially as there was in existence no Order in Council providing *in general terms* for the establishment and perpetuation of the Committee.[1] On the other hand, there is evidence to suggest that that body, far from being moribund at this date, was taking on a fresh, and more purposeful, lease of life. Sir Francis Sandford, just after his retirement in 1884 as Secretary to the Department, stated that, as part of the arrangement under the Order in Council of 1856 by which the Department was directed to assume certain duties in connexion with the poor law schools, the workhouse schools, the reformatories, and the naval and military schools, a number of designated Officers of State were appointed *ex-officio* members of the Committee. These were the Chancellor of the Exchequer, the Home Secretary, the President of the Local Government Board, the Secretary of State for War and the First Lord of the Admiralty. If this was indeed the case, then it is hard to account for the absence from the Committee of the Secretary for War in the Derby Administration of 1858 and of the President of the Local Government Board under Salisbury in 1886.

When the subject came up for debate in Parliament – for the appointment of a Vice-President to provide representation in the Commons required a statute – members from each House questioned the necessity for the continuance of the Committee of Council. It appeared to Lord Derby 'worthy of consideration, whether it would not be well to supersede the Privy Council altogether . . . and to have a Minister as the head of a Department who should have no other duties to perform, and who should be, in fact, responsible for the education of the people'. For one thing, 'the President of the Council had various other duties to perform', for another, 'a single responsible Minister was much more

---

[1] PRO Ed. 24/55. Memorandum relative to the business of the Privy Council Office, Appendix A., 18 November 1867.

efficient than a Board, however respectable and able the Members constituting that Board might be'. Lord Monteagle expressed the view that the Committee of Council was in constitution and principles one of the worst modes of administration. The members were ill-assorted; some could not attend for want of time; others had not the knowledge or opportunity of understanding the functions that nominally devolved upon them;[1] and as a result the real power was in the hands of subordinate persons. Other speakers argued that the new arrangement of having a minister in each House, far from improving the system, might lead to confusion and inefficiency. The Earl of Ellenborough felt that if their Lordships 'wished to have a department well conducted, they should rather place it in the hands of one than of two ministers, however able . . . It was quite enough work for one man, and that work would never be well done until it was confided to one man only'. And while criticism of the Bill was generally directed towards its details, some members contended that the whole measure was uncalled for, since the new minister would find very little to do that would occupy his time or justify his salary.

The government's case was lucidly expounded by Sir George Grey during the second and third readings. It rested on two main grounds. There was in the first instance a need for individual, in place of collective, political control; in the second, it was felt desirable, in view of the substantial increase in the grants since the Committee of Council was formed, 'that the educational department should be enlarged, and that it should be represented by an influential minister in the House of Commons'.

Brief and comparatively uncontroversial, the Vice-President of the Committee of Council on Education Bill passed quickly through its various stages to receive the royal assent on 27 June 1856, thereby enjoying the distinction of being the first piece of legislation relating to English elementary education to reach the statute book. It sanctioned the appointment of a minister of state, who must be a member of the Privy Council, to assist the Lord President, to act for him in his absence, and to represent the Committee in that House of Parliament where the Lord President might not happen

---

[1] When Lord Lonsdale became Lord President in 1852, one newspaper described him as a person 'whom no one ever heard of in connexion with education, but all may [have] heard of in connexion with the turf'. *Leeds Mercury*, 12 June 1852.

to sit.[1] It was, like most of the other measures, past and future, dealing with education, a compromise; as such it failed adequately to meet the demands of the situation. In some ways, indeed, it created as many problems as it solved, giving rise to a state of affairs in which 'the Vice-President was not a first-class Minister; the President was not a first-class educationalist. Therefore the Vice-President put on the steam and the other put on the brake'.[2]

Hence, it was singularly unfortunate that in the years following, additional duties, often unrelated to the education of children, were placed upon the Vice-President, partly perhaps because it was thought that his educational responsibilities were insufficient to keep him fully employed,[3] partly because the Privy Council throughout the nineteenth century, was 'used as a kind of potting shed for new administrative plants' of different varieties.[4] In 1858, for instance, the Public Health Act provided that, of the Lords of the Privy Council charged with its administration, the Education Vice-President must always be one. Arrangements of this sort, whereby the latter was made the repository for a heterogeneous collection of duties, were to become customary, leading, in the course of time, to a situation in which the Vice-President's responsibilities included the detection of diseases among imported cattle and the control of rinderpest in the Isle of Man.

To many members, the 1856 Act was seen as a mere tinkering with the steering mechanism, when what was required was a major overhaul of the entire educational machine. None was more aware of the need for a searching diagnosis of its faults than Pakington, who had also been largely instrumental in securing the creation of the Vice-Presidency. Conscious that the system as it stood was failing to provide education sufficient in quality and quantity for working-class children, he was at the same time anxious lest the country might be drifting towards a situation in which the elementary schools, through their dependence on state

---

[1] The first Vice-President, appointed 2 February 1857, was William F. Cowper, who later as Cowper-Temple was to win himself a place in English educational history as the author of the celebrated clause in the 1870 Act.

[2] E. M. Sneyd-Kynnersley, *HMI. Some passages in the Life of one of HM Inspectors of Schools*, 1910, p. 119.

[3] Gladstone, for example, voiced his opposition to a 'State functionary' such as the Minister of Education, 'an officer with a salary of £2,000 a year, and nothing to do'.

[4] Quoted in M. Wright, *Treasury Control of the Civil Service 1854–1874*, 1969, p. xxix.

aid, would find themselves under the centralized control of a government department. In this respect he was expressing the views of those who were growing increasingly hostile towards what was described as 'the Whitehall tyranny': the dispensation of large sums of public money, by non-elected and virtually irremovable officials, according to regulations they themselves laid down. He therefore moved, in February 1858, for a commission to be appointed 'to inquire into the present state of Popular Education in England . . . and to consider and report what changes, if any, are required for the extension of sound and cheap Elementary Instruction to all classes of the People'. The motion was carried by a two to one majority, and accepted by the government, which was probably relieved to see the thorny problem taken, at least temporarily, out of its hands, and to be provided with an excuse for imposing a standstill on the educational front.[1] In June a Royal Commission began its investigations under the chairmanship of the Duke of Newcastle, fresh from his resounding failure as Secretary for War during the Crimean campaign.

In the course of their lengthy deliberations, the Commissioners, naturally, examined the working of the Education Department. Indeed, one might say that, while their brief was to inquire into the state of elementary education, the conditions of the bureau itself became a central issue in their discussions. One of the first discoveries they made was that 'though various departments of Government were in possession of much information respecting detached portions of the subject, none could furnish a complete account of the state of education of any class of the population, or of any district in the country'.[2] They felt that a single central authority responsible for all forms of state-aided education was desirable on two counts: 'There is . . . an obvious convenience, and there will probably be a saving of expense, in placing our whole system of public education, so far as it is connected with Government, in the same official hands'.[3] Unfortunately, this observation was expressed almost parenthetically and was not included in the

[1] Limited in conception though the terms of reference may have been, they also revealed how far Parliament had travelled, in less than a generation, on the matter of education. The need for something approaching a national system had been recognized, and that it should be, at least in part, financed – and therefore superintended – by the state, had been implicitly accepted.

[2] *Report of the Newcastle Commission*, vol. 1, p. 7.

[3] *Ibid.* p. 475.

major recommendations, although the Commission did make some proposals designed to achieve a certain measure of integration.[1]

A second discovery, emerging from the extensive, if incomplete, investigations carried out in the course of the inquiry, concerned the nature of the schooling then provided. This was found in the main to be inadequate as regards both quantity and quality, owing partly to poor attendance by the children and partly to inefficient instruction by the teachers. On the basis of the limited evidence obtained (evidence which was later found to have grossly underestimated the deficiencies), the Commissioners concluded that 'the system has not effected . . . a general diffusion of sound elementary education among all classes of the poor'.[2]

The next logical step was to determine whether that system was capable of expansion sufficient to meet future demands, as well as present needs. It was at this point that the Commissioners made their third, and crucial, discovery, which appertained to the amount and nature of the work devolving on the Education Office. Here, the testimony of the Secretary and late assistant secretary was of decisive importance. Lingen, particularly, painted an alarming, if dispassionate, picture of an administrative machine on the verge of seizure. He showed how two main factors were responsible for this situation. The first stemmed from the Committee's policy of grant-appropriation, which was 'not to pay large sums of money in gross to the managers, but as far as possible to allot to certain specific purposes whatever money is to go out to the schools'. A block grant would have saved much time and trouble, for

the machinery which is necessary to insure that appropriation is of course an extremely complicated one. If you may have a school in any of the fifty-two counties of England and Wales, and if it may belong to either of four different denominations, and if the money which you send down to it may be for four or five different objects each of which has its own conditions and is subject to its own questions, a system of that sort is of enormous complication.[3]

The other factor arose from the denominational character of educational provision. No fewer than seven different sets of

---

[1] That part of the Newcastle Report dealing with charitable endowments is discussed in chapter 10.

[2] *Ibid.* p. 295.   [3] *Ibid.* vol. 6, q. 552.

officers had to be supplied to inspect schools in England and Scotland.[1]

Then, of course, all your books have to be kept under this seven-fold division; you have to consider in every single grant which is issued, not only where the school is, but what religion it is of; and that in addition to appropriating the grants to specific objects. You get this seven-fold division of denominations introduced into every account whatever which you have to keep; it adds largely to the labour of administration.[2]

Assistant Secretary Harry Chester, called attention to one of the disadvantages that flowed from all this complexity.[3]

A great evil in the amount of work has been . . . that the office has been so absorbed by the day's work that there has been very little time to consider what improvements might be made in the [education] system; and of late years there has been no attempt whatever to combine different religious bodies, or supply what was defective in the system as a general system, and to lay the foundation for something really like a national system of education. It is impossible for a person worked as the Secretary . . . is, to have time at his disposal to enable him to consider those questions properly.[4]

Having procured the basic evidence – the extent of educational deficiency in the country, and the intricacy of the machinery at the centre – the Commissioners proceeded to weigh it. The problem crystallized itself in the form of a single question: If the present system were to be extended to include the whole country, could it be managed by the Whitehall Office? Lingen expressed the gravest doubts; he would not go so far as to say that such extension was an administrative impossibility, but he did believe it would prove a matter of extreme difficulty and that the consequential increase in the establishment, both at headquarters and of the inspectorate, would be likely to 'alarm Parliament and the public'. He had one suggestion to make: 'The only way in which you could extend the

---

[1] From the outset, the Committee of Council had been responsible for supervising the application of the education grant in Scotland, as well as in England and Wales.

[2] *Ibid.* q. 500.

[3] His retirement, while the Commission was sitting, provided another. It was caused through ill-health brought on by overwork.

[4] *Ibid.* q. 703.

system would be by simplifying the payments . . .' Chester concurred with this view, but was more explicit:

I do not see how it is possible to relieve the Committee of Council on Education from the multiplicity of details which are involved in the present system, unless you give up the plan of inspecting the schools, and ascertaining that the work is done before you pay the money, and substitute for that a system of simply testing by examination, and paying by results.[1]

He was not prepared to claim that this scheme would be as effective as inspection on a small scale, but it would certainly relieve the Committee of nearly all the details, and would, therefore, be capable of application on a very large scale.

What Chester was suggesting as one means of surmounting the problem was by no means novel. The Commission sat at a time when examinations were à la mode, so to speak. This was the period when the Civil Service Commissioners, as we have seen, the universities, the public and preparatory schools, and numerous professional bodies were adopting this method of testing efficiency and gauging potential. It was then, too, that payment on the results of instruction was being tried out with a gratifying measure of success by another central authority for education: the Science and Art Department; and, by accident or design, a paper demonstrating the progress made under that system was published in 1861 when, in the words of the prime mover, 'it was thought that it might be useful and interesting to those who advocated its application to general education'.[2] Moreover, the Education Department itself had, in 1853, proposed, as a condition of the capitation grant, the passing of an examination by three-quarters of the pupils, though as it happened the scheme remained a dead letter; and some inspectors advocated the introduction of examinations as a means of securing improved teaching in elementary schools. What *was* new about Chester's proposal was that payment by results was being put forward for the purpose, not of raising educational standards, but of extricating the Department from the administrative tangle in which it had become ensnared.

At all events the Commissioners found the evidence of the permanent officials convincing enough to permit the drawing of

[1] *Ibid.* q. 716.
[2] H. Cole, *Fifty Years of Public Work*, 1884, vol. i, p. 303.

certain conclusions. They declared that the Education Office, as then constituted, was unique among government departments in several respects; in, for example, the minute details which the method of assigning grants to specific objects demanded, and the trouble involved in conducting the business between the Office and six or seven thousand independent bodies of school managers. And when it was borne in mind what these unusual features entailed –

the amount of vigilance required by a central authority in controlling a grant locally administered; the constant demands for additional aid upon special grounds, which have each to be separately considered; the liability to mismanagement and fraud in appropriating the grants and the care required for their transmission; the disputes which must often arise between managers, inspectors, and the Committee of Council, with regard to the payment or the withdrawal of grants; and further, that these intricacies of arrangement, which have proved so great already, would be quadrupled if the work of the office embraced the whole of England –[1]

when all this was taken into account, the Commissioners did not think that the Secretary's opinion as to the difficulty of making the system applicable to the entire country was overrated.

But they went further than deciding that the load on the Department could not reasonably be increased; they were also of the opinion that it ought to be lessened. 'There surely can be little doubt that any plan which should relieve the Committee of Council of some of this mass of minutiae, and should enable them to look to the principles of education instead of scrutinizing its smallest details, must improve their whole power of dealing with the subject.'[2]

The problem posed itself in these terms: How could grants of public money be so arranged as at one and the same time to protect the Treasury from excessive claims, to reduce the pressure on the Department, to foster local interest in education and to preserve the denominational character of the schools? In an attempt to resolve it, the Commissioners proposed the creation of elected boards of education in counties and in boroughs of more than 40,000 inhabitants. These boards would have the power to levy rates, to examine children in the three Rs, and to pay grants on the results of these tests. The purposes which, it was hoped, would be served

---

[1] *Report of the Newcastle Commission*, vol. i, p. 322.　　[2] *Ibid.* p. 325.

as a result of these changes were then spelt out: 'first, to maintain
. . . the quality of education by encouraging schools to employ
superior teachers; secondly, to simplify the business of the office
in its correspondence and general connexion with schools in
receipt of the grant; thirdly, to diminish the rigour and apparent
injustice of some of its rules.'[1]

And, lest there be any doubt as to the reason which prompted
them to make their proposals, the Commissioners stated: 'Our
principal object in . . . recommending that . . . the grant to all
schools in connexion with the Committee of Council shall be paid
in one sum [via county and borough treasurers] to the managers,
rather than appropriated . . . to particular objects, has been to
relieve the office of a great part of its connexion with the internal
management of schools, and thus to simplify its business . . .'[2]

On receiving the Report, the government lost no time in adopting those recommendations which promised both to be productive
of 'sound and efficient' elementary education and to present
minimal difficulties as regards their implementation. Unwilling
to risk another storm of sectarian indignation over local rating, it
decided to sweep away the multiplicity of separate grants, consolidating virtually all payments to each school into a single
capitation grant, payable to the managers alone and based on the
results of the individual examination of pupils and on their
attendance. Once again, this radical change in policy required no
statutory sanction; a departmental Minute sufficed. It was,
however, considered important enough to warrant a debate; and
the Revised Code of Regulations,[3] which incorporated the new
scheme, was presented to both Houses of Parliament on the same
day – 13 February 1862.

While it may be conceded that the government acted as it did
because it was genuinely alarmed at the spiralling costs of educa-

---

[1] *Ibid.* p. 337.   [2] *Ibid.* p. 334.

[3] The rules that regulated the proceedings of the Committee of Council
had been embodied in Minutes. In April 1858 an abstract of all former Minutes
was moved by Adderley, the then Vice-President, and published as a parliamentary paper. Two years later Lowe issued the same material, arranged in
chapters according to subjects, which acquired the title of 'The Original Code',
and which served as a framework on which all succeeding Codes were constructed. The 'Revised Code' was the first of these amended versions. These
documents became, as it were, the rule-book of the Department, governing its
conduct and controlling its relations with the schools. In time they took on the
character of Holy Writ itself, and were venerated – at least by officials – as such.

tion and because it believed that, on a cost-efficiency basis, this expenditure was excessive, there is little doubt that its primary purpose was to ease the burden on the central office. Ample proof of this is provided in the ministerial speeches at the time, and Lord Granville was to admit as much a few years later. 'The Revised Code . . .', he stated, 'partly originated from the Report of the Commission of the Duke of Newcastle . . . and partly from the facts which were observable in the working of the constitution of the business of the office.'[1]

However deplorable may have been some of the repercussions following upon the introduction of the Revised Code, there can be no doubt that it achieved one of its purposes. Taking the office establishment as a crude yardstick of its effectiveness in securing administrative economy, we find that in the decade 1861–70 the total 'indoor' staff increased by only four, and that from 1864 to 1870 the figure remained stationary, and this despite a growth in the region of 40 per cent in the number of schools, of children and of teachers.

But whether payment by results was introduced as an exercise in economy, or as a device for improving popular education, or as an administrative convenience, its institution had a profound and long-lasting impact on the structure, as distinct from the quality, of English education. For, as the passage of time has revealed, the measure effectively decentralized the educational system, thereby preserving it from some of the drawbacks that have been encountered in those continental countries where devolution in educational administration has not, to any appreciable extent, taken place.

A second incidental benefit concerned the status of elementary school teachers. Following the 1846 Minutes, a significant part of many teachers' salaries came directly from state funds, and, in addition, their qualifications and conditions of employment were regulated by the Committee of Council; hence, there was a tendency for teachers to regard themselves as civil servants and to claim the privileges attaching to that type of employment. The higher officials in the Whitehall Office were anxious to reverse this trend, and the opportunity came with the introduction of the Revised Code, for under it government grants were to be made, not personally to teachers as hitherto, but to the managers. Thus the

[1] *Report of the Select Committee on Education*, 1865, q. 2312.

teacher ceased to be, in any respect, a state employee, and became instead merely the servant of his managers who were now under no obligation – as they had previously been – to observe a recognized proportion between the salary they paid him and the amount of the grant earned from the Department, but might drive with him the best bargain they could negotiate. Curiously enough, however, the loss of such limited security and rights that teachers had originally expected or claimed ultimately redounded to their advantage; for had they been permitted to retain their civil servant status then they might well have failed to achieve the degree of freedom which they now enjoy as local government employees. Again, it can be argued that, in the long run and at the expense of a whole generation of school children, payment by results produced a reaction against tight bureaucratic control – a swing of the pendulum that gave impetus to the movement favouring a more liberal concept of the curriculum.

Yet another unexpected result of the new Code was that it led, directly or indirectly, to two further inquiries into the working of the Education Department. The first derived from the suspicion that the reports of those inspectors who opposed payment by results and placed their views on record, were being systematically pruned of any remarks critical of official policy. This suspicion was translated into an accusation in April 1864 when Lord Robert Cecil moved

That, in the opinion of this House, the mutilation of the Reports of Her Majesty's Inspectors of Schools, and the exclusion from them of statements and opinions adverse to the educational views entertained by the Committee of Council, while matter favourable to them is admitted, are violations of the understanding under which the appointment of the Inspectors was originally sanctioned by Parliament, and tend entirely to destroy the value of their Reports.

Upon the motion being carried, both Granville and Lowe tendered their resignations to the Prime Minister, though there is some evidence to suggest that the target of the resolution was not the political but the permanent head of the Department. A jealous Commons strongly objected to Lingen playing the role of a Grey Eminence; while managers, inspectors and teachers alike resented his brusque and condescending manner. In the event, Granville withdrew his resignation after Palmerston had persuaded him that no stigma attached to the Lord President as head of the Privy Council Office; but Lowe, feeling that he had been the subject of a personal censure, adhered to his decision and requested the appointment of a committee to examine the charges made against him.

Although the terms of the resulting select committee were restricted to inquiring 'into the practice of the Committee of Council on Education with respect to the Reports of HM Inspectors of Schools', the inquiry ranged over a wide area. Lingen was closely interrogated on the extent of his Department's jurisdiction. He confessed that he was unaware of the existence of any document defining the powers of the Committee and distinguishing between what it might or might not do without parliamentary approval. He believed, however, that the Committee would be compelled to seek such authority for any change which involved the expenditure of public money or for any substantial modification of the policy previously submitted to Parliament in the form of Minutes.

Both the Lord President and the Vice-President were questioned as to their respective powers and functions. Granville stated that he considered himself responsible for the whole action of the Department, and that 'a general understanding' existed between him and the Vice-President that no new rule should be established and no alterations be made without his (Granville's) sanction. 'But', he added, 'it was a matter of discretion with the Vice-President what matter should be brought before me.' Lowe's evidence, if it did not actually conflict with that of his superior, at the very least seemed hardly to coincide with it. He maintained that 'a very large portion' of the work of the Department did not come under the cognizance of the Vice-President, adding that the annual grants (by far the largest single item of business, and the most important) formed part of this category. He was occupied 'more with the building grants, and with any particular question which [might] be brought before him as presenting difficulties in any of the other departments'.

Remarks like these were hardly calculated to reassure those Members of Parliament who had hoped that the 1856 Act would supply their House with an authoritative spokesman on educational affairs. But the scepticism engendered by such testimony was only one facet of a widespread disquiet felt during this period about the whole question of the administration of the education grants.

The promulgation of the Revised Code just before Parliament rose in 1861, brought matters to a head. Many members felt, in the words of Granville's biographer, 'that changes so considerable ought to have been embodied in a Bill; and that so large an exercise of legislative powers by a public department, even though not *ultra vires*, was nevertheless objectionable, and went beyond what Parliament had intended when it confided those powers to the Privy Council.'[1] This resentment became crystallized into a fierce objection to what was regarded as a 'new despotism' wielded by faceless bureaucrats in Whitehall virtually immune from Parliamentary control.

The first attempt to secure an appropriate investigation was made by Sir John Pakington in May 1864 on the occasion of the debate on inspectors' reports. He called for an addition to the government motion proposing a select committee into their handling, so that its terms of reference would be broadened to include an inquiry into the constitution of the Committee of Council and 'how far their mode of conducting the business of the department is consistent with the due control of Parliament over the annual education grants'. He asserted that 'a deep feeling of dissatisfaction and distrust of the administration of the Educational Department prevails throughout the country'.

On this occasion the government successfully resisted the amendment, but the day of reckoning was not postponed for long. Pakington returned to the charge in February the following year by requesting the appointment of a select committee to inquire into the Education Office. The debate on the motion was chiefly remarkable for some very outspoken criticism of the Department. Pakington himself doubted whether there had ever been, in the whole range of our system of government, any department of state at all organized on such principles, and in such a manner, as the Committee of Council then was. In his opinion the organization of the Department was so defective that it was open to very grave objections, and that it could not possibly act with that degree of efficiency, and, above all, with that sense of responsibility, which the Legislature had a right to expect in every department of the Executive. Adderley, with Vice-Presidential experience behind him, said that the Committee of Council was 'anomalous in this respect, that a subaltern was the ordinary administrator, and that

---

[1] Fitzmaurice, *Lord Granville*, pp. 427–8.

the nominal head of it interfered only as much as he was inclined, and was appointed for other purposes, and without reference to his fitness or turn for the Education Department'. Moreover, whenever the President did interpose, the effect was to diminish the interest which the Vice-President took in his work.

Lowe, defending the existing arrangement, took a somewhat different view. He asserted:

There is one Minister who is responsible, and that Minister is the Lord President of the Council. There is no divided responsibility . . . one Minister is responsible for every administrative act of the Committee of Council . . . There is a legislative body, which is composed of a Committee of the Cabinet . . . ; and the administrative power is vested in the Lord President, assisted by the Vice-President who is under his direction.

As to the powers of the Department, Lowe maintained that it had no initiative; it merely followed the lead of voluntary and private enterprise. As for the reasons why the head of the Department should be in the Lords, Lowe argued that one was that the educational grant was distributed mainly among members of the Church of England, and that bishops of that Church had seats in the Upper House.

When Cecil rose to speak he exposed point by point the weakness and dangers of the present system. He felt that the minister who was responsible for the preponderant expenditure of a Department ought to have a seat in the Commons. But the problem went deeper than that. 'There is no doubt', he claimed, 'that the feeling exists far and wide that the responsibility of the Education Department is a sham – that the practical power is centred in a permanent officer.' Fastening on Lowe's remark that the Education Department possessed what amounted to powers of legislation, Cecil retorted:

I can hardly conceive that anybody could have expressed more clearly . . . the precise nature of the objection that we . . . have to the constitution of that Department. We do not like a quasi-legislative power – this *imperium in imperio*. There is one legislative power in the kingdom and that is . . . Parliament; and any other power which interferes with that is dangerous to the State and perilous to the liberties of the subject . . . I should have thought that a system so intensely unpopular and so complex that no one could understand it was a legitimate subject of inquiry by the House of Commons.

The House concurred, and on 14 March the committee was nominated. For the significance of the ensuing investigation it is fruitless to search for any improvements in the system to which its deliberations gave rise – there were none; it is to be found instead in the extraordinary diversity, not to say conflict, of opinion regarding that system which it revealed. The committee concentrated its attention on two main issues: the functions of the Committee of Council, and the respective powers of the Lord President and Vice-President.

As regards the former, several interesting pieces of information emerged. Its composition was not fixed, the members being chosen entirely upon the Lord President's authority, and by virtue both of the offices they held and of their interest in educational questions. One or two ministers selected themselves, however little they cared about education: the Chancellor of the Exchequer, because almost every Minute involved the expenditure of money, and the Home Secretary, because his appointment was a 'matter of propriety'; otherwise there was no absolute necessity for any other office to be represented. Only the Chairman could summon the Committee. The Marquess of Salisbury 'thought he did so' on three or four occasions. It was generally ill-received when he proposed it, and, in the event, none of the members attended, so he acted on his own responsibility. Lingen believed that three was the quorum necessary for the transaction of business, although he added that since 1856 the Lord President and Vice-President had proceeded on the assumption that they had the powers of the Committee of Council without necessarily convening that body. In any case no record of the attendance of members, or how often they met, or who came, was preserved. Indeed, unless Minutes were passed, no account was kept of any of the Committee's discussions.

Upon the major issues of functions and powers, the views of no two witnesses coincided; frequently they contradicted one another, and occasionally themselves. Lingen, for example, referred to the Committee of Council as 'deliberating' on questions of importance; later he was to say that it was simply a consultative body whose sole function would be 'negative'. Subsequently he agreed that it only met to ratify decisions previously made by the Lord President and Vice-President; in his very next answer he said that the Committee was often called together to advise on some educational matter engaging the public attention. He thought that it would be impossible for the Committee to initiate any measure. This was not Earl Russell's experience. He attested that he himself, as an ordinary member of the Committee, had proposed the capitation grants.

Lowe, in his turn, repeated that the Committee possessed powers of legislation, and both he and Granville maintained that it had no responsibility for administration, although the former added the lawyer-like caveat that its powers had never been defined and that while technically it was the depository of the whole power, it delegated all the executive and administrative functions to the Lord President. Granville approved of the Committee, and had found it of great use, and the practical working of it of much importance; nevertheless, it had absolutely no responsibility, and he declared that he would not be bound by the majority if he differed from it on a matter of principle. Russell believed it to be useful; but, dissenting from Granville's view, he considered it to have responsibility, though it would be difficult to define its extent, and he was of the opinion that a majority of its members might over-rule the Lord President. Lowe justified the retention of the Committee on the ground that it was a check against individual corruption or indiscretion. H. A. Bruce, the then Vice-President, thought that the assistance of the Committee had been helpful on two occasions during his period of office. Adderley, however, said that it was not only perfectly unnecessary but mischievous; and, having pronounced it 'useless and worse than useless', he called it 'an encumbrance' and 'a farce'. He complained that when it met he had to instruct the members on the question about which they were to be consulted.

Counsels were hardly less divided when the select committee examined the respective positions of the Lord President and Vice-President. Lingen felt difficulty in deciding whether the latter was a responsible minister or not, though he had no doubt that the Committee was irresponsible. He considered the Lord President, in whose hands rested the whole patronage of the Office, to be the superior officer, but estimated that 'nine-tenths' of the business of the Department was transacted by the Vice-President. Interrogated further, he assented to the view that the latter, in the absence of the Lord President, would appear to have co-ordinate authority with that minister on all educational matters, though he (Lingen) was unable to offer any definition of the word 'absence', which was capable of diverse interpretations. Lowe said that during his term of office he had regarded himself as neither more nor less than an under-secretary. Salisbury, on the contrary, believed that the Vice-President had rather more responsibility than a minister of such rank normally exercised. Bruce thought his position as Vice-President to be very different from that of an under-secretary. The latter was responsible only to his own chief, whereas the Vice-President was directly responsible to the House of Commons.

When questioned about the office of Lord President, Lowe maintained that that minister had numerous duties to perform and that those connected with education occupied a comparatively small portion of his time; Salisbury, on the other hand, said that the Lord President had very little to do apart from the business of the Education Department. Granville held the Lord President to be entirely and absolutely responsible, and the Vice-President to be completely subordinate to his chief. Russell was less dogmatic. While admitting that the Lord President was primarily responsible, he expressed the opinion that the Vice-President was also responsible, 'but in such a manner that he is far more responsible in certain cases than in certain other cases'.

With such an abundance of diverse material to sift and pronounce upon, it was scarcely surprising that the select committee was unable to reach any conclusions before the close of the parliamentary session of 1865. Unfortunately, when its members came to resume their deliberations the following year they found themselves unable to agree on a report. The chairman did, in fact, draw one up on his own initiative, but before it could be fully considered, the government fell and the committee dispersed. However, Pakington's draft merits some attention, both for its critical analysis of the central authority, and for its recommendations which anticipated certain provisions of the Education Acts of 1899, 1902 and 1944.

Referring to the Committee of Council, it began with the observation, commendably restrained in the circumstances, that the system was 'peculiar', and that it was more than doubtful whether any advantage was derived from it. The conclusion was

that the agency of the Committee of Council ... is anomalous and unnecessary; that it tends to diminish, on the part of the Education Minister, that sense of individual responsibility which is the best security for efficient discharge of official duties; and that in those rare cases in which the Minister requires advice from his colleagues, it would be better that the whole Cabinet should be consulted.[1]

Allusion was made also to 'the inconvenience that communications from the Education Office are written in the name of "My Lords", whereby perplexity, if not ridicule, is caused; the majority of those who receive such communications, have little idea who "My Lords" are, and know not with whom they are corresponding, nor under whose authority they are acting.'[2]

The second question to be asked and, if possible, answered was: Who was the Education Minister? or perhaps it should be: Was there one Education Minister or were there two?

No doubt the Lord President is theoretically the Minister, but it seems doubtful whether, in practice, the Vice-President has not the better claim to be so regarded; and there can be no doubt that the position of the Vice-President does not at all fulfil the objects of those whose repeated suggestions that popular education should be promoted by the appointment of a Minister, were at last met by a Bill, appointing a Vice-President, in 1856.[3]

After all the conflicting testimony supplied on these two issues, the Chairman was probably relieved to record that there was general agreement among witnesses on two points: first, 'that the present system is partial, incomplete and too highly centralised'; secondly, 'that the Education Department, as at present constituted, is not well adapted for the administration of a system so reformed as to reach every part of the country'.

The Draft Report ended with a series of recommendations which, had they been implemented, would certainly have accelerated the pace of educational reform and might well have prevented the confusion in educational administration that grew worse as the century wore on. The main proposals were: first, 'that the Committee of Council on Education, as being no longer adapted to the purpose for which it was formed, should cease to exist'; secondly, that there should be a Minister of Public Instruction, whose duty it should be both to regulate and control the whole subject of national education, and to propose to Parliament, with the concurrence of the Cabinet, of which he should be a member, such measures as the extension of education might require; thirdly, that

---

[1] *PP* 1866, VII, 124.   [2] *Ibid.*   [3] *Ibid.*

the Education Department should be so constituted as to be able at least to attempt a remedy for the evils of centralization and neglected districts;[1] for this purpose there should be established local organizations in connexion with the Department which itself should be 'suggestive', that is, it would have the statutory authority to *promote* education; and fourthly, 'that the numerous educational endowments, now almost useless, should be reformed, and made available'.[2]

Although the Chairman's Report was, for all practical purposes, pigeon-holed, it did succeed in stimulating some activity within the Department and utimately inside Parliament. Towards the end of 1867 three memoranda relating to each of the central authorities mainly responsible for the administration of educational funds, were drawn up at the direction of the Lord President. The document dealing with the Whitehall Office could hardly be described as revolutionary.[3] With respect to possible improvements that might be made to the constitution of the central authority for elementary education, its originator had only one positive suggestion to make, and that concerned the Committee of Council, the membership and functions of which might be formalized, though not necessarily rationalized. For the rest, the document consisted largely of a description of, and justification for, the existing arrangements.

But if departmental officials were complacent, Earl Russell was not. The creator of the Committee of Council had long been convinced that that body had served its purpose and ought now to be superseded by some central authority more appropriate to current requirements. On 2 December 1867 he moved four resolutions dealing with various aspects of educational reform. The last called for the appointment by the Crown of a Minister of Education, with a seat in the Cabinet, 'who would be capable of taking into consideration all affairs relating to education, and whose whole attention should be devoted to the furtherance and improvement of our educational system'. Answering for the ministry, the Lord President, the Duke of Marlborough, said that he personally had very great objections to such an appointment, though the only

[1] 'Neglected districts' were defined as those 11,000 or more parishes, with a population probably exceeding six millions, which derived no assistance, in the form of education grants, from the Exchequer.

[2] *Ibid.* 130.

[3] One of the memoranda, however, was highly significant. See pp. 222–3.

reason – or perhaps 'excuse' is a more suitable term – given for the government's opposition to the proposal, was that it might prove, if past experience was anything to go by, administratively inconvenient.[1] On the assurance being given that Her Majesty's ministers had the question of public elementary education under their consideration, the resolutions were negatived.

Then, by one of those political somersaults which the cynic is inclined to regard as opportunist and the party faithful as statesmanlike, the government completely reversed its position.[2] Less than four months after his rejection of Russell's suggestion, the Duke of Marlborough was himself moving the first reading of an education Bill which had as its purpose the appointment of a Secretary of State who should have the whole range of educational matters under his consideration and control, who would promote the cause of national education, and who would be armed with the powers necessary to enable him to initiate such measures as might be for the benefit of the country. The Lord President thought that 'the appointment of a responsible Minister of Education, capable of dealing with the subject in a comprehensive spirit, and of framing measures with the view of consolidating and uniting the different branches of primary and secondary education into one great whole, would be likely to be productive of the greatest possible advantage.'[3]

The Bill received a less than rapturous welcome from his fellow peers, but there was little outright opposition. Russell gave his approval, although he felt that the government, in creating a Minister of Education prior to establishing a system of local rating, had put the cart before the horse. Granville thought that the proposed minister would not have enough work to occupy him, while Lord Kimberley was at a loss to know what was to become of the Lord President if the latter were relieved of his educational duties. Answering the last point, Marlborough said that a notion seemed to prevail that the President of the Council had little or nothing to do but administer the education grant. That was not so, and to prove his point he recited a list of his own responsibilities other than those relating to education. It was, of course, precisely these extraneous duties of the Minister of Education to which objection was made by those who held that education was a matter of

---

[1] See below pp. 81–2.   [2] See also pp. 175–6 and 222n.l.
[3] *Hansard*, 3rd ser., cxci, col. 1326.

sufficient importance to warrant the undivided attention of that minister; and the error was compounded by the fact that not only the Lord President but the Vice-President also had to devote his time to non-educational matters.

In any event, this nineteenth-century version of a demarcation dispute remained unresolved, for the government, by virtue of pressure of business, found itself unable to proceed with the Bill. Gladstone's administration, which took office at the end of 1868, declined to follow its predecessor's initiative, deciding that its educational priorities should centre on the endowed schools and the neglected districts. The nation had to wait almost a century before the political head of the central authority for education was accorded the rank and dignity of a secretaryship of state.[1]

The following year, and on the eve of great events, the Department was thirty years old. During the preceding decade, thanks mainly to the Revised Code, its indoor establishment remained, numerically speaking, almost static, although the range of its activities widened. To a large extent, the causes of the growth in the work of the Committee of Council were beyond the control of the officials or ministers in charge, simply because the annual vote for education was in essence an offer to all accepting the conditions laid down to claim a share of it; moreover, the whole purpose of the grant was that this number should be as large, and increase as rapidly, as possible, the grant-regulations being justified as guarantees of efficiency rather than as checks on expenditure.

In 1869 the total staff (excluding inspectors) numbered seventy-three, consisting of the Secretary, two assistant secretaries, ten examiners, fifty-six clerks and a private secretary to the Vice-President; in addition there were three specialists – an advising counsel, an architect and an accountant. Such plain facts, however, reveal nothing about the men upon whose shoulders rested the task of administering the elementary educational system. Unfortunately, because very little has survived in the way of documentation concerning the activities of the Education Department in the mid-nineteenth century, the picture must necessarily remain incomplete. Nevertheless, it is possible, by piecing together such

[1] Ironically, the first holder of the newly-created office was a peer of the realm, the then Lord President of the Council, and a minister whose many and varied functions had occasioned much critical comment and some ridicule. The likelihood is that he was appointed more for party political than for educational reasons.

fragments of information and opinion as are available, to sketch a pen-portrait of the most important of the permanent officials: the Secretary to the Department himself.

Ralph Lingen's first contact with the Office came in 1846 when, as a young man of twenty-seven loaded with academic honours, he was selected as one of the three Commissioners appointed by the government to inquire into the state of education in Wales. In some ways it was a curious choice, since he was, like his two colleagues, totally ignorant of the Principality's traditions, institutions and native tongue. Despite their being barristers, the Commissioners, in the course of their investigations, committed serious errors in procedure, but perhaps *because* they were barristers, they appeared to imagine that their brief was to draw up a bill of indictment. Published towards the close of 1847, their Report amounted to a severe criticism of Welsh education; it also conveyed, with a singular lack of charity, an extremely unsavoury impression of moral and social conditions in the Principality. Needless to say, it created bitter resentment there and was regarded as part of a conspiracy to stamp out the language, religion and nationality of the Welsh. Indeed, the 'treachery of the Blue Books', as it became known, soured relationships between England and Wales, particularly in educational matters, for generations afterwards.

Notwithstanding this controversial initiation into the sphere of popular education, Lingen was offered a provisional appointment as an examiner under the Committee of Council when, in July 1847, the government agreed to Kay-Shuttleworth's request for additional staff to supervise the distribution of the annual grant. Two years later he found himself in charge of the Department.

Probably much to his own surprise, in view of the avowedly temporary character of the office, Lingen remained Secretary to the Committee of Council for over twenty years, which amounted, in fact, to more than a third of its existence as the central authority for elementary education. As Secretary, he came to wield considerable power, sometimes determining, always influencing, educational policy. There were several reasons for this growth of extra-parliamentary control. In the first place, the constitutional position of the Department was such that, for most of its existence, consistent and effective political direction over it was seldom exercised. Following the first Reform Act, the executive became much more answerable to the legislature, and its activities subject to scrutiny by the House of Commons. This development gave rise to problems for M.P.s who could not call non-political civil servants to account and, conversely, for civil servants who could not defend themselves if attacked in Parliament. The solution, as Kitson Clark has pointed out, was for the government to devise a system whereby each of its principal functions would be unambiguously superintended by a minister who could take responsibility for the actions of his officials. Initially, however, the difficulty was not recognized, and when the state began to intervene in earnest over an increasingly wide area, governments continued to create departments in which there was no minister to assume responsibility – as in the case of the Charity Commission – or in which uncertainty prevailed as to which minister was responsible – as in the case of the Committee of Council on Education, and, incidentally, the Science and Art Department. Eventually, the appropriate remedy was applied, but this process took time, 'so that during a critical period various important civil servants were not under effective political control'.[1] Lingen was one of these officials.

Secondly, the distribution of ministerial ability among the various departments of state was decided too much by the erstwhile importance of the offices and too little by their current significance, so that it came close to an affront to offer a talented statesman any of the supposedly 'inferior' departments, of which the Education Office was one. In such circumstances the permanent head was almost inevitably bound to fill the partial vacuum created. This tendency was accentuated if, as in the case of the Education Office, the departments were compelled by events to devise novel and complex techniques of administrative control. And the influence of the civil servant increased still more when there was a division of or a confusion over ministerial responsibility, when the 'ministers of education' – to employ a convenient anachronism – were required to devote part of their time to matters entirely unconnected with education, when the Department experienced a rapid turnover in its political management,[2] and when those politicians technically accountable for the provision of elementary education were

[1] G. S. R. Kitson Clark, *An Expanding Society. Britain 1830–1900*, 1967, p. 145.
[2] In the twenty year period 1849–69 there were eight different Lord Presidents of the Council, and in the thirteen years between 1856, when the office was created, and 1869 there were seven holders of the Vice-Presidency.

indifferent to, or ignorant of, the educational needs of the poorer classes.[1] Certainly, by 1864 at the latest, Members of Parliament were expressing their concern over the way in which the authority that properly resided in the executive and legislature was being usurped by 'tyrants in Whitehall'. Addressing the Commons in May of that year, during the debate on the inspectors' reports, Lord Robert Cecil protested that nobody seemed to know who was responsible for educational policy.

The House passed a resolution condemning the Government. The Government said 'Oh no! It is the Privy Council'. The Privy Council was represented by the Lord President, but the Lord President said it was the Vice-President. The Vice-President resigned and proved that he was innocent, and they inquire further, and find out it was the secretary.

As for Lingen himself, he entertained no doubts as to where the real, as distinct from the apparent or titular, authority lay. When appearing before a Commission of Inquiry, and on being asked whether some change which he suggested would not throw the government of the country into the hands of the permanent officials, he is said to have replied, 'I have yet to learn that the government is *not* in the hands of the permanent officials'.[2]

The weight of evidence suggests, then, that within broad limits – for instance, providing legislation was not required, which it seldom was – the effective control of the Education Department, not merely its day-to-day administration, resided with the Secretary. It is pertinent therefore to ask: What use did Lingen make of the authority he exercised, and in what ways did he influence the course of educational development? These questions can conveniently be considered in respect of two broad areas of activity: the relationships between, on the one hand, the Department and, on the other, those primarily involved in the work of the schools – the teachers, managers and inspectors; and the relationships between that same central authority for elementary education and

---

[1] During Lingen's rule, the office of Lord President was held by two dukes, two marquesses and four earls; and while nobility did not automatically disqualify a man for the work of superintending the education of the 'lower orders', neither did it render him particularly eligible for it.

[2] Quoted in the *Manchester Guardian*, 25 July 1905.

those agencies concerned with other constituent parts of the educational system.[1]

From all accounts Kay-Shuttleworth had, by the time of his retirement, established a cordial working partnership with the professional educators, their employers and advisers. It seems equally clear that during Lingen's tenure of office this friendly atmosphere changed gradually into one of coolness and ultimately into one of hostility – a transformation that cannot be ascribed simply to the fact that the growth in the amount and complexity of departmental business rendered the informal contacts of the earlier period more difficult to maintain.

There is little doubt that the crucial factor in this evaporation of mutual goodwill and confidence between the Department and those immediately responsible for the education of working-class children was the introduction of payment by results. While Lingen himself may not have initiated this development, it can be argued that he was indirectly to blame, in that he failed to put his own house in order before complaining to the Newcastle Commission about the administrative burden that was threatening to overwhelm his hard-pressed staff. As a contributor to one educational journal put it: 'For what the schools could not effect, teachers were held responsible; but the defects and anticipated failures of "the office" were not attributable to the workers but to the work given them to do.'[2]

Once the principle of payment by results had been approved, Lingen was given the task of implementing it. In his own revealing words, he drew up the Revised Code 'just as, if I had remained at my old profession, I might have drawn a man's will or his marriage settlement'. And when the new regulations came into force, Lingen found ample opportunity to utilize his legal training again (this time in the cause of economy), to such good effect that *The Saturday Review* was led to describe him as 'the ingenious Sphinx who propounds the recondite enigmas which he calls minutes, more inscrutable than cuneiform inscriptions, under which so many curious devices for hampering and annoying philanthropic educationists are concealed'.[3]

[1] For the Department's connexion, through the inspectorate, with other government departments having educational responsibilities, see below pp. 80–2; for its contacts with secondary schooling, see below p. 218n.l.

[2] 'Privy Council Administration', *The Educational Guardian*, 1 November 1862.

[3] *The Saturday Review*, vol. XLII, 5 April 1862.

More serious, however, than the irritations caused by the obscurity of the official language in which the regulations were couched was the exceptional exactitude with which they had to be observed. Many years before, Lingen must surely have been advised by his tutors that hard cases made bad law, and he was evidently determined, when discharging what he conceived to be his duty, not to be swayed by sentiment. One or two of the Secretary's rulings in the 'case law' that grew up around the administration of the new Code survive to illustrate the point.

In August 1863 an inspector wrote to Whitehall for advice.

Sir, A brief experience in examining schools under the Revised Code leads me already to ask guidance in the several cases noted below. 1. Children suffering from physical infirmity must be examined how? e.g. the Reading of one with impeded utterance, or writing with hand lamed by a whitlow? . . . 3. What course should the Inspector follow when the examination schedule has not been filled up before his arrival at the time fixed for the examination?

Lingen personally pronounced judgment:

1. As to reading, the inspector must satisfy himself that the child can itself understand what it reads. If the impediment does not permit this much to be ascertained, not to pass. As to writing, it must be performed within a sufficiently short time for practical use, and must be legible; if the impediment does not permit this much to be ascertained, not to pass. *In all cases where the infirmity is not self-evident* require a certificate signed by managers and teacher. 3. Proceed with the inspection of the school and report the fact to the Committee of Council. The managers will lose the grant for examination.[1]

In his autobiography, George Kekewich, the future Permanent Secretary to the Committee of Council, describes the Department's *modus operandi* when he entered it as an examiner in the spring of 1868. His book, so far as the closing years of his term of office are concerned, must be treated with caution, but, in view of the corroborative evidence available from various other sources, there is no reason to doubt the veracity of his sketch of the earlier period or to suppose that it is much exaggerated.

Under the Revised Code . . . deductions from the miserable grants were not only allowed, but freely imposed, with a severity that I suppose was considered by the official martinets of that day to be the best way to

[1] PRO Ed. 9/4. Secretary's Minute Book. Letter dated 15 August 1863. (Lingen's italics).

encourage the managers and teachers to do better. The heavier the fines we imposed, the greater credit we got from our superiors . . . I remember that once after I had suggested a deduction of two-tenths of the grant, Mr. Lingen, who happened to see the recommendation, sent for me and reproved me for not inflicting a larger fine. He then took his pen and wrote: 'My Lords have ordered a deduction to be made from the grant of five-tenths for faults of instruction, and have suspended the certificate of the teacher.' He added, addressing me: 'There; I think that will do for them!' I should think it probably did. That performance was typical of the Education Department towards the managers and teachers of schools in those days.[1]

In view of this kind of treatment, it is hardly surprising that the Department in general and Lingen in particular were feared and hated by the other elements in the educational 'partnership'. On the occasion of the inspectors' reports controversy, one influential journal complained:

If rumour does not much belie him, Mr Lingen is quite as powerful [as Mr Lowe] and a good deal more offensive. It is from Mr Lingen that all the sharp snubbing replies proceed, which have imprinted upon half the rural parishes of the country a deep conviction that the Education Department is their natural enemy, whom it is their first duty to elude, baffle and disprove to the utmost of their power.[2]

Specifically, Lingen was accused of a lack of any humanitarian feelings and of refusing to consult the professional educators before introducing measures which deeply affected them. Thus, on the first count, this 'prince of red tapists' was said to be 'animated by no popular sympathies, ignorant of, or sceptically disregarding the powerful sentiments by which communities are influenced, and moved only by considerations of official convenience and statistical uniformity . . .';[3] while, on the second, it was postulated that Lingen might have avoided all the 'inconveniences and annoyances' that stemmed from the application of the Revised Code 'if he had happened to have had practical acquaintance with Schools and Schoolmasters'. 'But', this exasperated correspondent continued,

he has sat for so long on his stool in Downing Street that I very much question if he has for very many years been inside any of those Schools for which he is legislating in so crude a fashion; and with infatuated

---

[1] G. W. Kekewich, *The Education Department and After*, 1920, pp. 10, 11.
[2] *The Saturday Review*, 16 April 1864.
[3] *The Educational Guardian*, 1 November 1862.

blindness he obstinately declines to accept the information which the more experienced and able Inspectors are longing to impart to him. If he had known more of the country, and less of the Department, he would have understood better how to have obtained increased efficiency at much less cost than he has done.[1]

What must have been so infuriating, at least for the teachers, was the knowledge that Lingen was setting double standards in the demands he made; there was, as it were, one law for the school staff and quite another for the Office personnel. For example, teachers might have felt justifiably aggrieved that, while they were forbidden to have private pupils, keep a night school, or have any other work besides that of the daily school, under penalty of forfeiting the advantage of having pupil teachers, apparently no objection was raised to the senior civil servants in the Department indulging in a variety of extra-mural activities. Pre-eminent among these officials was F. T. Palgrave, who during his examinership, compiled the celebrated *Golden Treasury*. At least four other examiners of the period, Sir Henry Craik, Walter Severn, A. J. Butler and W. J. Courthope, all produced important publications during their stay in Whitehall.

There were at least two other anomalies. Whereas Lingen rigorously insisted that examinations were appropriate, indeed essential, instruments for the purpose of assessing the efficiency of teachers, he successfully resisted their use as instruments for estimating the potential efficiency of the higher officials in the Department. While the other branches of the civil service were abandoning the practice of nomination in the appointment of candidates in favour of limited or open competition, the Education Office continued to recruit its examiners and inspectors through the exercise of patronage. As one authority has caustically observed: 'Being experts in examinations, the Education Department refused to adopt that fashion of recruitment for important grades, whatever the rest of the Civil Service did.'[2]

But the most glaring discrepancy concerned pay and produc-

---

[1] 'A letter on the Administration of the Parliamentary grant for the promotion of education in Great Britain addressed to a member of the House of Commons by a school manager in the North.' *Education Miscellanies*, vol. 10, Archives of the Department of Education and Science.

[2] J. Craig, *A History of Red Tape*, 1955, p. 156. For an explanation of this paradox, see Lingen's testimony before the Select Committee on Civil Service Appointments, 1860, qq. 3145, 3149-51.

tivity. Teachers were paid, under regulations laid down by the Secretary, strictly according to the results they achieved. If one eye-witness is to be believed, it could hardly be said that Lingen in turn applied that same principle of remuneration to those subordinates for whose 'output' he was himself personally responsible. Long afterwards, Kekewich recalled the routine followed by his colleagues when he joined the Department. Those examiners whose duty it was to scrutinize inspectors' reports were

aggregated in one room (a very pleasant arrangement for social intercourse), and they guarded against over-work by settling for themselves the number of school reports that they could be expected to deal with in a day . . . At the time when I first entered the Office the number of [these] reports . . . which the Examiners agreed to regard as a day's work was, I think, eight. When the schools to be dealt with were small, these might represent an hour or an hour and a half's work, and unless they were exceptionally large, eight reports were not exactly backbreaking, as they could usually be got through on an average in three hours or less, without any undue pressure on the brain . . . I remember that once, when there was a considerable arrear, I despatched seventy of these 'cases' (as they were called) in a day, a fact which may perhaps be taken to indicate the measure of the severity of the ordinary day's work. When any of us had completed the tale of reports he had allotted to himself, he betook himself to other pursuits, with the happy consciousness that he had done his duty. Under these circumstances, as might be imagined, we had plenty of leisure, and we came late and left early . . . The hour for attendance was eleven o'clock, but it was not often that any of us put in an appearance before half-past eleven or twelve; and we were supposed to leave at five, but most of us usually disappeared long before that hour. Included in the day's attendance was, of course, the necessary period for reading the *Times* . . . In fact, we attended practically as much or as little as we liked . . . sometimes . . . a full holiday was taken on French leave without discovery.[1]

Kekewich also described the examiners' methods of dealing with correspondence:

there was at no time any hurry about answering letters. If a man had the temerity to write to the Office, we felt that he ought to take his chance of an answer, and the greater the difficulty he was in, . . . the less likely he was to get it. Besides which, we considered that an early reply would be an inducement to him to continue the correspondence – a result which was naturally regarded by us as undesirable.[2]

[1] Kekewich, *Education Department*, pp. 14–16.   [2] *Ibid.* pp. 21–2.

And the examiners' superiors apparently provided no better example:

In the rooms of the assistant Secretaries and Secretary . . . might be seen many piles of papers strapped together, waiting for some sudden access of energy on the part of the official responsible for their despatch . . .[1]

Doubtless all the higher administrative staff were thankful that they were not, so far as their salaries were concerned, subject to the Draconian Laws that *they* imposed upon teachers. Doubtless, too, it was this general failure to practise what he preached that made Lingen, and the Department he led, so intensely disliked by the people to whom he dispensed rough justice.

If to what has been briefly mentioned here about Lingen's relationships with the schools, are added his attitude towards inspectors[2] and his isolationist policy towards other elements[3] that comprised what, for want of a more appropriate term, must be called the country's educational system, then his influence as Secretary was profound, and demonstrably injurious. *How* he came to exert that influence has already been indicated; *why* he chose to exercise it in the manner that he did remains to be considered. Part of the explanation, no doubt, lay in his occupation and training. As a bureaucrat he abhorred administrative untidiness and resisted outside interference; as a lawyer he wished to see the management of elementary education based upon a few clear principles, governed by 'case law', and controlled by precedent.

But the causes went deeper than this, and ultimately derived from what Lingen's concept of the purpose of the Education Department was, and how he regarded his own function within it. Where Kay-Shuttleworth had seen his role as being essentially creative and dynamic, his successor took a negative and narrow view. Kay-Shuttleworth, in the absence of definite political direction, believed his responsibility to be the promotion and extension of education; Lingen, in contrast, felt bound to act within the letter of the law – or rather the Order in Council which had created the Committee of Council and which had confined its powers merely to the superintendence of the application of all grants made by Parliament for the education of the poor.

Translated into practical terms, this meant that, at first, Lingen's

---

[1] *Ibid.* p. 22.   [2] See below pp. 83–4.   [3] See below p. 218n.1.

aim was to 'hold the ring' between rival contestants for educational grants. Later, however, he came to see himself as the custodian of the public funds and as the arbiter of precisely how those funds should be distributed.

Mr Lowe highly prized Lingen's power of saying 'No', with an emphasis and determination which repelled the most obstinate and most ingenious of petitioners . . . It was often alleged against him that he was too apt to insist on tying up administrative business in the bonds of red tape. Rightly or wrongly, he was very ready to insist on technicalities as a defence against what he considered to be improper inroads upon the public resources in the interests of sections or individuals.[1]

And, in a biographical sketch, one acquaintance declared that Lingen's 'strength lay perhaps not so much in his capacity to make changes as in his ability to negative claims upon the public purse'.[2]

But administrative and fiscal considerations were not the only factors that determined Lingen's attitude towards the elementary educational system he superintended. Unlike some of his contemporaries – politicians such as Brougham, Roebuck, Wyse and Russell, or public servants Kay-Shuttleworth and Matthew Arnold – he did not regard the education of the poorer classes as a challenge, a noble cause or a moral imperative. He thought of it more in terms of the correctly-balanced ledger, the neatly-filled form and the inerrant rule-book. He reduced it to a mere commercial undertaking, conducted in accordance with closely-prescribed legalistic formulae. In the words of one writer: 'The Committee of Council became the Board of Directors for the Education Department, Ltd., Manager, R. Lingen, Esq., paying on a commission basis, with a standardized system of bookkeeping in all its branches, producing a very limited type of product and quite without a Sales Promotion Department.'[3] Moreover, to Lingen, as he himself admitted before the 1865 Select Committee, the whole business was somewhat tedious. His barely concealed disdain for the work he was expected to perform met with a sharp rebuke from the chairman: 'The duties which you call "drudgery" . . . consist in superintending the education of England . . .'

[1] *The Times*, 24 July 1905.
[2] *Dictionary of National Biography*, article on Lingen.
[3] W. F. Connell, *The Educational Thought and Influence of Matthew Arnold*, 1950, p. 241.

In a sense, Lingen was the victim of his own upbringing, for he had no experience of failure and he knew virtually nothing of the more tangible aspects of social distress – poverty, hunger, disease, ignorance and squalor. Fundamentally, he was not interested in the education of the lower orders, or rather he was concerned lest there might be too much of it. He believed that the teachers might legitimately pass on to the rising generation of workers a safe minimum of rudimentary facts and skills appropriate to their station in life; but that done, the schools' function was discharged. This much is clear from his evidence given in 1887 to the Cross Commission. Asked whether he thought that 'the standard and idea of what should be included in elementary education was pitched a little too high' at that time, he replied in the affirmative; and later he declared that, if he had his way, he would sweep out of the Elementary Code all that variety of subjects which had been added to the curriculum since the introduction of the Revised Code a quarter of a century before.

It would, however, be wrong to suggest that Lingen's influence was wholly malign. During his Secretaryship he became deeply disturbed over what he called the 'fragmentation' of education among the various religious bodies responsible for its provision. The schools, he felt, were much less educational than denominational institutions, and he grew convinced that there was only one solution to this problem, '*viz.*, to separate secular and religious instruction and in effect to take the former out of the hands of the congregations, making it a purely civil matter'.[1] There is little doubt that when the time came in 1861 to revise the education code, Lingen saw it as a golden opportunity to impose this solution, for he must have realized that, by attaching the grant only to the three Rs, the existing emphasis on religious teaching must be undermined. The Rev. Francis Close, a prominent Evangelical, suspected as much. He asked Kay-Shuttleworth 'How far is your friend Lingen at the bottom of this? He is a secularist . . .' And earlier Lingen had shown his determination to rid the denominational system of what many considered to be one of its less defensible features – the petty proselytizing of pupils against the wishes of their parents. In the Minutes of 1853 the Committee of Council insisted that the trust deeds of schools aided by public

[1] PRO Ed. 24/53. Memorandum on the Representation of the Education Department in the House of Commons. 6 June 1855.

funds must include a clause which would enable parents to obtain for their children complete exemption from all religious instruction. For the insertion of this proviso Lingen seems to have been largely responsible.[1] Finally, it is fair to add that, at least during his late twenties and early thirties, Lingen took an active interest in the movement for university reform, and that, when the Schools Inquiry Commissioners were investigating secondary educational provision, he lent his support to the campaign for devoting some of the nation's charitable endowments to the education of girls.

Nevertheless, on balance, Lingen's contribution to the growth of English education can hardly be described as beneficial, although it was unquestionably significant and far-reaching in its effects. His secretaryship makes one regret the more the early retirement of his predecessor, whose passionate concern, human warmth and breadth of vision he so signally lacked. While it would be unjust to call Lingen a failure – in certain respects he succeeded only too well – he was something of a tragedy.

In the space of less than a generation the Department had changed considerably, and arguably for the worse. Its political control resided ambiguously in two ministers whose respective spheres of influence were ill-defined, who stood in an uncertain relationship with the Committee of Council which had originally exercised the sole responsibility, and whose functions ranged far outside the management of the education grants. The administration of the latter was conducted by officials who, by all accounts, knew little and cared less about the education of the poorer classes and who, on the admission of one of their number, treated elementary schools with contempt.[2] And over them presided a man who had alienated the managers and ignored the inspectors, had reduced the teachers to the level of ciphers in a vast exercise in accountancy, had come to regard children as so many grant-earning units, and had won for the Department he personified an unenviable reputation for arrogance, meanness and inefficiency. It was upon a Department such as this that fell the task of grappling with the immense problems created by the Education Act of 1870.

---

[1] See, for example, H. J. Burgess, *Enterprise in Education*, 1958, ch. 11; *The National Society's Monthly Paper*, January 1870, No. cclxxviii; and *The Times*, 24 July 1905.

[2] Kekewich, *Education Department*, p. 11.

HM INSPECTORATE

During the period 1849–69 four major developments affecting the character and role of the inspectorate took place. The first was an effort to use it as a means of introducing some unity of purpose, if not control, among certain of the numerous agencies making educational provision, followed by a reversal of that tendency due to the administrative difficulties it entailed. The second was a deliberate attempt both to constrict the independence of the inspectorate and to prevent it from influencing educational policy. The third was a sudden change in the function of the inspectorate from being an advisory and supervisory body to one mainly concerned with examining children and hence assessing teachers. The fourth was a move to obtain inspection on the cheap without, as it were, debasing the coinage.

These trends, however, did not emerge until some time after Kay-Shuttleworth's departure. At first such changes as took place were due simply to an increase in demand necessitating a corresponding increase in supply. Thus, the steady growth in the number of schools and in the volume of work resulting from the inauguration of the pupil-teacher system involved, in 1850, a substantial enlargement of the inspectorate. By that date the cost of inspection had begun to alarm the Treasury, and so the Committee of Council adopted the expedient of appointing assistant inspectors at half the normal salary. They were co-ordinate, as distinct from subordinate, inspectors whose duties were to assist HMIs in the various districts. Additional appointments to both grades became necessary when, in 1851, evening and ragged schools were permitted to apply for aid, and in 1853 when capitation grants were introduced. By the latter date the inspectorate, excluding HMIs responsible for Scottish schools, was thirty strong.

That same year saw an inquiry into the inspectorate by the Treasury Committee which had been carrying out an investigation of the Privy Council Office as a whole. Its members paid particular attention less to the *quantity* of HM Inspectors than to their *quality*. They made two firm recommendations: first, that 'no one . . . unless a graduate high in honours at one of the Universities, should be selected without passing an examination, which should be of a searching character'; secondly, that as 'a full trial of the fitness of the Inspectors for their duties is so important, . . . the term of probation should in their case extend over the first three years'. Reading between the lines, one may detect an implied criticism of the methods of selecting and training hitherto employed. While accepting the fact that appointment to the inspectorate, as also to the class of examiners, formed part of the Lord President's patronage, the committee of inquiry was yet concerned lest the right of nomination should be abused. Almost certainly it was aware that several inspectors owed their positions to having influence in high places. Nor could the committee have been happy at the thought that the only induction most newly-appointed inspectors received was one designed to enable them to complete the necessary official forms.

Yet, in spite of (the defenders of patronage and amateurism would say 'because of') their exemption from any qualifying examination, and their lack of both relevant teaching experience and adequate training, all the evidence suggests that the inspectors of this early period performed their twin roles of missionaries and watchdogs with considerable energy, skill and understanding. These qualities were to be severely tested in the years to come.

Providing the first challenge was the gradual widening of their duties until these embraced the inspection of numerous groups of educational establishments in addition to the elementary schools with which they were originally and mainly concerned. It was a challenge that the inspectors met, but one to which the officials in Whitehall proved sadly unequal.

On an earlier page[1] mention was made of the inclusion in the inspectorate of a number of Poor Law Inspectors. Their presence requires a brief explanation. One of the duties of the Commissioners appointed under the Poor Law Amendment Act of 1834 was to ensure that the Boards of Guardians provided some kind of education for pauper children in workhouses. In consequence, the Commissioners became supporters, and thereby inspectors, of district schools, purpose-built institutions for such children from several Poor Law Unions. Doubtless owing to Kay-Shuttleworth's influence, the Committee of Council began in 1842 to grant-aid two of these schools which therefore became liable to inspection by HMIs. At first the Committee was prepared to allow this inspection to be conducted by officials responsible to another central department, the Home Office; but this arrangement proved

[1] See above, p. 36.

doubly unsatisfactory, since it entailed a kind of dual control and since the Poor Law Inspectors were required to inspect the whole workhouse establishment, not merely the educational component. To remedy this situation, the government in 1846 decided to place district schools under the supervision of the Education Department, which in turn appointed four inspectors with authority to examine the condition of the schools and to ascertain the character and qualifications of the teachers therein.

During the same period the Committee of Council likewise assumed responsibility for the inspection of industrial and reformatory schools; and then, in 1856, as has been noted previously, an Order in Council was issued recommending that the Education Department should thenceforth inspect regimental and naval schools also.

All these promising developments were regrettably short-lived. One, in fact, was still-born, in that the War Office declined the Department's offer to inspect army schools. The Admiralty, however, agreed to transfer its control of inspection to the Committee of Council, though not for long, for even as it did so the tide was beginning to flow against this kind of experiment. As early as 1857 the Department, having found that 'a two-fold inspection, and a two-fold administration of public money, by separate departments of State'[1] was difficult to operate, relinquished its share of responsibility for industrial schools. It continued for a short while to inspect the remaining three categories of schools, but 'it became evident, as experience accumulated, that the educational business of each Department was an integral part of its functions, and could not, without conflicting or superfluous administration, be shared with any other Department'.[2] Accordingly, between 1860 and 1864, the inspection of first the reformatory, then the workhouse and finally the naval schools was transferred to the Home Office, the Poor Law Board and the Admiralty respectively. An unspecified official commented on these developments: 'Of the administrative soundness of this result, no one acquainted with the practical working of the contrary system can doubt'.[3] The tone of self-justification suggests that not everyone was convinced of its *educational* soundness. It is at least

---

[1] *Report of the Committee of Council on Education*, 1858–59, p. xxxvi.
[2] PRO Ed. 24/55. Memorandum dated 18 November 1867.
[3] *Ibid.*

arguable that the separation had unfortunate consequences. As one writer has said:

It seems a pity that this [Poor Law] Inspectorate did not survive; had it done so, the Education Department would probably have extended its supervision to all special types of schools as they appeared; and the twentieth century might have escaped some of the anomalies of a situation in which a whole group of schools are under the control, not of the Ministry of Education, but of the Home Office.[1]

At all events, the episode clearly illustrates the Education Department's inclination, during Lingen's reign, when confronted by a choice between alternative courses of action, to favour what was administratively convenient rather than what was educationally desirable.

Alongside this reduction in commitments went a tightening of discipline. When Adderley became Vice-President in 1858 he learned that the inspectors were continuing to meet annually in London to discuss educational matters. The custom had originated with Kay-Shuttleworth in 1846, and both he and Lord Lansdowne had set great store by these meetings as affording an opportunity for discussing common problems. Gradually, perhaps inevitably, the inspectors came to use them as a forum for expressing opinions on departmental policy, and by the mid-fifties it had become the practice to put controversial issues to the vote, even if this involved passing collective judgment on executive and administrative decisions. Both Adderley and Granville, the Lord President, deprecated this procedure on the ground that inspectors, as civil servants, ought not to arrogate to themselves the right, as a body, to criticize official policy; and the Vice-President forbade the practice. Lowe, in 1859, took the matter a stage further and stopped the annual conferences altogether. They were not resumed, even in a modified form, for over twenty years, and consequently the very men whose duty it was to have an intimate knowledge of educational practice were prevented from offering a collective view as to its defects or how they might be rectified.

This was not all. In 1858 Lowe and Lingen discontinued the unabridged publication of inspectors' reports, deciding instead simply to quote selected passages from them. In many cases this censorship was thoroughly justified as some inspectors were inject-

---

[1] N. Ball, *Her Majesty's Inspectorate 1839–1849*, 1963, p. 195.

ing religious propaganda into their reports, but it laid the Department open to the charge that it was tampering with the latter in order to show itself in the most favourable light. The whole question was brought into the open in 1864 when Lowe was accused of mutilating the reports by expunging from them all adverse references to the views which the Revised Code embodied.

At the subsequent inquiry Lowe was exonerated from all blame. The select committee, in a carefully worded Report, came to the conclusion that 'the supervision exercised in objecting to the insertion of irrelevant matter, or mere dissertation, and of controversial argument, is consistent with the powers of the Committee of Council, and has, on the whole, been exercised fairly, and without excessive strictness'.[1] On the other hand, it felt bound to add that

the knowledge, or even a reasonable suspicion, that the Inspectors' reports are subject to alteration, either directly or indirectly, at the instance of the Department, has, without doubt, a tendency to lower their value, if they are to be regarded as independent sources of testimony in matters of opinion or controversy touching the educational views or policy of the Committee of Council.[2]

At the same time the select committee reached the verdict that inspectors could not be permitted to enjoy unfettered freedom to state their views so long as they remained servants of the Department to which they were by loyalty bound. The Report ended:

Whatever may have been the understanding under which the appointment of Inspectors was originally sanctioned, Parliament cannot be presumed to be ignorant (since the year 1858 at latest), that the heads of the office have exercised a censorship over the Inspectors' reports as to the insertion of argumentative or irrelevant matter; and your Committee are of opinion that some such power is essential to the effectual working of the Department so long as it retains its present constitution and functions.[3]

The effect of this Report was to identify HMIs more clearly as civil servants owing the allegiance appropriate to that calling.

It was one thing, however, for the Education Office to require that inspectors abide by departmental decisions once they had been made, and quite another to refuse to consult those inspectors over the formulation of policy. Yet the testimony taken before the select committee of 1865 suggests this was indeed the case. All

---

[1] *PP* 1864, IX, 17.   [2] *Ibid.*   [3] *Ibid.* 18.

the inspectors examined stated that their advice had not been sought on any major questions. HMI Tufnell declared that most of the experienced inspectors had complained to him that they had never been consulted on the most important measures of the Privy Council Office. The result was that all significant changes were made simply upon the theoretical knowledge of the officials in Downing Street, none of whom had had any inspectorial experience. Proof of this could be found in the nature of the measures they introduced. Tufnell thought that the effect of giving up the practice of conferring with inspectors had been to throw an enormous amount of power into the hands of the secretariat, especially as the political chiefs were themselves without any appropriate firsthand knowledge.

The select committee must have found difficulty in believing that the Department would deliberately insulate itself from expert advice in this way. The chairman asked the Rev. William Kennedy, who had been an HMI for seventeen years: 'During that interval [five or six years] since they [the annual conferences] ceased, are the Committee to understand that you, although one of the most experienced inspectors, have never been consulted by the heads of the department?' Answer: 'During that period I have never been consulted.' Kennedy added that if the Department had kept in closer sympathy with managers and inspectors, it could easily have become the most popular instead of the most hated of state departments. Thus the Office, in addition to ridding itself of the collective counsel of its inspectors, chose to disregard their individual wisdom as well.

It also succeeded in transferring some of the odium it had incurred in recent years, to the inspectorate, for as a result of the Revised Code, the inspector ceased, for the most part, to be a constructive adviser, becoming instead 'the harsh dispenser of an all too meagre government grant whose size he determined'.[1]

Another by-product of the Revised Code was the abolition of the grade of assistant inspector. The twenty-four members of that rank became full HMIs, so making possible a sub-division of the large districts in which they had been employed, the intention being to operate the Code without adding to the size, and therefore the cost, of the inspectorate. But it was soon apparent that HMIs, with thousands of scripts to mark, would require help of some

[1] E. L. Edmonds, *The School Inspector*, 1962, p. 81.

kind. In 1863, therefore, the Committee of Council instituted a class of inspectors' assistants. Stringent rules as to their qualifications and the nature of their appointment were laid down. An inspectors' assistant had to be a successful elementary school headmaster, recommended by an inspector and approved by the Department. In addition to other requirements he had to pass a civil service examination. His duty was to assist the HMI in the mass of routine work which accompanied the annual examination, but he was not himself allowed to examine except in the presence of, or by a written order from, an inspector. Indeed, the inspectors' assistant was left in no doubt as to his lowly status, for, quite apart from his receiving a considerably smaller salary than his senior officer, he was informed: 'It is only by your thoroughly comprehending the limited and subsidiary character of the assistant's duty that you will repel the imputation of setting a young man to judge his elders, and often his superiors, in the art of school-keeping'.[1]

It could hardly be said, then, that the teachers had won more than a minor concession in the campaign they were prosecuting to persuade the Department to appoint inspectors from among their ranks. Perhaps little more could have been expected at this stage considering the uncompromising stand taken on this issue by the Newcastle Commissioners. Schoolmasters they declared, were unfit for the office of inspectors who should be equipped, by previous training and social position, to communicate and associate upon terms of equality with the managers of schools and the clergy of different denominations.[2]

Actually, the Commissioners appeared to be much more concerned about the social standing of inspectors than with their professional suitability, and the discovery that there was, in Lingen's words, 'no actual preparation before-hand which is prescribed for these gentlemen' (i.e. the Assistant Inspectors), did not appear unduly to have disturbed them. But it was this very point – that men with no, or hardly any, practical understanding of elementary school work were appointed to the inspectorate – which led to

---

[1] *Minute of the Committee of Council* dated 19 May 1863.

[2] The Commissioners also rejected the proposal that women be appointed, although this refusal was scarcely surprising in view both of the extremely limited degree of female emancipation in society at large, and of the hazards to which an unaccompanied woman travelling in lonely or insalubrious districts might be exposed.

increasing friction between HMIs and the teachers whose performance they assessed and whose salaries they determined. Since
teachers themselves were expected to be trained for their vocation,
their resentment was excusable. They could with some justice
claim that, on grounds of equity, if not common-sense, those who
sat in judgment over them should be at least similarly qualified.
It could, perhaps, be argued in mitigation of an otherwise in-
defensible state of affairs that most of the inspectors were at least
men of high intellectual calibre from cultured backgrounds. As one
educational historian commented: 'The fact that they were so has
been the salvation of the situation, otherwise it would indeed have
been a case of the blind leading the blind. Actually it was a case
of blundering intelligence leading blundering ignorance.'[1]

The Newcastle Commissioners had observations to make also
on the denominational character of the inspectorate, which they
stigmatized as wasteful and inconvenient. For, as a result of the
successive Concordats, there were three distinct sets of inspectors,
and this entailed a threefold division of the country into districts.
They would have liked to recommend the adoption of a local instead
of a denominational distribution of inspectors, but they felt unable
to do so because they were convinced that the managers of the
great majority of schools would object to being placed under an
inspector of a different communion from their own.

Accepting this advice that no immediate change could be contemplated in the organization of the inspectorate, the Committee
of Council continued to abide by the agreements previously made
with the different religious groups. But towards the end of the
decade it became increasingly restive about the administrative
difficulties involved. Its Report for the year 1869 was outspoken
in its criticism.

It is unnecessary to dwell at any length on the extravagance of a system
of inspection under which three, or in Scotland four, different inspectors
may have to waste their time and energy in travelling to some out-of-the-
way district for the purpose of reporting on a scanty attendance of
children in each of a few denominational schools.

These schools, it was suggested, could in all probability be easily
visited by a single inspector at a cost of a third of the time, labour
and expense required by the existing arrangement. Additional

---

[1] H. Holman, *English National Education*, 1898, p. 137.

benefits would flow from such a modification; it would produce 'greater uniformity in the standard of examination applied to the various schools in each district' and it would probably 'lead to a general improvement in education throughout the country, from the concentration of the efforts of the promoters and managers of schools in individual localities, which might be expected to ensue if they were brought under the guiding influence of a single mind'. And it would certainly furnish the Committee with more definite and connected information than was then obtainable respecting the educational work and requirements of each district.

Although appearances might indicate that the Department was pleading a case, in truth it was justifying a decision already taken; for, at the time the Report was written, Parliament had under consideration the Elementary Education Bill, which contained proposals for ending denominational inspection. Now while this particular reform did shortly ensue, the wider hopes expressed in the Report remained unfulfilled. One obstacle to the reorganization of the inspectorate to meet changing conditions was about to be eliminated; but until such time as its structure had been improved, its functions radically re-defined, and questions concerning the qualifications, experience and training of its members satisfactorily settled, there could be no substantial progress made towards the formation of what was becoming increasingly necessary: a co-ordinated body of expert educational advisers which would also be acceptable to the teaching profession.

5

THE EDUCATION DEPARTMENT:
THE YEARS OF EXPANSION, 1870–85

No serious educator could have invented the present system so fatal to
instruction and to inspection.

                    – Witness before the Cross Commission.

The five years between 1865 and 1870 were of crucial importance
to the future of English education in general and of the Education
Department in particular. It was apparent to many perceptive
observers that far-reaching changes in the elementary educational
system were imperative as a condition of national survival. Judged
simply in terms of its own limited objective – that of providing
working-class children with rudimentary skills and knowledge –
that system was failing lamentably. Voluntary effort, even if
supported by state aid, could not meet the needs of the rapidly
growing industrial areas; while the Revised Code was, in some
ways, hampering rather than assisting that effort. Indications
that the problem was earnestly engaging Parliament's attention
may be found in the attempts at legislation made in 1867 and 1868.
These endeavours came to grief on the rocks of sectarian rivalry, a
rivalry that might have impeded progress indefinitely but for the
advent of certain external pressures which undermined traditional
attitudes. Abroad, the triumph of the well-schooled Prussian
soldiers over the Austrians, and the victory of the better educated
Federal troops over the Confederates, suggested there was a causal
connexion between military superiority and educational efficiency.
In the commercial sphere, manufacturers, alert to the challenge
of foreign competition, looked to education to raise industrial
productivity and the standards of British workmanship. At home,
the incentive to act came with the widening of the franchise in
1867. It was not merely that with the extension of the suffrage to
the urban working man went the corollary that he must be educated
for his new responsibilities. The Reform Act, as Dover Wilson
has pointed out, had wider implications than this. It meant that,
for the first time since the Commonwealth, the balance of political

power tilted in favour of nonconformity. As a result, not only did 'the masses' begin to lose their dislike of state action as a form of upper class paternalism, but the Dissenters no longer needed to regard state education as being predominantly Anglican.[1] Indeed, even the extreme Voluntaryists, who had opposed every extension of government assistance to education, were by then acknowledging defeat in the struggle to provide schools from their own resources. Significantly, their most influential campaigner, Edward Baines, informed his followers in 1867 that their cause had run its course and that his 'revised judgment' now obliged him to support state education. Furthermore, the general election of 1868 returned the Liberals to power with a strong working majority and a mandate for reform. In no state department was the government's intention to carry out that mandate made more plain than in the Education Office, where the Radical, W. E. Forster, was given the post of Vice-President.

Soon after his appointment, Forster indicated the direction in which his mind was working. In a speech to a national conference on education at Manchester early in 1869, he declared his government's determination 'not to destroy anything in the existing system which was good, if they could avoid it'. He wanted 'to establish a system that would embrace the whole of the country, and leave no child without a chance of education, whilst at the same time making the best of the existing machinery'.

This declaration of intent was made explicit in Forster's introductory statement to the Commons in February 1870 on the occasion of the first reading of his Elementary Education Bill. He proposed 'to complete the present voluntary system, to fill up the gaps, sparing the public money where it can be done without, procuring as much as we can the assistance of the parents, and welcoming as much as we rightly can the co-operation and aid of those benevolent men who desire to assist their neighbours'.

In the course of his address Forster revealed the dimensions of the gaps he meant to fill.

We have about 1,500,000 children more or less imperfectly educated in the schools that we help; that is, they are simply on the register. Of the children of the working classes only two-fifths between the ages of six and ten years are on the registers of the Government schools, and only one-third of those between the ages of ten and twelve.

[1] J. Dover Wilson (ed.), *The Schools of England*, 1928, p. 23.

Moreover, only half the parishes in England and Wales contained schools earning Privy Council grants.[1]

To ascertain more precisely the location and degree of the deficiency that had been revealed in various surveys, the government proposed that the country should be divided into 'school districts'. The Education Department would be empowered to investigate the educational provision in each district and to determine whether that provision conformed to certain prescribed standards. If it failed to do so, the voluntary agencies would be allowed a period of grace, until the end of the year 1870, in which to supply the deficiency. If they were unable or unwilling so to act, a new local authority, the school board, would be set up for this purpose; it would be given powers to levy rates, build and maintain schools, provide teachers and, if necessary, enforce the attendance of children.

After thirty nights of vigorous debate, in which various aspects of the religious problem loomed large, the Bill as amended passed the Commons on 9 August 1870. Once it became law it changed the whole relation of the state to education. Hitherto, the business of the Education Department had been mainly concerned with administering the annual grant in aid of voluntary effort. Henceforth, the Department was to be an executive body, with powers to secure the provision of efficient elementary schools throughout the country.

Strangely enough, although the qualifying adjective 'elementary' was included in the title of the Act, no attempt was made in the statute to define the meaning or scope of the term (perhaps because it was considered to be self-evident), nor did Parliament or the Courts subsequently provide any authoritative explanation of what was meant by it. The vagueness proved something of a blessing for it subsequently enabled the Department to encourage comparatively advanced studies in elementary schools. On the other hand, the mere inclusion of the word in the Act set the seal of statutory approval on the notion that 'elementary' education differed from 'secondary' education in kind as well as in degree.[2]

---

[1] One writer has recently suggested that Forster's inspectors and official advisers may have deliberately falsified the figures they produced 'because they had a vested interest in the expansion of their own department'. E. G. West, *Education and the State*, 1965, p. 145.

[2] Forster's earlier attempt at legislation had, in fact, been titled 'The Education of the Poor Bill'.

Curiously, too, the interpretation of the measure, and of the grant regulations which constituted an important element in its operation, was, owing to a late amendment, entrusted to auditors primarily responsible to another government department.

At all events, the legislation necessarily involved the Department in much extra work. Requests from voluntary bodies for building grants had to be dealt with, applications for the establishment of school boards considered, regulations for school board elections drawn up, school board by-laws approved, and arrangements for the transfer of voluntary schools to school board management settled.

In order to cope with this additional business, the complement of examiners was doubled, and six of the original ten were raised to the new rank of senior examiner. At the same time, two more assistant secretaries were appointed, making four in all. Forster's choice of his private secretary, Patrick Cumin, to fill one of these posts occasioned some resentment among the higher staff who thought that one of their number should have been promoted, certainly not a newcomer. However, the Vice-President had good reasons for his choice. He needed an assistant secretary to handle legal matters arising out of the 1870 Act, and as Cumin was a lawyer and had reputedly drafted some of its more important provisions, the latter's preferment was eminently sensible.

Foremost among the urgent tasks confronting the officials was that of finding out how much school accommodation, if any, was required in every school district. To ascertain this, the Department was ordered to call for returns concerning the state of education in each locality, and it was empowered to appoint sundry Inspectors of Returns, whose statutory duty would be 'to inquire into the accuracy and completeness of any one or more returns . . . and into the efficiency and suitability of any school mentioned in any such return, or which ought to have been mentioned therein, and to inspect the scholars in every such school'. The Inspectors of Returns were to submit their findings to the Department which would then make its decision regarding each district.

Since these investigations entailed a considerable amount of legal business – a semi-judicial discretion had to be exercised on, for example, the question as to whether the injunctions of the Act were being fulfilled – the Department generally chose as its Inspectors of Returns barristers-at-law. They were, however, to be 'supervised' by HM Inspectors, and as their services would not be required once all the returns had been scrutinized, their appointments were to be of a temporary nature. As it happened, of the sixty-three recruited, several were later selected to be examiners and a number eventually became HMIs.

The method of their recruitment is reminiscent of that employed for inspectors' assistants. Normal civil service examination requirements were dispensed with, each HMI being asked to submit the names of three men possessing certain academic qualifications, from whom the departmental chiefs would select one. Into this category of successful nominees came a young lawyer who was later to recall the circumstances of his appointment.

About Easter [1871] there came a letter to my father from our old friend . . . H. Sandford, who was a cousin of Sir Francis Sandford, Secretary of the Education Department, and had become a Senior Inspector. He premised that certain officers were to be appointed to make enquiries under the new Education Act – men who had graduated with honours at Oxford or Cambridge – and that the nomination of these was in the hands of the District Inspectors. He went on to enquire whether my father had a son with the necessary qualifications. Now at that time, I was a briefless barrister of something less than two years' standing.[1]

Mention of Sandford draws attention to another event of 1870. Early that year, Ralph Lingen, who for over two decades had ruled the Education Department, at long last relinquished his position as Permanent Secretary. On balance, his tenure of office had not been a happy one for those dedicated to the educational cause, and there can be little doubt that his departure was unmourned by teachers, managers and inspectors alike. He was a man of high intellect, possessed of pronounced financial acumen, considerable administrative ability and an educational philosophy of sorts; he was, nevertheless, a man unsuited by training and by temperament to the task of guiding the educational fortunes of the country during those crucial twenty years. As a lawyer he brought an impassive and inflexible mind to bear on the problems of education; as a civil servant he was inclined to view those problems in administrative rather than in human terms. The education of the people was far more a cross to be borne, far less a crusade to be

[1] Sneyd-Kynnersley, *HMI. Some passages*, pp. 2–3.

fought. In the words of one commentator, 'He was resolutely determined that the expenditure of public money should be severely checked, and his temptation was to look with a suspicious and grudging eye upon every claim involving an increase of outlay . . .'[1] It was, indeed, his reputation as a strict economist and a watchful guardian of the taxpayers' money that brought him to Gladstone's notice when the Prime Minister was seeking to fill the vacancy caused by the retirement in 1869 of the Permanent Secretary to the Treasury. At the close of that year the position was offered to and accepted by Lingen. Thus, by an ironic twist of fate – or rather by virtue of his proved capacity to control expenditure – Lingen, although no longer directly responsible for educational policy, continued for another fifteen years to influence its development; for it was at just about this time that the Treasury began more forcefully to exercise its right to determine what the various departments of state might spend and in particular to control their staffing.

In his place, Francis Sandford, who had previously been first an examiner, then an assistant secretary, was appointed. It seems, in some respects, a curious choice. During the following fourteen years, he assumed responsibility for the administration of the statute which both increased the power of the state over, and lessened the hold of the voluntary agencies upon, national education. Yet he strongly disapproved of the extension of state control and he devoted his years of retirement to campaigning in support of denominational schooling. Impartial as civil servants are reputed to be in the discharge of their duties, it is hard to believe that he carried out his responsibilities as Permanent Secretary with any great conviction or enthusiasm.

1870 was, in more ways than one, an *annus mirabilis* so far as the Education Department was concerned. In July, when the fate of the Bill hung in the balance, there was a government reshuffle and Gladstone invited Forster to join the Cabinet. His promotion was as much a recognition of the growing importance of education in national affairs as it was a tribute to the Vice-President's personal qualities as a statesman.[2]

Forster swiftly proved to be a master of the 'trade' to which he

[1] *The Times*, 24 July 1905.
[2] The earliest instance of a Vice-President enjoying Cabinet rank from the moment of appointment was that of Edward Stanhope in 1885.

had been assigned; he had, in addition, to be a jack of several others. His biographer writes:

For some inscrutable reason he [the Vice-President] is also the minister who has to look after the health of the cattle of the country; and accordingly, during [the] year 1869, when his mind was so fully occupied with the great question of the nation's schooling, Forster had to spend no little portion of his time in coping with an outbreak of cattle-disease, and in passing a measure designed to stamp out a threatened plague.

To Forster himself, the explanation for his having to deal with questions relating to quarantine and the like was simple rather than obscure. 'Somebody had to deal with them, and it was thought ... that he [the Vice-President] might as well have them as anybody else.'

That minister was relieved of some of his multitudinous duties in 1871 when a newly established department, the Local Government Board, took over the supervision of local authorities in sanitary matters. This was just as well since that year was an exceptionally heavy one as far as Forster was concerned. Over and above the work involved in the implementation of the 1870 Act and the 1869 Endowed Schools Act (q.v.), there was, first, a Scottish Education Bill to be conducted through Parliament providing for the creation of an independent department of the Education Office for the management of Scottish business; secondly, another occurrence of foot-and-mouth disease calling for legislative and administrative action; and finally, the Ballot Bill which the Vice-President was deputed to pilot through the Commons. Forster's task was hardly made easier by the prolonged absence of the Lord President who had been chosen to go to the United States as leader of the British side of the Joint High Commission set up to resolve the Alabama Claims.

There was yet another event occurring in 1870 that affected the Education Department. This was the Order in Council of 4 June which set in motion a general overhaul of the home civil service, and which introduced into it more of those reforms that the Northcote-Trevelyan Report had recommended sixteen years before. Informed public opinion was now clamouring for an end to patronage. The articulate and influential middle classes were tired of corruption, both because it produced inefficiency and waste, and because it reserved the fruits of office to a favoured few.

Moreover, this same bourgeoisie were becoming increasingly aware of the social and commercial value of education, so that the new scholastic establishments created to meet the resultant demand had a keen interest in seeing entry to the civil service thrown open to all comers. In 1870 the government was prepared to act since, by that date, patronage was no longer essential for the management of the Commons.

The Order in Council laid down two important principles. Open competition was to be the normal method of entry into the civil service, and the personnel of each department were, broadly speaking, to be organized in two divisions: the higher grade would be employed on intellectual and administrative work, the lower on mechanical and clerical duties. There were, however, exceptions to the rule that certification by the Civil Service Commissioners was to be a condition of admission. Examination could be dispensed with in the case of a situation for which qualifications 'wholly or in part professional, or otherwise peculiar, and not ordinarily to be acquired in the Civil Service', were considered to be necessary by the head of the department concerned and by the Treasury. Included in this category were those officials exempted under the Superannuation Act of 1859, which meant that the Lord President retained the right to nominate inspectors and examiners. Unconvinced as to the necessity for the continuance of this privilege, the Treasury suggested to the Committee of Council that the post of examiner should be removed from Schedule B (the list of exempted situations) and filled from among the competitors at the Class 1 examination for higher-grade staff. No action was taken by the Committee. It pointed out, in extenuation, that were it to recruit through open competition, it would get only the 'Treasury leavings'. This was because the 'prizes' in the premier department were so numerous, and because the average rate of pay there far exceeded that offered in the Education Department.

The renewed attack upon patronage which the Committee strove to withstand was not, be it noted, an isolated attempt at reform; it formed part of a wider effort to overhaul the entire central administrative machinery of government. The growth of collectivism during the mid-Victorian period pointed the need for a unified and co-ordinated civil service operating under the general supervision of the department ultimately responsible for the expenditure of public moneys. In 1866 came the Exchequer and Audit Act which perceptibly increased Treasury control by requiring that all departments should prepare their accounts in conformity with a more or less uniform plan. To this end the statute authorized the Treasury to nominate an officer in each department with personal and pecuniary liability for all its financial affairs.[1] Two years later a Minute was circulated defining the extent of the power which the Treasury would expect to exercise, and stipulating that its prior approval would be required 'for any increase in establishment, of salary, or of cost of service, or for any additional works or new services which have not been specially provided for in the grants of Parliament'. About this time, too, the Treasury also issued regulations governing the staffing of Government offices, but, since most of the latter had their own ideas on the type of employee most suitable for the particular work involved, these instructions were largely ignored.

Apparently, all these endeavours to improve the service both financially and structurally produced little immediate response, for in 1873 a select committee was appointed 'to inquire into whether any and what reductions can be effected in the expenditures for the civil service'.

Although the committee's aims were to secure economy of administration and standardization of procedure, it failed to produce a report which promoted either of them. But the defects of the existing organization were so glaring that the government felt compelled to institute a more searching and comprehensive investigation. In 1874 a Commission was constituted under the chairmanship of Lyon Playfair with instructions to consider, *inter alia*, the methods of selecting civil servants, the question of transfer of personnel from office to office, and the possibility of grading the civil service as a whole.

The Civil Service Inquiry Commission issued its first Report, which dealt with the ordinary clerical establishments, in January 1875. In essence, the 'Playfair Scheme' as it became known, recommended the division of the service into two branches, one of which was to be composed of men who had passed a stiff competitive examination with a view to their performing intel-

---

[1] In due course, and in accordance with Treasury policy subsequently formulated, the duties of Accounting Officer in the Education Department were assigned to its Permanent Secretary.

lectually demanding work, the other of less highly educated clerks who could carry out routine duties.

So far as the Education Department was concerned, the chief interest of the Playfair inquiry lay in the discontent it revealed among the lower ranks of the Office. Their main grievance was that 'all the better appointments are reserved for direct nomination, and are guarded from the approach of ordinary civil servants by an impassable barrier'. It was claimed that the examiners at that period, whatever they might have been in the past, were not 'educationists' in any real sense of the word. Their functions were solely administrative and such as a higher class of clerks could discharge; and if indeed the examiners *were* the body of 'specialists' they were reputed to be, then it was remarkable that their number should have increased, between 1870 and 1874, by 92 per cent, while that of the assistant clerks had grown by only 11 per cent. In effect, the clerks were complaining that the Department had recently appointed a great many examiners who were engaged in tasks which they themselves could carry out.[1] Questioned on this point, Cumin, one of the assistant secretaries, agreed that the Department employed, in proportion to the clerical body as a whole, a very large number of these 'highly intelligent officers' (i.e. examiners). In explanation he disclosed that the Department had decided to make an interchange between the inspectors and examiners, so as to enable the one to become the other, and that the Treasury had agreed to the heavy influx of examiners during the current year on the understanding that they might subsequently go out as inspectors possessed of a sound knowledge of official duties. The Playfair Commission's verdict was that, although open competition was generally desirable, nomination could not be condemned outright, with the result that the Lord President proclaimed his determination to retain the latter method in the appointment of examiners. Needless to say, this continued dispensation of patronage in the Education Department at a time when it was gradually disappearing from the rest of the civil service, served but to deepen the resentment of those who were thereby denied entry to the administrative grades, and to foment

---

[1] Kekewich observed that there was 'a wide gulf of caste' between the clerks and the examiners. For this reason the former were never promoted, 'though they were constantly agitating for promotion, on what might possibly be thought the legitimate ground that they checked and supervised the work of the Examiners on the Inspectors' reports'. Kekewich, *Education Department*, p. 32.

part of that discontent within the Office which marked the last few years of its independent existence.

While the Treasury was endeavouring to make the civil service generally a more adaptable and effective instrument, efforts were being made, from both without and within, to bring greater unity of control to the Education Department *per se*. Since 1856 this had been, to all intents and purposes, *two* departments: one operating from Whitehall and dealing with elementary education, the other stationed in South Kensington and concerned with technical instruction. But the twain never met, their only real point of contact being that they were both under the ultimate direction of the Lord President. Otherwise they went their different ways, each pursuing its own independent policy and possessing its own separate administrative machinery.

For several years this Dual Monarchy of the educational world worked tolerably well, largely because the spheres of action of the two departments were sufficiently distinct to render conflict of interest or duplication of effort unlikely. But as the elementary school curriculum broadened to permit the teaching of science and drawing, a strong possibility arose that the two provinces might overlap. That the authorities were alive to the problem is shown by an article in the Code of 1871 which stated that no grants were to be given for examination in those subjects on which grants had been paid by South Kensington in the preceding year.

It was soon realized, however, that this kind of prohibition was no substitute for a coherent over-all policy. An opportunity to embark upon the process of amalgamating the two establishments came in 1873 with the resignation of Henry Cole from the secretaryship of the Science and Art Department. In April the following year, Francis Sandford, while retaining his position as Secretary at the Whitehall Office, was appointed to the vacancy, and for the ensuing decade a single official controlled both branches.[1] But the experiment was not a success, for when Sandford retired in 1884 his successor was relieved of the responsibility for the Science and Art Department which again received its own Permanent Secretary. Why the amalgamation proved unsuccessful is not clear; the reasons were sought in vain

[1] Actually, Sandford's educational empire extended beyond even these wide bounds, since in 1873 he had been appointed Secretary to the Scottish Committee on Education also.

when some fifteen years afterwards discussions were taking place
on recombining the departments.[1]

To a few members of the Legislature, however, it seemed obvious
that mere administrative action, even at the most exalted level,
would not satisfactorily resolve the 'uneasy dichotomy' prevailing
between the two authorities; only political action could achieve
an effective union. Hence the attempts made during 1874 to
re-open the question of ministerial responsibility for education
which some six years before had been within striking distance of
solution, only to be shelved.

In May Lord Hampton (the former Sir John Pakington) asked
the Upper House to resolve 'that it is desirable that the Committee
of Council on Education should be superseded by the appointment
of a Minister of Public Instruction, who should be entrusted with
the care and superintendence of all matters relating to national
encouragement of science and art and popular education'. Unfortunately for the noble Lord, the Tory Party had undergone
another change of heart. The Lord President explained why. He
acknowledged that the previous Conservative administration had
introduced a Bill for the appointment of a Minister of Education
but, he argued, the state of things in respect of education had
altered entirely since then. 'At that time', he went on, 'the
Department had to overtake all the work of education throughout
the country; but the Act passed . . . in 1870 had relieved it of
much of that work.' In other words, it was felt that the state,
having imposed educational duties on local bodies, could safely
leave them and the religious organizations to make the necessary
provision free from undue interference by a central authority.

The government was equally unsympathetic towards a less
ambitious proposal made in the Commons by Lyon Playfair some
three weeks later. He moved that a select committee be appointed
to consider how ministerial responsibility, under which the votes
for Education, Art and Science were administered, might be better
secured. In the course of a long and closely argued speech,
Playfair – a former Secretary of the Science and Art Department –
criticized the existing system on three main grounds. First, the
dual control exercised by the Lord President and Vice-President
was, by definition, unsatisfactory. Proof of this could be shown,
for example, by the circumstance that the Vice-President, who

[1] See PRO Ed. 24/8. Correspondence dated 24 April 1884 and 26 June 1899.

was answerable to the Commons for efficient administration, could not appoint a single officer to make that administration efficient. Secondly, the mutually exclusive independence of the Whitehall and South Kensington branches resulted in waste and disunity. 'Each is afraid of the other, and they run on two contiguous and parallel lines of rails, with few crossings, lest they should come into violent collision.' Thirdly, there was a lack of co-ordination among the several central departments responsible for different forms of elementary education. 'The Lord President', Playfair observed, 'does not take charge of all the primary schools, for there are outlying votes for the purpose scattered among various departments.' 'In this country', he concluded, 'there is no Minister of Education. There is only a Lord President of the Council, who is content to remain the manager of a very low order of primary schools and of a few disjointed schools of Science and Art.'

Replying for the government, the Prime Minister expressed the opinion that nothing would be gained by precipitate action. 'Any rash attempt at reform, by a Resolution or by the disturbing process of Select Committees . . . can only irritate the public mind, and create obstacles which might otherwise not exist to the improvement which might be carefully brought about.' In the wake of this cautious pronouncement, Playfair withdrew his motion. To be sure, no one could subsequently have accused the Disraeli administration of 1874–80, or yet that of Gladstone which succeeded it, of undue haste. Not until 1883 was the very moderate request for the appointment of a select committee granted, and even then its terms of reference were no wider than those Playfair had suggested nine years before.

In 1879 occurred the Education Department's fortieth anniversary. The considerable expansion of elementary school provision following the 1870 and 1876 Acts[1] had led to a corresponding growth in the central office. Between 1869 and 1879 the permanent

[1] Lord Sandon's Elementary Education Act of 1876 placed every parent under the legal obligation of seeing that his child should receive 'efficient instruction in reading writing and arithmetic'. Until that date no child need attend school unless he or she happened to be a pauper, a criminal, employed in a factory or to have a soldier as a father. The Act further provided that in districts where there were no school boards, the appropriate local authorities might appoint School Attendance Committees which could exercise the same powers in enforcing attendance as did the school boards.

establishment more than doubled. The increase, from 73 to 174, fairly reflected the changing national picture. In statistical terms alone, the decade was one of impressive achievements:

	1870	*1880*
Number of inspected elementary schools	8,281	17,614
Number of scholars on registers	Under two million	Nearly four million
Percentage of pupils in average attendance	65	70
Number of certificated, assistant and pupil teachers	28,341	71,202
Education Department grants	£894,561	£2,487,667

All this activity involved the Department in a great deal of extra paper work, the correspondence increasing in complexity as well as volume, with the result that many of the communications addressed by the Education Office to the Treasury contained requests for additional staff. It is evident from the replies that the latter department was becoming ever more perturbed at these frequent and heavy demands. There was irony in a situation where the former Permanent Secretary to the Education Department found himself writing to his successor in this vein: 'My Lords cannot but view with uneasiness the apparently unlimited extension which is being allowed, year after year, on one plea or another, to the numbers and cost of the Education Department.'[1] Doubtless it was this apprehension which in 1883 induced the government to accept the need for an inquiry into the administration of the education grants.

An interesting side-light on the relations between the Department and the Treasury is revealed in the memoirs of Lord George Hamilton who was Vice-President between 1878 and 1880. The incident he describes also serves to demonstrate how unsatisfactory were the lines of communication within the Department, and how the Committee of Council was still functioning, albeit in an erratic and unconventional way.

Soon after his appointment it seems Lord George 'somewhat rashly' described himself as the 'Minister of Education', in the belief that his transfer from the India Office was by way of being a promotion. This unwitting self-aggrandizement was resented

[1] PRO Ed. 23/71. Letter dated 2 January 1879.

by the Lord President who complained to the Prime Minister.[1] Beaconsfield thereupon invited Hamilton to an interview, at which he pointed out that the Lord President was technically and legally head of the Department. Admittedly, the relative positions of the two Education Ministers presented something of an anomaly, but as things stood the only advice he felt able to give was that Hamilton must get on with the Lord President as best he could. If, however, he experienced any real trouble, he was to bring the problem to his (Beaconsfield's) attention.

Following this conversation, Hamilton 'entered into an understanding' with his superior, whereby the latter should deal with questions of policy and be consulted on certain other matters, leaving the whole of the remainder of the work to the Vice-President. For a while this *modus vivendi* operated reasonably well, due in large measure it seems to the fact that the two Ministers were near relatives, but in 1880 a serious difficulty arose. It stemmed from the government's decision, in view of the economic and political situation, to pare down departmental estimates as much as possible. Hamilton and Sandford trimmed the forecast of expenditure on education to the barest minimum and submitted it to the Treasury. A few days later Sandford informed Hamilton that, after the Cabinet meeting at which the estimates were discussed, the Chancellor of the Exchequer had told the Lord President that the reductions were not sufficient, and had persuaded him to agree to a further cut – without reference to the Vice-President. The latter remonstrated with his chief, who refused to retract his undertaking to the Chancellor. It was then that Hamilton recalled the Prime Minister's invitation. On learning the nature of the complaint, Beaconsfield asked if there was not a thing called the 'Committee of Council upon Education' and if he himself was not a member of it. Both questions being answered in the affirmative, he instructed Hamilton to tell the Lord President that the Committee was to be summoned im-

[1] The Lord President in question, the Duke of Richmond, was apparently rather sensitive about his position. Some years before, he had taken exception to the implication underlying Lord Hampton's request for the appointment of a Minister of Public Instruction. 'There exists', he asserted, 'a Minister of Education, and I have the honour to be that Minister.' The force of that declaration was somewhat diminished when later in his speech he remarked, 'I do not think the time has arrived for appointing a Minister of Education'. *Hansard* 3rd ser., CCXIX, cols. 690, 692.

mediately. The members of 'this heterogeneous body' duly assembled and Hamilton was called on to state his case. Beaconsfield then declared, 'I do move that the Committee of Council upon Education do agree with the Vice-President'; and the meeting ended abruptly.[1]

As it happened, this was not the first time that Hamilton had had a dispute with the Treasury. Soon after taking office, he resolved to cut down unnecessary expenditure. He therefore went carefully through the education estimates and rigorously pruned them, sending on to the Treasury only what he believed to be absolutely necessary. He recalls what followed:

I received a reply from the Treasury to the effect that the estimates must be reduced by £10,000. I wrote back pointing out that I had already reduced them by more than that amount, and I asked on what ground this demand was made. In reply I was informed that it always had been the practice of the Treasury to cut down education estimates by £10,000, and to that rule they intended to adhere.[2]

Accordingly, the next year he put up the estimates in order to give the Treasury the satisfaction of cutting them down.

In spite of these lively exchanges, Lord George Hamilton found his work at the Education Department the opposite of stimulating. It was, he writes,

terribly meticulous and dull after the India Office. I had to administer about three Acts of Parliament under a code. That code consisted of 150 regulations and 7 schedules. It dealt with the minutest detail connected with school life, and so tied the managers and teachers with red-tape regulations that all individuality or initiative was knocked out of them.[3]

Unfortunately, the Revised Code also seems to have paralysed the Vice-President who, despite his condemnation of the system, made no attempt to improve it.

Hamilton was succeeded, in 1880, by A. J. Mundella, a politician who possessed all his predecessor's independence of mind and considerably more imagination. Immediately on taking office he set about strengthening the law relating to attendance at school. His Education Act virtually completed the machinery created in

[1] Lord George Hamilton, *Parliamentary Reminiscences and Reflections (1868 to 1885)*, 1916, pp. 151-4.
[2] *Ibid.* p. 304.   [3] *Ibid.* p. 156.

1870 and modestly improved in 1876. Hitherto school boards and school attendance committees had only been *empowered* to frame by-laws enforcing compulsory school attendance. The result had been that many authorities, fearing the effect such regulations would have on juvenile employment, declined to exercise their powers. Mundella's statute instructed them to do so 'forthwith'; in the event of refusal or inability to comply by the end of the year, the Department itself would frame the by-laws.

Mundella's next action – leaving aside those measures concerned with technical and Welsh higher education – was to announce his intention of bringing in a new Code. The importance of this decision lay not so much in the changes that were effected as in the procedure that was devised for determining what those changes should be. Previously, the practice had been for the Department to take note of any difficulties arising from, and any complaints made about, the Code then in force. These observations were then considered by the Lord President or the Vice-President or the Secretary, before a decision was reached as to what alterations were necessary and/or desirable.

Mundella resolved to institute a less autocratic method. To begin with, he invited school boards and other bodies interested in education to submit suggestions for the improvement of the Code. An analysis of these proposals revealed certain broad guides to action which were circulated to twenty or thirty of the principal inspectors for their critical comment. These papers, in turn, formed the raw material for a draft report which was examined in detail by a departmental committee especially constituted for the purpose. This first Code Committee, as it came to be called, consisted of the Secretary, two of the assistant secretaries, the three inspectors for training colleges, and Mundella, who presided. Finally, the amended report – or Code, as it had by this time become – was reconsidered by an enlarged committee comprising, in addition to the seven original members, four more senior inspectors, and the Lord President who took the chair. The new Code that emerged from this last refining process was then laid before Parliament to permit discussion prior to its enforcement.

Although it must be said that the body of regulations resulting from the elaborate procedure just described did not satisfy everyone so far as its educational merits were concerned, there was general approval for the democratic methods by which it had been produced. To some extent this willingness on the part of the central office to consult and debate, rather than arbitrarily to impose its edicts, marked the turning of the tide in the duologue between the Department and the schools. The master-servant relationship of the Lingen regime gradually gave way to the concept of a working partnership, as later ministers and secretaries saw the advantages to be derived from enlisting the co-operation of the teaching profession, inspectorate and local authorities.

For this reason Mundella kept the Code Committee in being after it had completed the task for which it had initially been formed. It became a permanent consultative body, maintaining a watching brief over the practical application of the Code, and modifying, from time to time, those articles that proved unsatisfactory. It was nevertheless, found to be a somewhat unwieldy body as originally constituted, and by 1895 the inspectorial contingent had been replaced by a single officer: the Senior Chief Inspector.

Mundella's efforts at reform[1] were helped considerably by the fact that his nominal chief, Earl Spencer, not only gave him a free hand but also supported his actions when the need arose. This self-abnegation on the Lord President's part did not go unnoticed. At South Kensington, where they were often seen together, the wags would remark: 'Here come Lord Mundella and Mr Spencer'.[2] Paradoxically, Mundella's position was strengthened rather than the reverse when, in April 1882, the Lord President, while retaining his seat in the Cabinet, was appointed Viceroy of Ireland; for now the Vice-President was in undisputed command, since Lord Carlingford, who acted as the deputy Lord President, left Mundella very much to his own devices. His authority was not greatly affected even when Carlingford succeeded to the Lord Presidency in March 1883, for the latter combined the office with that of Lord Privy Seal, which meant that opportunities for interference must have been limited. Moreover, when on one noteworthy occasion Carlingford did attempt to assert himself, Mundella proved powerful enough to override him.

While Mundella's record of achievement is impressive, he did experience one failure, or perhaps it would be fairer to say 'partial

---

[1] See also pp. 115–17, 183, 240n.l.
[2] H. E. Roscoe, *Life and Experiences*, 1903, p. 288.

failure' in view of subsequent events. During his tenure of office he became increasingly impatient to be rid of those non-educational duties which not only detracted from the dignity that he felt ought to attach to the position of Minister of Education,[1] but also rendered more difficult the efficient discharge of that Minister's responsibilities.

It so happened that at that time the Opposition was pressing for the creation of an Agricultural Department which would include among its functions the administration of the Acts relating to contagious diseases in animals – precisely those functions that Mundella regarded as an irrelevant encumbrance. In March 1883, therefore, he seized the opportunity to approach Gladstone on the subject, urging that the veterinary department should form the nucleus of a Department of Agriculture under the nominal direction of the Lord President, and that the Education Department should be detached from the Privy Council. To add weight to his argument, he submitted a memorandum from the Permanent Secretary approving the suggested separation of the educational duties of the Vice-President from his other obligations.

The Prime Minister's reactions were discouraging. There was still a possibility, however, that Parliamentary pressure might succeed where a personal approach had failed. In June, Mundella's friends, led by Sir John Lubbock, tabled a motion in the Commons calling for a separate Department of Education. Lubbock summed up in two sentences his objections to the prevailing arrangements:

If the Vice-President of the Council ... was really the Minister of Education, then we had the anomaly that the Minister of Education was not Head of his own office, and was under the Minister of Agriculture. On the other hand, if we were told that the President of the Council was the Minister of Education, then we were in this extraordinary position ... that the Minister of Education undertook none of the duties of his office.

Gladstone opposed the motion on two counts. He deprecated, on principle, the proliferation of Government departments, particularly with regard to the adverse effect it might have on Cabinet efficiency. He felt, too, that the occasion had not arrived to make such a change. But, although he closed the door, he carefully refrained from bolting and barring it. He was prepared

[1] He must have found particularly irritating, and perhaps offensive, the nickname that he was given about this time – it was 'Trichinosis'.

to concede that even if the times were not propitious for making a decision, they might be ripe for instituting an inquiry. The half-loaf was accepted, and a select committee, under the chairmanship of the Chancellor of the Exchequer, was appointed 'to consider how the Ministerial responsibility, under which the Votes for Education, Science and Art are administered, may be best secured'.

While this Committee was gathering evidence, a minor commotion disturbed the Education Department. Early in 1884 Francis Sandford vacated his post as Secretary. During his last years in office he found his work becoming increasingly uncongenial. He had long been aware of how difficult it was for the permanent head to serve two masters – the Lord President and the Vice-President – even when they were in agreement; when they were in conflict the task became almost impossible. He was feeling the strain, too, of trying to administer simultaneously two separate and dissimilar establishments with different traditions, organizations and functions. Moreover, he was unsettled by Mundella's dynamism, and unsympathetic to many of his reforms.

The choice of a successor lay with the Lord President who, whichever of his other rights might have been whittled away over the years, still exercised that of patronage within the Department. Carlingford's nominee, probably on Sandford's recommendation, was a distinguished inspector. But Mundella had his own ideas on the subject. He was determined to secure as his lieutenant someone who could be relied upon to support the school boards. Such a man was assistant secretary Patrick Cumin, and it was he whom the Vice-President insisted should be appointed.[1] Carlingford refused to withdraw his choice, whereupon Mundella threatened to submit his resignation to the Prime Minister. Conscious of the political damage such a gesture would inflict, Carlingford capitulated.

This matter of patronage was, inevitably, one of the topics that exercised the minds of the select committee members who, in 1884, investigated the administration of the education grant.[2]

[1] Cumin's partiality towards the school boards is strikingly demonstrated by the appearance during the 'eighties of the Higher Grade Schools, to the potential illegality of which lawyer Cumin turned a blind eye.

[2] For the findings of the select committee on questions appertaining primarily to the Science and Art Department and to the Charity Commission, see chapters 9 and 12 respectively.

Their interrogation clearly indicated that they considered ano-malous a situation in which the Minister who did practically all the work ('nineteen-twentieths' in Lord George Hamilton's opinion) had no say in the appointment of the agents who acted under him. But this particular problem was seen to be only one element in the complex constitutional question of ministerial responsibility as a whole.

On this central issue there was general agreement among wit-nesses that, while the Lord President was the Minister of Educa-tion *de jure*, the Vice-President was the Minister *de facto*.[1] By and large, this arrangement worked tolerably well, but only because the two ministers were good friends or because the Lord President voluntarily renounced much of the power given him by law. There was, in fact, at least one distinct advantage to be derived from this dual control. It meant that the Department was represented in the Lords by a minister of the very highest rank and necessarily a member of the Cabinet, and in the Commons by a minister who was automatically a Privy Councillor and whose status was some-what superior to that of an Under-Secretary of State. Mundella, for instance, asserted categorically that he would rather be a Vice-President with a Lord President in the Cabinet, than be a Minister of Education outside the Cabinet, lacking any representation with-in it. This argument, however, contained a major flaw since the practical consequence of it was that the acknowledged, if not accredited, Minister of Education was generally excluded from the Cabinet and therefore prevented from personally exercising any influence at the seat of political power. Moreover, even if the government and the Department were not particularly disturbed by this division of responsibility, the school authorities were, for they did not know who actually was the Minister of Education. But at least the situation was not further confused by the inter-position of the Committee of Council, which by this date seems to have receded into the background. According to Sandford, the

---

[1] The Vice-President's advancement in status was ascribed to the circum-stance that that minister was invariably a member of the House of Commons, whereas the Lord President was almost always in the Lords. This convention took on a new significance when, after the 1870 Act, interest in educational questions centred on those relating to local bodies. The House of Commons, because of its representative character, devoted considerably more attention to such questions than did the House of Lords.

Committee was rarely convened save when legislation was in prospect; it might, perhaps, meet once a year.

Two witnesses regarded the ministerial position as being so unsatisfactory that it ought to be changed. Forster felt that the first need was to get rid of the term 'Vice-President', the very name being inconsistent with the fact of his being chief. Hamilton's suggestion was that, following the precedents of the Board of Trade and the Local Government Board, the Vice-President should be made President of the Education Department. And it is interesting to note that Carlingford used the precise title of the future Minister of Education that was adopted in 1899, i.e. 'President of the Board of Education'.

The Select Committee members in their Report agreed that changes were both necessary and desirable. They were of the opinion that the existing arrangement, in which power was divorced to some extent from responsibility, was neither 'logical nor convenient'. They could see no adequate reason why there should be any more natural connexion between the Education Department and the Privy Council than between the Board of Trade and the Privy Council; but, as it might be advantageous for the Minister of Education occasionally to have the assistance of other Privy Councillors specially summoned for consultation with him, they recommended that 'a Board of (or Committee of Council for) Education should be constituted under a President, who should be the real as well as nominal Minister, in this respect holding a position like that of the President of the Board of Trade'.[1] In proposing this, the Committee did not deny that there were objections to the constitution of an administrative department in the form of a Board which had no genuine existence. Although they could not make firm recommendations as to whether the Minister should always be a member of the Cabinet or of the House of Commons, or as to what his salary should be, they thought that his duties should be recognized as being not less important than those of some of the Secretaries of State. They were not, on the whole, in favour of adding to or subtracting from the Department's powers. Specifically, they saw no reason for altering the existing responsibility for workhouse schools, or for primary schools connected with the army, the navy or the marines; and they

---

[1] *Report from the Select Committee on Education, Science and Art (Administration)*, 1884, p. iii.

refrained from inquiring into the administration of reformatory and industrial schools on the ground that these had recently been investigated by a Royal Commission, the Report of which had just been submitted to Parliament; but they did propose that the Scottish Education Department should have its own Permanent Secretary, although they considered that 'Primary Education in England and Scotland should be under the control of the same Minister'.

For a few weeks the fate of these proposals hung in the balance. The main opposition to their adoption seems to have come from Carlingford who, as Lord President, would have been the minister most directly affected by them and whose acquiescence was vital. Gladstone himself expressed much dissatisfaction and some surprise that the select committee had favoured the appointment of a Minister of Education. He nevertheless endeavoured to overcome Carlingford's resistance by offering him the choice of two embassies. The Lord President, however, was adamant. 'The education department would lose its connection with the cabinet', he wrote to the Prime Minister in a letter stating his objections.

In the end Carlingford had his way, for doubtless Gladstone's pressure was never more than half-hearted; and another fourteen years had to pass, a high-powered Royal Commission had to pronounce judgement and the logic of events had to make itself felt, before the main recommendation of the Childers Committee was finally implemented.

One change only flowed from the investigation: the complete detaching of Scottish educational administration from English control. In 1885 a Secretary for Scotland was appointed. He replaced the Vice-President as the chief executive on the Scotch (later renamed Scottish) Committee of Council for Education, which at the same time received its own Permanent Secretary. This separation almost certainly benefited the Scots who, freed from the tangled administrative web in which the educational system south of the border was becoming enmeshed, were enabled to develop their own distinctive pattern of schooling.

The Scots were wise to dissociate themselves from the Education Office in Whitehall. In spite of Forster's efforts and Mundella's reforms, its standing in the educational world was still unenviably low. At the end of this third phase in its history, Edward Thring felt constrained to castigate it in these terms: 'The present exponents of Education in London won't do. As far as I know them, they are the strangest mixture of red tape, crude dissatisfaction, narrow sciolism, revolutionary fumes, unworkable old, and unworkable new, kneaded up into an infallible pudding that can be imagined.'[1]

The Headmaster of Uppingham was not, of course, an unbiased observer – indeed, he had a personal interest in denigrating the Department; yet his assessment was, in all probability, fairly close to the truth. Ministerial weakness, parliamentary indecision, and the maladroitness of permanent officials in the past, had all contributed to making the Department the subject of suspicion and dislike by those who were affected by its decisions, and of derision and contempt by those who were not.

Nevertheless, hopeful signs were emerging. Mundella's Vice-Presidency, which ended in 1885, not only witnessed extensive improvements in the structure and working of the educational system, but, more important, began the long, slow process of transforming the climate of opinion within which that system had to operate.

HM INSPECTORATE

The Act of 1870, which made such a profound impact on so many other aspects of the educational system, also produced, immediately or ultimately, important changes in the inspectorate. The most obvious difference between the inspectorate of 1870 and that of 1885 was a purely quantitative one. At the earlier date there were some seventy-five full inspectors, aided by a mere twenty-three assistants; fifteen years later the number of HMIs had risen by nearly two-thirds to 121, while the army of inspectors' assistants had increased more than six-fold to total no fewer than 152; and these figures do not include the thirty-one officers of an intermediate grade that was introduced during the period.

But of more significance for the future development of the inspectorate than this purely numerical growth, were the changes in form and structure that accompanied it. Three of them stemmed more or less directly from Forster's measure. By Section 7 (3) of the Act, HMIs were relieved of the duty of reporting on religious

---

[1] G. R. Parkin, *Life and letters of Edward Thring*, 1910, p. 436. Letter to H. C. Brown, dated 31 October 1885.

instruction. In this way the Concordats negotiated in the 1840s came to an end, and the inspectorate as a whole could thenceforth be organized territorially instead of according to the sectarian nature of the schools. The country was therefore divided into districts, and each HMI became responsible for the inspection, within his district, of all schools, whether provided by voluntary bodies or by school boards. This reorganization led both to a saving of staff and to a more effective use of inspectors' local knowledge. It also enabled the Department to attempt the introduction of a long-overdue reform: the co-ordination of standards of inspection. To this end the districts were grouped into eight divisions over each of which a senior inspector presided. He was made responsible for the supervision of his suffragan inspectors and for securing uniformity of procedure. Unfortunately, the system, which looked sound enough on paper, failed to work in practice. For one thing, the senior inspectors often neglected to carry out their duties; for another, even when they did, the senior inspector's standard was framed according to his own personal view and was not correlated with that of his colleagues.

Another innovation belonging to the period immediately following the 1870 Act, though in no way attributable to it, was the appointment of a Professor of Music as the first specialist inspector. The Treasury was clearly reluctant to sanction the creation of what might prove to be an expensive precedent, for the Department was, at the outset, permitted to retain Mr Hullah's services on a year-to-year basis only.

The rapid growth in the inspectorate during the 'seventies gave cause for some misgivings both within the Treasury and in Parliament. The former was primarily disturbed by the increasing cost involved. Basically, the difficulty was that most of the expenditure was automatic, varying with the size of the school population; control could therefore be exercised only by altering the method of grant allocation. On this subject the Treasury submitted a series of proposals to the Department. The first of these intimated that a change might be necessary in the system of payment by results which, having been introduced to solve certain administrative problems, was itself producing others.

The much more serious question must . . . at no distant time arise whether grants of proportionately fixed amount, in the nature of grants in aid, subject to public inspection of the schools receiving them, must not supersede a great part of the highly centralized scheme, whereby all the details of individual examination are brought to Headquarters. So long as the grants are unlimited in amount, such a system may be necessary, but it tends to break itself down by the ever increasing number of officers which it requires for its safe administration.[1]

Lingen, it would seem, had been hoist by his own petard.

To devise a solution along these lines would take time; so the Treasury, in an attempt to relieve the immediate pressure, requested that the Department should make more effective use of its existing establishment. 'My Lords do not consider that the evidence before them is sufficiently convincing that the present staff of Inspectors and Assistants is unequal to the discharge of the duties of Inspection now falling to be performed . . .'[2]

Failing to persuade the Department that such an expedient was practicable, and faced with apparently never-ending requests for extra staff, Lingen resorted to a third stratagem: economy through a saving on salaries. 'Would it not be feasible', he inquired, 'to increase the number of Inspectors' Assistants in a greater proportion than at present to the increase of Inspectors?'[3] This idea, too, proved unacceptable. In the end the Department devised its own answer to the problem.

It was not merely the size of the force that gave the Treasury cause for concern. As early as 1875 Lingen had written to his opposite number in the Education Department:

My Lords have no wish to interfere with the discretion of the Lord President in regard to the selection of candidates, but they feel that His Grace and the Lords of the Committee will agree with them that the very large increase in the number of these officers in recent years, renders it more than ever desirable to act on a system which will secure that in every case of nomination to an appointment in the Education Department there is clear and sufficient evidence of the possession by the nominee of qualifications fitting him for the post he is to occupy.[4]

Reading between the lines, one may detect a note of disquiet over the suitability of at least some of the successful candidates.

[1] PRO Ed. 23/71. Treasury Correspondence File. Letter dated 2 January 1879.
[2] Ibid. Letter dated 3 January 1880.
[3] Ibid. Letter dated 31 March 1880.
[4] Ibid. Letter dated 14 January 1875.

Little, unfortunately, is known of the methods employed for the selection of HMIs during this period. There is, however, contained in Sneyd-Kynnersley's autobiography a revealing account of one probably not uncommon way in which aspirants to the inspectorate reached the Lord President's 'short list'.[1] Apparently, Sneyd-Kynnersley's father knew a member of the Cabinet who was prevailed on to use his influence with the Lord President. Some horse trading between the two ministers took place and the application was approved. Later in his memoirs, the author recalled the circumstances of his initiation. 'When on my appointment I received my instructions from the Secretary, he said that, looking to my experience gained as Inspector of Returns, it was not necessary that I should serve any further apprenticeship.'[2]

Perhaps not all appointments were engineered in so blatant a fashion as this, and perhaps – for Inspectors of Returns formed a special category – not all fledgling HMIs were given so cursory an induction into the service; nevertheless, there existed sufficient uneasiness over these matters for questions to be raised in Parliament. In 1878, William Rathbone, the Member for Liverpool, drew the Commons' attention to the very inadequate training given to the inspectors prior to their being entrusted with full responsibility. Then, early in the following year, he moved that 'arrangements ought to be at once made to provide that, in future, before being appointed to an independent post, newly-appointed School Inspectors should have one year's training under an experienced Inspector, unless they have been previously engaged in the education of children for a sufficient time to make this unnecessary'.

In a forceful speech, Rathbone drew attention to the defects of existing practice. He attributed the great variation in inspectors' standards and methods to their lack of training, and he argued that young men who knew nothing about children or about elementary education must almost certainly fail properly to discharge their duties. He asked whether it was not a monstrous absurdity that, whereas a much longer apprenticeship than one year was con-

---

[1] A list of eligible candidates for the posts of inspector and examiner was handed down from one Lord President to another. So far as prospective HMIs were concerned, it consisted in 1884 of between 200 and 300 names.

[2] Sneyd-Kynnersley, *HMI. Some Passages*, p. 106.

sidered necessary to make a man a good cobbler or a good joiner, men were expected to do satisfactorily, without any previous training, such highly skilled and technical work as school inspection; and he inquired whether it would not be well that some of the best of the elementary teachers should be made inspectors. Mundella, incidentally, strongly supported this last suggestion, complaining that the most competent persons were not allowed to become inspectors, because there was no promotion from the ranks.

Lord George Hamilton, the then Vice-President, objected to the motion (which, despite ministerial disapproval, was carried) on account of the additional expense – some £2,000 per annum – entailed. In any event the proposed scheme was, in his opinion, unnecessary, since all freshly-appointed inspectors had to serve a certain term of probation (the minimum period was a fortnight) with the senior inspector of the district to which they were assigned.

Shortly after this debate the Conservative government fell, and Mundella became Vice-President. Without delay he set about the task of making the inspectorate a more effective educational instrument. Having decided that 'nothing could be so mischievous as turning upon the schools young and inexperienced inspectors', he appealed to the Lord President 'not to appoint another inspector without good reason; indeed, without its being proved absolutely necessary, and without our having some better guarantee of his possessing the necessary qualifications for an inspector'.[1]

With the introduction of this stand-still agreement, Mundella secured, in numerical terms, a stable inspectorate, and was therefore able to concentrate his attention upon its reorganization. He had long been aware of the gap that separated the HMIs, who were often appointed on account of *whom* they knew, from their assistants, who were selected by virtue of *what* they knew. In an attempt to bridge that gulf, he instituted, on the revision of the Code in 1882, an intermediate class of sub-inspector. Sub-inspectors were to be recruited from among the inspectors' assistants after some years' approved service in that capacity, and they were entrusted with many of the responsibilities of full HMIs. They could, moreover, entertain the prospect of promotion to the higher ranks. At the same time, Mundella changed the method of

---

[1] *Report from the Select Committee on Education, Science and Art (Administration)* 1884, q. 1054.

appointing inspectors' assistants. Whereas, previously, HMIs had been authorized to nominate an assistant, henceforth the Department would assume exclusive powers of selection. By the end of 1885, twenty-nine sub-inspectors had been appointed, and, by attaching each of them to an HMI, it became possible to enlarge many districts and so economize on the number of district inspectors.

The introduction of the new Code supplied Mundella with the opportunity of issuing to inspectors fresh instructions on the performance of their duties. Considerable stress was placed on the need for better co-ordination throughout the service. Conferences of senior inspectors were to be held as required, and each senior inspector was instructed to arrange annual meetings with the district inspectors within his division. At these, the senior inspector would discuss with his colleagues any difficulties that might have occurred during the year, or any of the grant regulations which they thought might be improved; the senior inspector would then submit to the Department a report, the salient features of which would be considered by the Code Committee. In addition, the position of the senior inspector was more clearly defined, his duty being to secure uniformity of standard in the examinations and to see that the various instructions issued from time to time to the inspectorate were duly carried out.[1]

The following year (1883) is notable for the appointment of the first woman inspector. This female incursion into what had always been an exclusively male preserve owes its origin to the growing interest in girls' education which characterized the second half of the nineteenth century, and more particularly to the demand for some practical work on the distaff side in schools. This pressure, reinforced by evidence supplied to the Royal Commission on Technical Instruction (1881-4), resulted in the introduction of cookery into the Code of 1882 and in an increased emphasis being laid upon the importance of needlework. Recognition of the incompetence of the average male to examine the latter subject led to the provisional appointment of Miss Emily Jones as the first Directress of Needlework. She was not, however, accorded the title of HMI, and she acted solely as an expert in her subject. She was to remain the lone representative of her sex on the inspectorate for seven years.

[1] The title senior inspector was changed to that of chief inspector in 1884.

The most intractable, and for this reason the last, problem that Mundella tackled was that of ensuring that HMIs were suitably prepared for their vocation. In his final year of office he issued another set of instructions, one of which declared that uniformity of standard would be further secured by means of the special training that all future inspectors would be required to undergo. The intention was to place a newly-gazetted inspector under the direction of an experienced HMI by whom he would be trained before being given charge of a district.

In a sense, Mundella had both shelved and, to some extent, solved the problem by his moratorium on the creation of full HMIs and by his introduction of the class of sub-inspector. This is borne out by Sandford's evidence before the 1884 select committee. Asked if there had not been a complaint that inspectors had been appointed who lacked any practical knowledge of teaching, he replied: 'Such a complaint has been made, but in the selection of Inspectors of late years, somewhat more attention has been paid to that'. But he went on to point out that this previous experience was by no means an essential attribute for inspectors to possess. 'An Inspector's duty is . . . not so much to interfere with methods or systems of instruction, as to report on the results arrived at, tested by examination of the scholars.' So long as this limited conception of the inspector's role remained paramount, so long would the inspector find difficulty in gaining the confidence and respect of teachers, and so long would he find it impossible to become what Kay-Shuttleworth had intended he should become: the teacher's guide, philosopher and friend.

6

THE EDUCATION DEPARTMENT:
THE FINAL PHASE, 1886-99

Our system, if so it deserves to be called, is the product of growth, not of manufacture . . . What we have achieved in the department of public education has been gained by a process of gradual evolution, by experiment, by opportunities, by successes and failures, by compromises and concessions, and not by any predetermined plan or clear forecast of the future.

– Sir Joshua Fitch, HMI

By the middle of the 1880s the contest between the school boards and voluntary bodies had developed, for the former, into a struggle for supremacy, for the latter, into a struggle for survival. With each year that passed, the balance of power was tilting more and more in favour of what were erroneously called the 'State' schools. It was a situation which no Tory Party worthy of the name – whether 'at prayer' or otherwise – could regard with equanimity; and in the general election of 1885 the educational battle became a political issue.

The outcome of the campaign was decided by the Irish vote. To secure it, the Conservatives promised Cardinal Manning that, in return for Roman Catholic support, they would appoint a Royal Commission to review the existing state of education in England. Their astuteness won them a narrow victory which, though short-lived, enabled them to redeem that particular pledge. In January 1886 the Government nominated the members of the Commission which was presided over by Sir Richard, later Viscount, Cross. Its terms of reference were 'to inquire into the working of the Elementary Education Acts' and to make recommendations. Consequently, the field of inquiry was vast, and, in order to render their task more manageable, the Commissioners prepared 'a syllabus of points for inquiry' which listed a number of more or less distinct items requiring examination. The twelfth, and significantly last, topic dealt with the Committee of Council – the specific question being: 'Is the present constitution of the Educa-

118

tion Department satisfactory?' The lowly position accorded to this aspect of the inquiry was reflected in the interrogation of witnesses, in which little attention was paid to the central authority for education, and in the subsequent Reports, which made no reference to it. The Commissioners even neglected to endorse the recommendation of the Childers Committee for the appointment of a genuinely responsible Minister of Education. It was, perhaps, this failure to come to grips with one of the most vital educational problems of the day that prompted Sir George Kekewich to comment

That Royal Commission, like others, had the usual effect during the period of inquiry of delaying all change for the better. The Department, when attacked upon its administration, could, and did, always use the fact of the Royal Commission's existence as a reason for doing nothing; and I well remember how greatly it relieved Mr Cumin from even considering proposals for improvement coming from any quarter.[1]

Yet it would not be true to say that the Commissioners totally ignored administrative matters. They evinced some interest in the duties of examiners, and their attention was drawn to the ever-growing complexity of the grant regulations, to the 'tremendous detail' involved in examining and reporting on every school in the country, and to the pressing need to unburden the central office of much of this minutiae. In the light of these representations, the Commissioners came to the conclusion that

if, in the impending reorganisation of local government of the country,[2] education were recognised as one of the most important branches of that local government, and arrangements were made for gradually connecting it, more or less, with the civil administration of each locality ... such an arrangement would ... tend to decentralize the present system ..., relieving the Education Department of innumerable administrative details, and largely reducing the cost of its staff, while retaining for the Education Department powers of general control, which have been of the greatest value in the past.[3]

This eminently sound advice went unheeded at the time (owing admittedly, in part, to differences of opinion within the

[1] Kekewich, *Education Department*, p. 36.
[2] By the Local Government Act of 1888, county and county borough councils were brought into being.
[3] *Final Report of the Cross Commission*, 1888, p. 195.

5

Commission as to how the system of local government should be conducted) and fourteen more years were to pass before it was taken.

One other subject appertaining to educational administration was touched upon in the course of the investigation. A recently-retired HMI expressed the opinion that, in the higher administrative positions in the Department, the element of practical experience was wanting. He thought that if the senior officials were examined, few of them would be found to have had much opportunity of gaining first-hand knowledge of the schools. His suggestion was that a Chief Inspector should be made an assistant secretary whose duty would be to advise on all points connected with the actual work of inspection; he would be the Department's educational adviser, just as one of the assistant secretaries was the legal adviser. He felt also that there was much to be said for having attached to the Office an ex-schoolmaster who knew the educational process thoroughly and who would be able to exercise an influence upon the framing and application of the Code. Cumin, however, was much opposed to the idea, contending that the difficulties encountered by the Office were mostly those of a kind to be solved by persons of legal training rather than by educational experts. In any case, he placed much faith in the Code Committee which had been designed to achieve the necessary liaison between the central department and the schools.

In judging the merits of the proposal, the Commissioners found Cumin's argument the more convincing.

The Secretary, wisely as we think, deprecated a measure which would practically tie the hands of the Office in dealing with the whole body of inspectors, and might easily stereotype the special views of a single expert, liable himself, by withdrawal from personal contact with schools, to lose touch with the varying conditions of education. Already according to present arrangements the political and permanent heads of the Department are free to seek the best advice they can command on educational matters from any member of their staff, whether in or out of the office.[1]

These remarks begged several important questions. What evidence, for example, had the Commission for suggesting that an assistant secretary could impede his departmental and political chiefs? Was the danger of stereotyping the 'special' views of a

[1] *Ibid.* p. 71.

single expert worse than that of stereotyping the views of several theoreticians living in an ivory tower ? Why was it less desirable to bring into the Office a man who might lose touch than to rely on those who had never been in touch at all ? What guarantee was there that the Department would *seek*, let alone take, the advice they were free to call upon ? Indeed, the Commissioners must have been conscious of the frailty of their case, for they concluded by declaring that there was, possibly, 'no reason why a vacancy in the secretariat should not be filled by the appointment of an inspector'.

There is no need to dwell upon other parts of this massive document. The cleavage of opinion among the members of the Commission, which resulted in the issuing of majority and minority Reports, weakened the impact of such recommendations as were made. However, one suggestion at least was acted on. All the Commissioners felt that the system of payment by results then in force was carried too far and was too rigidly applied, and that 'it ought to be modified and relaxed in the interests equally of the scholars, of the teachers, and of education itself'. The desired modification was effected in the Code of 1890 which abolished grants in respect of the three Rs, making the capitation grant a fixed one, determined by school attendance. But whether this change, and those that followed, were the direct consequence of the Cross Commission's recommendations, or whether they were introduced for administrative rather than educational reasons, it is not easy to say. Certainly the Department was finding payment by results increasingly difficult to operate, so that any simplification in the allocation of grants must have commended itself to the officials concerned.

At the same time as the Cross Commission was inquiring into the working of the Elementary Education Acts, another Royal Commission, under the chairmanship of Sir Matthew Ridley, was investigating civil service establishments. The Playfair Scheme had been in existence for ten years, and the time seemed ripe for an inquiry into its effects. Under the procedure adopted by the Ridley Commission, each department was required to complete a questionnaire covering numerous aspects of staffing and organization. The returns showed the business of the Privy Council Office – with which the Education Department was still connected by a ministerial link – to be of a very varied character. This stemmed from the custom, prevalent throughout the nineteenth century, of making the Council Office the initial repository for every new duty of supervision over public services. So that by the 1880s its functions could only be classified alphabetically: it was responsible for assizes, burial boards, clergy returns, Dentistry Acts, Education Acts, foreign deserters, gas company amalgamations, etc. down to university statutes and Veterinary Surgeon Acts. Thus it fell to Lyon Playfair, when he became Vice-President in 1886, to carry through the Commons a Bill for the reform of the medical profession. Eventually, in 1889, Vice-Presidents were relieved of their responsibilities for the administration of such statutes as the Contagious Diseases (Animals) Act of 1867, by the creation of a separate Board of Agriculture under its own Minister. While this transfer of power simplified matters in one respect, it complicated them in another, for the new Board was authorized to grant-aid agricultural education, and to undertake the inspection of those schools, other than elementary, in which technical instruction in any way connected with agriculture or forestry was given. As a result, yet another central authority was added to those already involved in educational administration.

The Ridley Commissioners produced their Final Report in 1888. They made no startling proposals, being content to recommend the tidying up of the existing system, partly with the object of removing legitimate grievances among civil servants. No attempt was made to interfere with the higher division, which had gained for itself a powerful and privileged position. The result was that, while virtually all the lower division was recruited by open competition, many posts in the higher grades were still filled by patronage and limited competition. By this time, too, even the staff had a vested interest in nomination, for they were accustomed to receiving from ministers appointments for their sons and other relations. Among these officials were the examiners and inspectors of the Education Department who, Playfair complained, were 'too often like Nasmyth's hammers used for cracking walnut shells', and whose time was wasted on the performance of tasks far beneath their capabilities. But, in spite of Playfair's protestations and Treasury disapproval, Lord Presidents continued to exercise their prerogative by directly appointing these intelligent and highly-paid men to carry out what often amounted to little more than routine clerical duties.

In 1889 the Department celebrated its golden jubilee. In view of the steady growth of the elementary educational system over the preceding decade, it is remarkable that the Office establishment actually shrank during that period. This decrease in numbers from 174 to 169, despite a substantial increase in the numbers of schools and teachers, can be partly ascribed to the ever-tightening grip exerted by the Treasury over all government departments. From the late 1860s onwards, successive Orders in Council and statutory instruments enabled the Treasury to control more effectively civil service expenditure, and especially to regulate, within fairly narrow limits, the size of departmental establishments. Throughout the 1880s the Treasury brought considerable pressure to bear on the Education Office to moderate its demands for extra staff; and this reluctance on the part of Chancellors of the Exchequer to sanction additional appointments led the Department to institute an inquiry into 'the possibility of simplifying the system under which grants are ... made to promote Public Education'.[1] Apparently a small coterie of Treasury officials (still led by Lingen, incidentally) was a more potent instrument in persuading the Department to undertake a re-appraisal of the policy of payment by results than were the massed ranks of educationists.

Early in 1890 Patrick Cumin died. He had suffered increasingly from ill-health during his last years as Secretary. His term as Permanent Head of the Education Department bears some comparison with that of Kay-Shuttleworth in that the burdens of office seem to have exacted a similar grievous toll. One of his colleagues wrote: 'How Cumin ever got through the very heavy work of the Secretary was mysterious ... [He] had a great deal of disciplinary work to do; in the Education Department not only the official staff had to be kept in order, but teachers guilty of serious offences might have their certificates cancelled or suspended ...'[2] Evidently, the Department was still unable to create an internal organization which, by relieving the Secretary of disciplinary duties, would allow him to concentrate on matters of policy.

Cumin was succeeded by George Kekewich, then a senior examiner, to whom, if his memoirs are to be believed, the elevation

[1] PRO Ed. 23/71. Letter dated 9 February 1881.
[2] Anon. *Patrick Cumin, Secretary of the Education Department. A sketch*, n.d., p. 17.

came as something of a surprise, for he had not solicited the position nor was he one of the highest ranking officials. It may be that he was appointed 'on the express understanding [that] he would be more compromising than Cumin, whose golden rule had been never to admit he was wrong'.[1]

One of Kekewich's first duties was to administer the new Code which came into operation soon after he was promoted. By 1890, the grant system had again become excessively complicated, and the Department decided that it was desirable from both the educational and administrative standpoints to simplify it. The framing of these regulations produced what seems to be the last recorded meeting of the Committee of Council. This almost defunct body was summoned at the behest of the Lord President, Viscount Cranbrook, who considered the Code to be so revolutionary a document as to require the strongest possible sanction.

Describing what took place, Kekewich wrote:

> It was an extremely odd, and very perfunctory, proceeding. The Code, or part of it, was read out to the Committee by Lord Cranbrook, but apparently few of them understood it or took the smallest interest in it. Lord Salisbury, however, who was present, by way, I suppose, of saying something, criticized an article which provided that a proper supply of lavatories should be supplied for the use of the children. He insisted on a reduction of the grant if the school lavatories were out of repair. As he was Prime Minister, there was nothing for it but to gratify his wish, and the alteration was duly made. (But it was wholly opposed to the spirit of the Code, which had abolished all reductions of the grant, and was afterwards removed from it at the first opportunity.) Lord Cranbrook then took alarm, as he obviously feared that if the Committee began really to consider the Code in detail, they might from sheer ignorance play havoc with it. So he said that there was nothing more of importance, and as Lord Salisbury was in a hurry, the meeting ended.'[2]

The Committee of Council, which had taken the stage in circumstances of high drama in 1839, had now descended, in the closing period of its chequered career, to acting out a farce.

The following year another instalment of educational legislation was added to the statute book. It provided for the payment of a fee grant in place of, or in diminution of, school fees payable by

[1] W. H. G. Armytage, 'Patric Cumin, 1823–1890', *Bulletin of the John Rylands Library*, vol. 30, 1946–7, p. 276.

[2] Kekewich, *Education Department*, pp. 59–60.

parents of children in elementary schools. In doing so it virtually made instruction in such schools free. This measure, the new Code (which also made provision for the establishment of day training colleges), and the perennial increase in the school population all placed fresh demands upon the Department. Further duties were imposed by the Elementary Education (Blind and Deaf Children) Act of 1893, which compelled school boards to provide for the education of children so handicapped. Throughout the 1880s the Office had managed to cope with the growing amount of clerical labour involved in administering the grants without recruiting any extra staff, but there were limits to what it could, in the absence of additional assistance, be reasonably expected to absorb. Some idea of the quantity of paper-work handled annually by the Department can be gathered from the data submitted by Kekewich to the Treasury in support of a claim for a larger establishment. Between 1889 and 1892 the number of documents registered outwards had grown from 154,689 to 205,210, an increase of 32·6 per cent; whilst the number of inward registrations rose from 57,802 in 1886 to 137,672 in 1892, an increase of 138·1 per cent.[1]

The formidable array of statistics compiled by the Secretary served to suggest that the Department was gradually being submerged under an ever-rising flood of forms and correspondence. Merely for administrative reasons, the reorganization of local education authorities was becoming essential, irrespective of whether it was an educational desideratum. However, another ten years were to elapse before the needful reform was introduced. In the meantime ministers and officials had perforce to operate the educational system within the existing framework, hoping that the latter would not collapse beneath the weight of its own superstructure.

But if, to change the metaphor, there was no prospect of renovating the obsolete machinery without Parliamentary intervention, it was nevertheless possible to improve certain parts by administrative action, provided, of course, the minister possessed the

---

[1] PRO Ed. 23/71. Letters dated 14 December 1891 and 24 January 1893. Also tabulated were the figures for the establishment, which had grown from 124 to 153 in the period 1889–92. But Kekewich went on to point out that the staff increase was 'far more apparent than real, in as much as 24 out of the 29 represent Assistant Clerks who previous to their promotion had been employed as Copyists'.

necessary resolution and freedom of manœuvre. Both these pre-requisites to the improvement of departmental efficiency – and of inter-departmental relationships – materialized with the appointment of Arthur Acland to the Vice-Presidency in Gladstone's fourth administration. Acland was, in many respects, more fortunate than most of his predecessors. He was immediately given a place in the Cabinet and he enjoyed great independence in his conduct of affairs. For one thing, the Prime Minister, obsessed now with the Irish Question, no longer fettered his colleagues as had formerly been his practice; for another, the successive Lord Presidents Kimberley and Rosebery did little more than represent the Department in the Upper House, engaged as they were with the additional offices of Secretary for India and Prime Minister respectively. Moreover, whereas earlier ministers had been saddled with incongruous duties connected with agriculture and veterinary science, Acland, thanks to the legislation of 1889, was able to devote nearly all his energies to education.

An urgent, if not the most urgent, problem confronting him on taking office in 1892, was that arising from the lack of co-ordination among the central authorities responsible for the three main sectors of education: elementary, technical and secondary. Hitherto, the problem, when it had not been ignored, had been deferred, but the arguments against further indifference or procrastination were now incontrovertible. On economic and administrative as well as on educational grounds, the tripartite division of control was acknowledged as wasteful, confusing and inefficient.

Alive to the need for swift action, particularly in the sphere of post-primary education where the most pressing difficulties had arisen, Acland wasted no time in setting up a Joint Departmental Committee consisting of representatives of the Education Department, the Science and Art Department and the Charity Commission. Its function was 'to consider generally the question of a properly organized system of secondary education for England and Wales, and particularly the relation to one another of the three Departments represented on the Committee'.[1] The Vice-President soon realized, however, that a device operating at this level could bring but temporary relief; only a complete merging of interests and a unified command would provide the basis

[1] *Report of the Committee of Council on Education, 1893–4*, p. 9.

for a permanent solution. This was easier said than done, for such a radical reform necessitated legislation, upon which Parliament showed little inclination to embark. Acland, his hand strengthened by the deliberations of an important conference on secondary education held at Oxford in October 1893, was determined to break the deadlock. As a result of his persuasions, the government in the following March appointed a Royal Commission to investigate the problem.

The Bryce Commission's terms of reference – 'to consider what are the best methods of establishing a well-organized system of Secondary Education in England' – superseded the more general brief given to the inter-departmental committee. But the latter was kept in being to deal with the more particular. In this capacity it proved to be of considerable value, 'enabling the three Departments to keep each other readily informed of the attitude of each towards the many questions in which each is interested, and so to avoid contradictory or inconsistent action'.[1]

Having done what he immediately could to bring order to the chaotic realm of secondary education, Acland turned his attention to the hardly less unsatisfactory condition of the two departments for which he was primarily responsible. So far as the Whitehall Office was concerned, he was disturbed to find that it lacked the means both to gather and to disseminate useful educational information, that it gave too little guidance to local authorities and teachers, and that even the guidance provided tended to be based on inadequate research. With a view to remedying these defects, he asked the Treasury in December 1894 to sanction the appointment of a 'Director of Special Inquiries and Reports'.[2]

After this, events moved surprisingly swiftly. On New Year's Eve the Treasury responded, approving the proposal and defining the duties of the new branch. These were 'to keep a systematic record of educational work and experiments in this country and abroad, and also to obtain and supply information, and to inquire and report upon any special educational question which may be referred to the Director by the Lords of the Committee'. At Acland's insistence, it was agreed that the head of the section should have direct access to the Permanent Secretary to the

---

[1] *Ibid.*

[2] The letter as originally drafted gave the title as 'Director of Educational Intelligence'.

Education Department and thereby enjoy the status of an assistant secretary. He would, in addition, be provided with a small staff consisting of an assistant director and two clerks.

On 1 January 1895 Lord Rosebery approved the appointment of Michael Sadler as Director. Acland, who had for some time been anxious to find a place in the Department for this 'golden boy' of the educational world, gave him an almost completely free hand in the running of his section. Could the Vice-President have foreseen the consequences of his action, he might have had second thoughts.

It would be absurd to suggest, of course, that the internal conflicts which rent the Department during the years that followed were caused exclusively, or even predominantly, by Sadler's arrival. The seeds of dissension had been planted long before, and they were given the opportunity to flourish following a change of political control shortly afterwards. For some time the Office had not been a happy one. Kekewich's advancement was resented by several colleagues who had been senior to him either in rank or in length of service or in both, and his and Acland's efforts to galvanize the higher staff into activity cannot have been welcomed by the examiners, most of whom had been recruited in the immediate wake of the 1870 Act and were now middle-aged and set in their sedentary ways. Moreover, these officials were additionally aggrieved because, having entered the Department at about the same time, few of their number could entertain any hopes of promotion. To make matters worse, the clerical grades harboured two major grievances: the first-class clerks protested that, though they did work equivalent to, or more demanding than, that performed by examiners, they did not receive the same pay or enjoy the same privileges; nor, because of the 'caste system' prevailing in the Department, could they, or the second division clerks below them, ever aspire to the higher ranks. Over and above these sectional complaints, there were other grounds for discontent. The mounting pressure of work forced many members of staff to put in long spells of overtime, and this was in addition to an increase in the daily attendance from six to seven hours imposed throughout the service by the Treasury in an effort to alleviate the manpower shortage and reduce labour costs. Morale may well have been affected, too, by the fact that the Education Department had grown to be much the largest of all government offices, for its very size created problems of communication. Last but not least, working conditions within it were difficult almost to the point of being impossible.

Into this troubled and potentially inflammable atmosphere entered Sadler, a man brimming with energy and ideas and devoted to the cause of education. He was as indifferent to civil service traditions as he was impatient with bureaucratic methods. Possibly, the Department, in normal circumstances, could have assimilated without undue upheaval one such unusual recruit. But, by an extraordinary turn of fate, it found itself having to accommodate a second; for Sadler, in looking for a suitable assistant director to help him, chose an individual – Robert Morant – whose talents and ambitions matched, if they did not surpass, his own.

For many years to come these two stars of the first magnitude illumined the educational scene. To begin with, their courses ran parallel and during this period their combined brilliance shed light on many places which had hitherto been obscure or unexplored. Sadler attached, as he was probably meant to do, a very liberal interpretation to the terms of the Treasury directive under which he had been appointed. He conceived his task as the investigation of current educational practice, on a comprehensive and international scale, with a view to discovering ways in which English education might be improved. The main fruits of this research were published in book form under the title of *Special Reports on Educational Subjects*, the first of which appeared in 1897; yet, valuable as they were, these volumes represented only a part, and perhaps not the most important part, of the activities of the new branch. Some idea of the range, if not the depth, of its contribution to educational theory and practice was provided by Sadler himself in a memorandum submitted to the Board of Education in 1903.[1] Included in this document outlining the work of the Office of Special Inquiries and Reports were such activities as the collection, both in this country and abroad, of educational information for official use; answering general queries on educational matters received from local authorities, educational societies and individual students; assisting people at home or from overseas who were engaged upon comparative studies in education; inquiring

[1] 'Notes on the work and needs of the Office of Special Inquiries and Reports attached to the Board of Education,' Cd. 1602, pp. 39–40.

into the curricula, staffing, and attendance at public secondary and higher grade schools in a number of selected areas in England; running the Department's reference and lending libraries. All these and several other varied undertakings were carried out by a staff of six.

The fate of this Office is soon told. In 1903, as the result of a quarrel with Morant, who had become the Permanent Secretary, Sadler resigned. After his departure the Office was allowed to survive for a few more years in an emasculated form, and then quietly allowed to die. Some of its functions were transferred to other sections; many were discontinued completely. Following its disappearance, the central authority for education in England ceased to possess a separate research department until 1961, when a Research and Intelligence Branch was established in the Ministry.

However, one enterprise, namely the library, *was* permitted to thrive. Formerly housed at South Kensington, this collection of books, reports, periodicals and documents was transferred, at Sadler's request, to Whitehall at the end of 1896. To it were added a number of books which had been gathering dust in the cellars of the Department, and the whole library placed under the charge of the Office of Special Inquiries. At the same time, Sadler filed a request for the appointment of a person to manage the new enterprise. He asked that a woman be selected, both for reasons of efficiency and economy, and because 'many of the inquiries, which the branch is required to make, are concerned with the education of girls'.[1] The application was granted, and Miss Beard, who had helped Sadler in his University Extension work, became Library Assistant. After her arrival, the entire collection was catalogued, and a lending library, comprising official reports on education and selected works on educational subjects, was established for the use of HMIs and other members of the Department.[2] The present reference library of the Department of Education and Science was assuming a recognizable shape.

By a remarkable coincidence, at almost exactly the same time as Sadler and Morant were beginning their profitable partnership in the Office of Special Inquiries, a somewhat less beneficial associa-

---

[1] Draft of a letter from the Director to the Treasury dated 30 January 1897.
[2] Cd. 1602, p. 14. As long as the library was housed in Cannon Row, the books were distributed among the many rooms occupied by the officers of the Department; hence it was not possible to allow the public access to the shelves.

tion was in the process of formation at Headquarters. Following the general election of 1895, the Conservatives, in alliance with the Liberal Unionists, returned to power. Salisbury, the new Prime Minister, experienced some difficulty in forming his coalition government, having, in the allocation of offices, to take account of factors other than the suitability of the incumbent. Because of this, some departments received ministers whose talents or temperaments were not altogether appropriate to their responsibilities. In no case was this more true than in the Education Office. For reasons best known to himself, the Duke of Devonshire, having refused Foreign Affairs, chose to be Lord President of the Council. Kekewich characteristically complained that 'from the day he [Devonshire] assumed that position to the day he vacated it, he was profoundly ignorant of the system the Department had to administer, of its routine and of its duties';[1] and the Duke himself, on one occasion when he found the latter more than usually tedious, despairingly groaned, 'I can't understand how it is I ever got the reputation of an educational expert'.[2] Even *The Times*, in retrospect, could find little favourable to say about his ministerial aptitude.

It is now clear . . . that the present Government has no real interest in education. Lord Salisbury and Mr Balfour, to do them justice, have never professed any . . . while the Duke of Devonshire, placed by circumstances which probably surprise no one more than himself at the head of English education, can hardly be said to display undue enthusiasm for it . . .[3]

While, according to Halévy, Devonshire 'was known to cherish only one strong passion – that for his stud of race-horses'.[4] In this way the richest man in the country became responsible for the education of its poor.

The Vice-Presidency went to Sir John Gorst who, it must be said, *was* genuinely interested in education; unfortunately, this interest was too often subordinated to a desire for scoring off his

---

[1] Kekewich, *Education Department*, p. 93.
[2] Quoted in B. Holland, *The Life of Spencer Compton, 8th Duke of Devonshire*, 1911, vol. 2, p. 273. Remarkably, the index to this volume covering the Duke's seven years at the Education Department contains no separate reference to 'education'.
[3] *The Times*, 6 September 1900.
[4] E. Halévy, *A History of the English People in the Nineteenth Century*, 1951, vol. 5, p. 190.

political opponents and irritating his officials. Had either Devonshire or Gorst been prepared to let the other take command, the Department might have lived out its last days in comparative peace. As it was, this 'extraordinarily ill-assorted pair attempted to run in double-harness'.[1] The experiment was almost bound to end in failure, if not disaster, for Gorst 'soon found the Duke of Devonshire's somnolent dignity as intolerable as the Duke found his own headstrong cynicism'.[2]

One of the first tasks confronting these strange bed-fellows was to consider the findings of the Bryce Commission. Working with singular speed, its members produced their Report by August 1895, and they made a point of emphasizing the need for equally prompt action from the government.

The Commissioners had been charged with inquiring into the organization of *secondary* education. Their investigations, nevertheless, led them to examine the part played in this area by the Education Department which, by virtue of the title, if not the terms, of the 1870 Act, should have confined its activities to the provision of *elementary* education only. In spite of this limitation, it had over the years established certain links with secondary education. These were described to the Commissioners in a document supplied by the joint departmental committee which had been studying the question of the educational system at the secondary stage.

The committee pointed out that, while the Department had virtually no immediate or statutory association with secondary education as such, its connexion with the latter, though not direct or even acknowledged, was in fact real and extensive. This connexion was exerted both from below and from above, that is, upwards from the elementary schools and downwards from the training colleges and university colleges. As regards the former, the Committee revealed that school boards, despite the restrictions imposed by Parliament, were 'practically at liberty (subject only to the control of the district auditor which is not exercised on any uniform principle) to provide and conduct schools scarcely distinguishable from Secondary Schools, and to pay for their provision and maintenance out of the school fund'.[3]

---

[1] Kekewich, *Education Department*, p. 83.   [2] Halévy, *A History*, p. 190.
[3] PRO Ed. 24/7. Memorandum of the Joint Departmental Committee (Education), Paper C. Dated April 1894.

Between the Department and the university colleges there were two main points of contact: the Treasury grant and the day training colleges. The committee recalled that in 1889 the Treasury, when agreeing to make an annual grant of £15,000 in aid of certain colleges giving education of a university standard in arts and science, had recommended, *inter alia*, that each participating college should submit an annual report and statement of accounts to the Education Department, and that 'a person representing the Government' should inspect each college from time to time to ensure that the state obtained a reasonable return for the assistance it gave. Since then, the Department had secured the implementation of the first proposal, but had not yet taken any steps towards the inspection of the colleges, despite a Treasury reminder that such a safeguard was highly desirable.[1] So far as the second group of university institutions was concerned, the committee explained that under the Code of 1890 the Education Department had established a system of day training colleges for teachers to supplement the existing network of voluntary colleges. Relations between the Department and the former were exceedingly intimate; each college had to conform with the regulations laid down in the Code and each was annually inspected by one of the HMIs of training colleges, who made a special report on it.

In their own researches, the Bryce Commissioners found the *statutory* connexion of the Department with secondary education to be slight indeed. It stemmed from the working of the Endowed Schools Acts, whereby the Charity Commissioners had been brought into a 'definite, though incomplete, relation to the Committee of Council on Education'.[2] The schemes that they devised for the better utilization of endowments required the Department's approval, and if these schemes were subsequently laid before Parliament, they were considered to be in the charge of the Lord

[1] The English universities succeeded in remaining substantially independent of state control. In 1919 a University Grants Committee was constituted, consisting not of officials but of people with direct experience of the work and needs of the universities. It was to this body – not to the Board of Education – that the duty of allocating the Treasury grant was entrusted. But the decision almost went the other way. Eight years previously, agreement had been reached that all university grants were to be administered by a committee under the Board. Then the government changed its mind, mainly because it became aware of Morant's unpopularity in university circles.

[2] *Report of the Royal Commission on Secondary Education* [C. 7862], 1895, vol. I, p. 26.

President or the Vice-President. Nevertheless, the relationship between the Department and the Charity Commission (which was at that time the body most nearly approaching a central authority for secondary education) was tenuous and unsatisfactory, not least because the Department possessed no direct influence over the formulation of schemes, and because circumstances had, since 1874, tended on the whole to bring the Commission and the Minister less and less in touch with each other.[1]

The Bryce Commissioners further discovered that between the central authorities for elementary and *technical* education, there was also a link, albeit of a single strand. That link was supplied by the Vice-President, who was the political head of both the Education and the Science and Art Departments; apart from this personal connexion each was completely independent of the other.

It was against this background of divided control and over-lapping jurisdictions that the Bryce Commissioners made their recommendation for a unified central authority, comprising the Education Department, the Department of Science and Art, and the Charity Commission so far as its activities were concerned with educational endowments. This authority 'ought to consist of a Department of the Executive Government, presided over by a Minister responsible to Parliament, who would obviously be the same Minister as the one to whom the charge of elementary education is entrusted'.[2]

The Report also advocated that the local administration of secondary education should be reformed by setting up in every county and county borough a local authority for *all* types of secondary education, and this was the recommendation that the government attempted to implement first. Its decision was influenced by the concern that many Conservatives felt over the inability of the voluntary schools to compete with the rate-aided board schools. The Education Bill of 1896 therefore contained proposals aimed not only at improving local administration, but also at bringing relief to the church schools.

Owing mainly to the opposition of school board supporters and Nonconformists, this attempt to kill two birds with one stone proved abortive. But the debates on the Bill are instructive, and the after-effects of its failure significant. Introducing the measure into the Commons in March 1896, Gorst stressed that one of its

[1] See chapter 12.   [2] *Ibid.* p. 257.

virtues was that, by decentralizing the administration of the education grant, it would reduce the load falling on the central office. Illustrating the enormous size of this burden, he informed members that in the previous year the Department had inspected 19,789 day schools from each of which it had received returns containing 1,659 blank spaces. This meant that the Office had to scrutinize the information contained in 32,829,951 spaces, each document having to go through fifty-four different stages, before the amount of grant could be decided. Gorst pointed out that these transactions were not made any easier by the fact that the Department's offices were scattered over several acres, and his elaboration on this point drew laughter from the House. But the scene he conjured up had its serious as well as its ludicrous aspects, for the working conditions he described must have lowered staff efficiency and morale. By 1896 the problem had grown to such alarming proportions that a special committee was appointed to report 'on the defects of the buildings of the Education Department and the probable requirements of the Department in the future'.

The committee's report is, in one respect, a unique document, for it included an analytical survey of the work of each of the twenty-one sections into which the Department was divided.[1] What emerged was a picture of vast and intricate complexity. By 1895, for example, the number of documents entering and leaving the Office had exceeded the million mark. But even more astonishing than the size and nature of the administrative machine were the circumstances in which it had perforce to function. These the committee described in considerable detail. A few short extracts may serve to indicate the tenor of the report.

At present the Department is housed in five separate buildings at a considerable distance from each other . . . The rooms of most of the Sections cannot be properly grouped together even within the main building. E.g. [the Section dealing with] stationery and printing has one room on the ground floor, one on the third floor and one on the first floor, thus involving the laborious carriage upstairs of tons of goods. Another Section has charge of 27,770 portfolios, all of which have to be frequently consulted, but these are stored partly in a public passage and partly in four small rooms at the top of the building.[2] In Trafalgar Buildings . . . the lavatory is now turned into a library . . .

[1] See note p. 278.
[2] The portfolios contained inspectors' reports on schools.

But the main and pervading defect of the present chance-medley of the buildings is that they defy due organisation of the work. The large volume of public business cannot be properly arranged, supervised or directed because it cannot be put into due correlation. Sections which have immediately to deal with one another cannot be put into proximity. The clerical section, dealing with the bye-laws and elections of school boards is at Charing Cross; while the records of the letters of the school boards are one third of a mile away at Treasury Buildings ... The statistics which have to be gathered from every portfolio are collected and tabulated in King Street, whither about 28,000 portfolios have to be continually transported from Treasury Buildings from the Sections there charged with their custody. But more important is the separation of the financial administration of the Department, which assuredly ought to be under one roof and in contiguous rooms. It is at present in two divisions and half a mile apart. Fee Grants are calculated and paid at Charing Cross, the annual grants at the Census Buildings, while the Assistant Secretary who acts as Financial Secretary necessarily sits at Whitehall.

Such separation entails either excess in the number of the supervising staff or want of supervision. It involves damage to, and sometimes the destruction or loss of, bulky portfolios and papers, which have to be wheeled loose in hand-trucks through crowded thoroughfares; it also involves the employment of a considerable number of messengers and the absence of clerks from their own work in order to act as messengers in charge of important papers. Lastly, this state of dismemberment renders a very large and complicated administration more complicated still.[1]

Extensive comment is superfluous. The Report revealed a state of affairs so bizarre that one no longer feels that the Department officials deserved censure for their failure to run the educational system efficiently and imaginatively; rather one is astonished that they contrived to run it at all.

Gorst, meanwhile, was encountering such vigorous opposition to his Education Bill that the Cabinet decided to abandon it, before it ruined the parliamentary time-table or got lost in a flood of amendments. This was the famous occasion when the Duke of Devonshire was asked to convey the news, as tactfully as possible, to Gorst. His Lordship proceeded to the Vice-President's room where he delivered his message in the following terms: 'Gorst,

[1] Final Report of the Departmental Committee on the defects of the buildings of the Education Department, 1896. To make matters worse, there was still no telephonic system linking the central office with the outlying premises.

your damned Bill's dead'. After this incident, according to Kekewich, Sir John 'sulked and absented himself from the Office', spending most of his time at South Kensington plotting against the Whitehall officials. Consequently, the Board of Education Act was 'framed without his aid, and that fact caused additional friction'.[1]

Frustrated in its attempt to implement one of the two main recommendations of the Bryce Report, the Department explored the possibility of acting on the second. The Royal Commission, when emphasizing that the reform of the central authorities was a matter of urgency, had pointed out that there were no fewer than four such authorities empowered to provide or assist education in one form or another. Based, if that is the correct term, in Whitehall, the Education Department was primarily concerned with elementary schools; but, through the higher grade schools, the training of teachers and the evening schools, not to mention the approval of schemes for endowed schools, it was also involved in secondary education. From South Kensington, the Science and Art Department's influence extended to higher grade and evening continuation schools as well as secondary schools proper; in addition, it exercised some supervision over the administration of the Technical Instruction Acts. Yet a third body, the Charity Commission, was charged with the duty of framing schemes for the better management of educational endowments, and, though its principal functions lay in the sphere of secondary education, one category of elementary endowed schools also came under its jurisdiction. Finally, the Board of Agriculture possessed certain powers relating to the supply of agricultural education. And this list comprised only those central authorities whose educational responsibilities the Bryce Commissioners considered should be integrated. There were, in fact, another five government departments with fingers in the educational pie: the Admiralty, the Home Office, the Local Government Board, the Public Works Loan Commissioners and the War Office.

An 'administrative muddle' of such dimensions led not only to confusion but to waste and conflict. Feelings of jealousy were noticeably rife between the Whitehall and South Kensington Departments. They were, in the words of one legal authority, 'separate in name, separate in local habitation, separate in

[1] Kekewich, *Education Department*, p. 102.

constitution, and separately entrusted with public funds, to be administered by each department independently of the other'.[1] As such they vied with each other in their efforts to 'attract custom', as it were, or to extend the boundaries of their respective empires. In no case was this rivalry more apparent than in the provision of evening classes. Gorst, particularly, was disturbed by its effects, informing the Commons in July 1901 that:

In the great bulk of the towns of this country there is actual chaos in this evening school education system, and practically the same sort of instruction is being given in rival schools maintained at the expense of the ratepayer and the taxpayer, and efforts are being made to draw students from one another and injure each other's position.[2]

This example of free enterprise operating within the public sector illustrates the confusion that permeated the educational system during the late Victorian years. It was also symptomatic of a deep-seated malaise afflicting that system which only drastic surgery could cure. The government began tentatively to explore the problem, hoping perhaps that administrative action could supply a remedy. Soon after the failure of the 1896 Bill, two committees were set up to examine some of the difficulties connected with the oversight of secondary education. The first of these, under the Vice-President's chairmanship, was appointed to inquire into 'the mode in which the grants to Science and Art Schools . . . are distributed and to report whether any alteration should be made therein'. The second took the form of a joint conference between, on the one hand, representatives from the Incorporated Association of Head Masters of Secondary Schools, and of spokesmen for the higher grade schools on the other. Presided over by Sir George Kekewich, the conference was designed to attempt a resolution of the differences between the two kinds of school.

It soon became obvious, however, that if the Bryce proposals were to be adopted in their entirety – and nothing short of this would really meet the case – then legislation would be necessary. The amalgamation of the Whitehall and South Kensington Departments could be achieved merely by means of an Order in Council; but the placing of the educational part of the Charity

[1] *Manchester Guardian*, 21 December 1900. Law Report. Mr Justice Wells.
[2] *Hansard*, 4th ser., XCVI, col. 1177.

Commissioners' work under a different central authority would require parliamentary sanction. On 26 February 1898 the Duke of Devonshire submitted to the Cabinet a memorandum outlining his views on the form such legislation might take. This document marked the commencement of work on a measure which ultimately became the Board of Education Act of 1899.[1]

By the latter date the Department was sixty years old. Its establishment over the preceding decade had grown considerably. The administrative staff, now numbering thirty-three, consisted of the Secretary, five assistant secretaries, eight senior and eighteen junior examiners and an architect. These officers were supported by a host of clerks of various grades nearly 250 strong. The total permanent staff at headquarters, including the five members of the Office of Special Inquiries, amounted to no fewer than 284, and to this must be added another 225 temporary clerks and copyists, bringing the number of those employed in administering the elementary system to over 500. Three factors, at least, were responsible for this remarkable growth. There was the continuing rise in the school population, due partly to improved attendance and longer school life and partly to an increase in the birth-rate and a fall in infant mortality. There was the tendency for the Department both to widen spontaneously the range of its activities, and to have additional duties imposed upon it. And there was, on the Treasury's part, a less stringent attitude towards the Department's requirements. Quite possibly, a fourth factor was present in the shape of 'Parkinson's Law', a theorem stating that any bureaucratic organization tends naturally to grow in size each year at a rate which, given the necessary data, can be predicted. Although the formula is a jest, it probably contains a certain truth.

Just as the Education Department's career began in an atmosphere of disputation and turbulence, so did it end. But whereas in 1839 the causes were entirely external, stemming from political and religious disputes, in 1899 they were largely internal, and arose from the conflicting personalities of those running the Department. And, since the events of the period are intelligible only in the light of a knowledge of the individuals who fashioned them, a brief description of the leading characters seems appropriate at this point.

'It would be difficult to imagine', writes Eric Eaglesham, 'a

[1] For a survey of the events leading up to the Act see chapter 13.

more explosive administrative situation than that under the Duke of Devonshire's remote Presidential control in 1897–9.'[1] Not that the Duke himself was a combustible element. Indeed Kekewich, describing him as 'a living wet blanket', found him quite the reverse. The trouble was that the Lord President took no interest in elementary education, and the details of its administration bored him. These attitudes he shared with many of his predecessors; but while they were generally content to delegate their responsibilities, the Duke decided to rule as well as reign.

Sir John Gorst, the Vice-President, was cast in a very different mould. Clever, witty, resourceful, he might have achieved some eminence as a statesman but for a fatal flaw: his almost uncanny skill in making enemies. He even succeeded in moving the normally imperturbable Duke to anger, until eventually the latter was driven to ask Kekewich 'whether any inducement worthy of his [Gorst's] acceptance could be offered him to transfer his energies elsewhere'. Sir George suggested that a colonial governorship would be tempting. 'Said the Duke, slowly and deliberately . . . "I cannot imagine that the Government would offer Sir John Gorst the governorship of any colony that they desired to *retain*!"'[2]

After the abandonment of the 1896 Bill, Gorst harboured a grudge against Kekewich, and against Sadler who had helped in its drafting and whom he blamed for its failure. The quarrels became so bitter that the Vice-President had very little to do with the Department's administrative affairs between 1897 and 1901, while his last two years in office appear to have been spent in fomenting trouble between the branches at Whitehall and South Kensington. Of this period in his career, an anonymous writer commented, 'Sir George Kekewich . . . and Sir John Gorst have practically ceased to be on speaking terms with each other. Sir John, in fact, is hardly on speaking terms with anybody – even with himself . . . Lord Salisbury threw him the Education Department like a bone to a hungry dog. He gnaws it, and has pretty well destroyed it.'[3] These remarks probably magnified Gorst's destructive capacity; yet there is no doubt that Sir John was a divisive force within the Department, and an irritant of quite remarkable potency.

---

[1] E. Eaglesham, *From School Board to Local Authority*, 1956, p. 109.
[2] Kekewich, *Education Department*, pp. 94–5.
[3] *Truth*, 15 August 1901. Quoted by Kekewich, *Education Department*, pp. 335, 336.

The character of Permanent Secretary George Kekewich is revealed to some extent in his autobiography. It is the work of an angry old man, embittered at the treatment he received, disillusioned by his experience in the corridors of power, intent upon settling old scores. There is, however, too much corroborative evidence supporting his account of events for it to be dismissed as a mere fabrication or gross distortion. In happier times he might have made an exceptionally distinguished contribution to educational development. His greatest virtue lay in his conviction that the function of the Department was primarily to promote the welfare of young people; his greatest achievement lay in gaining the confidence of the teachers and in improving relationships between the schools and the Department;[1] his greatest misfortune was that he found himself in the grip of circumstances over which he could exercise little control. In the end he was crushed between the upper millstone of political indolence and spite, and the nether millstone of intrigue and ambition on the part of his departmental subordinates.

One of these was Michael Sadler, who saw his Office of Special Inquiries very much as a private show run exclusively by himself. In Whitehall today it would probably be called 'Sadler's circus' and would be equally resented by the other officials – the more so in Sadler's case because he was also regarded as an 'outsider' and an 'upstart'. After his first two years as Director he became increasingly unhappy. For a variety of reasons he was on bad terms with most of the senior staff who treated him with growing hostility. Gradually drawn into the policy-making side of the Department's work, he became involved in machinations which he found fascinating, and at the same time, distasteful.

The other officer in the Department with a strong sense of purpose was Sadler's assistant, Robert Morant. Morant is perhaps the most controversial figure ever to set foot on the English educational scene, and his complex personality would have made an interesting subject for psycho-analytical study. It is difficult to arrive at any impartial assessment of his services to education or of the methods he employed to secure the position whereby he could influence its progress. The likelihood is that soon after his arrival

---

[1] On his retirement, the National Union of Teachers, as a token of their appreciation for his work, conferred upon him the honorary membership of their association.

in the Department he became alarmed at the chaotic state of educational administration and was resolved to bring some order and sense of direction to it. This was no mean aspiration; and doubtless he felt, as he manœuvred his way to the seat of power, that the end in this instance justified the means.

It would, however, be inappropriate to close this account of the Department on a discordant note. The convulsions that shook it in its last years should not be allowed to obscure its very solid achievements. Beginning life as a minor branch of the executive concerned merely with the distribution of a paltry grant for assisting the construction of a few hundred schools for a few thousand pupils, it had grown into an important department of state accountable for the education of the vast majority of children throughout the country. In statistical terms alone its progress had been impressive. By 1901 it was responsible for the allocation of an annual grant of almost £9 million to over 20,000 schools which were attended by nearly six million scholars of whom some 82 per cent were in regular attendance and whose average school life extended over seven years. The quality of the teaching in the schools, the narrow conception of the term 'education', and the confused state of central and local administration, were less evidently matters for congratulation. But within the limits imposed from time to time by religious intransigence, political prejudice, Treasury parsimony and bureaucratic ineptitude, it had made a significant contribution to the promotion of national well-being. Its founder, Lord John Russell, would have been gratified to learn that his original proposal that the Department should be concerned with 'all matters relating to the education of the people' was gradually being adopted; and, although it had frequently departed from the principles he upheld, its architect, Kay-Shuttleworth, would in all probability have approved of the outcome.

HM INSPECTORATE

If, as has been suggested, the Cross Commission failed to conduct more than a cursory inquiry into the administrative side of the Department's work, it redressed the balance by subjecting the inspectorate to a searching scrutiny.

By and large the Commissioners found little to criticize adversely. Their opinion was that, though the system of inspection might be susceptible to improvement in certain particulars, the country on the whole had been well served. They expressed no dissatisfaction with the methods employed in the selection of HMIs or with their lack of expert knowledge. Apparently, the possession of a good honours degree furnished them with a sufficient qualification. On the one hand, graduates were judged capable of quickly acquiring familiarity with elementary school work; on the other, the requirement that inspectors should be men of high academic attainment might have proved 'a useful check on unsuitable appointments'. In support of their argument they quoted at length from the Committee of Inquiry of 1853, just as if the conditions and suppositions obtaining then had not changed in thirty-five years.

Cautious and qualified approval was given to two proposals several witnesses had advanced. The Commissioners saw some justice in the demand that elementary school teachers be admitted to all grades of the inspectorate, though their recommendation 'that it is neither fair nor wise to prevent elementary teachers from rising to the rank of inspectors', was couched in terms that fell short of outright enthusiasm. Also examined was the question of whether female rather than male inspectors 'should be employed to visit infant schools, to examine the lower standards and to inspect the whole work of those schools in which girls form the preponderating or exclusive element'. They felt that there were serious practical difficulties involved in the general employment of women on the inspectorate 'where much travelling is required', but they considered that 'in large towns the experiment might be tried of appointing sub-inspectresses to assist in the examination of infant schools and of the lower standards'. Such officers ought to have been teachers in elementary schools, or have had experience as governesses in training colleges.

A third recommendation concerned the problem of securing greater uniformity of standard among the inspectors – a matter to which the Department had itself been recently devoting much thought. The Commissioners believed that the requisite consistency would be rendered easier of attainment 'if the chief inspectors ceased to have charge of small districts of their own, and confined themselves to the large areas which they have to supervise, so that their whole time and attention might be given to such supervision'.

In their Final Report the Commissioners also provided a full and detailed description of the duties of HM Inspectors. The examination of children constituted only one of their many responsibilities. They had pupil-teachers to examine and training colleges to inspect. They were required to submit an annual report on the general efficiency of every school and teacher in their districts, and to 'pay visits without notice, for the purpose of observing and conferring with the managers and teachers on the general work and organisation of the schools, on the time-tables, and on the methods of instruction'. In addition, they had to keep a constant watch over the school supply of their districts and to advise the managers, not only on the accommodation required, but on 'the particulars of procedure, of law, and of the working of the Education Acts, as well as on the numerous non-educational difficulties which necessarily must arise in the management of the schools'. Finally, they were expected to advise the Department on questions of policy and administration, and to report the general feeling of their districts about those questions. In short, and to use modern phraseology, HMIs were regarded by the Department as its 'eyes and ears'.

Such were the principal findings of the Commissioners; but how did the inspectors themselves regard their functions? The testimony of one HMI, who later cast a critical retrospective eye on his experiences during this period, presents a less imposing picture. Recalling that part of his work connected with the conduct of the annual examination of children to assess the grant due, he wrote:

For me they were so many examinees; and as they all belonged to the 'lower orders', and as (according to the belief in which I had been allowed to grow up) the lower orders were congenitally inferior to the 'upper classes', I took little or no interest in my examinees either as individuals or as human beings, and never tried to explore their hidden depths.[1]

If this outlook was common to many inspectors, then the Cross Commissioners may have been mistaken in their belief that a university education generated 'wide and liberal' views; it could, and evidently did, also breed intellectual snobbery and unhealthy social attitudes.

[1] E. Holmes, *In quest of an Ideal*, 1920, p. 64.

Oddly enough, the first innovation introduced by the Department following the publication of the Report was one that the Commissioners had been at pains to deprecate. In their discussion of the role of female inspectors, they observed that 'the multiplication of inspectors for special subjects, such as needlework, cookery, domestic economy, drill, music, and the like, however desirable in the interests of these studies, is open to many objections and is obviously possible only within very narrow limits'.

But the Department found that strict adherence to a general policy of non-specialization in the inspectorate presented serious administrative difficulties, at least so far as distinctively female education was concerned. When, for example, cookery was to be examined, the inspector often had to call upon the services of any lady who could be persuaded to offer incidental assistance, sometimes only to discover that such a volunteer was as unknowledgeable as he himself. In 1890, therefore, a Mrs Harrison was enlisted to inspect cookery and laundrywork in schools. Although her appointment was on a temporary and experimental basis only, she was accredited, unlike her co-partner on the needlework side, with the title of 'Inspectress'.[1]

That same year Kekewich sought the Lord President's assent to a major reform: the appointment of a senior chief inspector. Administrative control of the inspectorate had for long rested with the chief clerk, an office that Kekewich himself had held immediately prior to his promotion. As such he soon came to recognize the need for some 'ultimate inspectorial authority' to coordinate standards and to act as an appeal court in the event of serious disagreements between inspectors and teachers or managers. Lord Cranbrook concurred with the proposal and, after a slight altercation with the Treasury during which the Lord President threatened to resign if financial sanction were refused, the appointment was approved.

The man selected for the new post was the Rev. T. W. Sharpe, who had been one of the Anglican inspectors gazetted before the 1870 Act and was now nearing the end of his career. However, his services proved so valuable that the Treasury was twice asked to permit his remaining in office beyond the normal retiring age.

[1] The Hon. Mrs Colborne, who succeeded Miss Jones as the Directress of Needlework in 1894, and Miss Dean, who followed Mrs Harrison in 1896, were both placed on the Department's permanent and pensionable establishment.

Kekewich, in justifying his request, pointed out that, apart from any other consideration, it would be very inconvenient just then to transfer Sharpe's work to other hands, since many developments were taking place in the field of inspection.

Among the more prominent of these may be mentioned the gradual abandonment in large measure . . . of the old system of examination and payment by results in Day Schools, and the substitution of a more intelligent system of inspection and appraisement of educational methods, under which the Inspector becomes the adviser of school managers and teachers, and does not continue, as formerly, to be merely their judge and critic. In the general introduction of this new order of things, which must of necessity take some few years to accomplish, Mr Sharpe's advice is invaluable.[1]

Sharpe stayed on until the close of 1897, and, during a period of change and experiment, his personal contribution as the first senior chief inspector appears to have been extremely important. But to begin with, the position itself as a means of securing the requisite degree of control and co-ordination proved less effective than had been anticipated.

Further reforms had to await the arrival of Arthur Acland. By promoting a number of sub-inspectors to the rank of full HMI he opened up the inspectorate to certificated teachers. Not that the lowering of this barrier, which was still social rather than educational in character, made much difference at first to the overall composition of the force, nor did it serve to remove the teachers' dissatisfaction. Almost certainly, as Dr. Edmonds has surmised, 'the root cause of the trouble was the principle of selection by nomination to HM Inspectorate and its operation in favour of 'Oxbridge' antecedents in three cases out of every four'.[2]

Whilst Acland was seeing belated justice done to the teaching profession, changes of nomenclature were introduced into the inspectorate. With the discarding of the principle of payment by results, inspectors' assistants could no longer perform the function for which they had originally been appointed. Consequently, in 1895, their title was altered to that of sub-inspector (second class),

[1] PRO Ed. 23/71. Letter dated 14 February 1894.
[2] E. L. Edmonds, *The School Inspector*, 1962, p. 145. In his book, Kekewich describes the method employed by the Duke of Devonshire in the selection of examiners and inspectors. 'The last man appointed was from Oxford, we had better have one from Cambridge this time.' Kekewich, *Education Department*, p. 155.

though the conditions of their appointment remained much the same. Concomitantly, sub-inspectors were to be known henceforth as sub-inspectors (first class).

Women, too, were beginning to benefit from the gradual relinquishment of long-lasting prejudices. The success of the specialist inspectresses in needlework and cookery, the clear lead provided by some school boards in appointing female organizers over a wide range of subjects, and the growing appreciation of the importance of girls' education, did much to enhance women's claims to more general recognition. Prompted also by the Bryce Commissioners' somewhat lukewarm recommendation that 'duly qualified women should be chosen where there is likely to be sufficient work for them',[1] the Department decided, towards the end of 1895, to appoint two women as sub-inspectors to assist their male colleagues in the work of reporting on the condition of girls' infant schools, or upon that of girls attending mixed schools. The Treasury, whose approval had to be obtained for any increase in establishment, showed characteristic caution in agreeing to the request, insisting on a designation – sub-inspectors (women) – which would not prejudge the conditions under which such officers might in future be promoted. In the rearguard action against female emancipation, it was clearly determined not to capitulate prematurely. Acknowledgement of ability was one thing, equality of opportunity was quite another.

Under Kekewich, the Education Department showed itself less attached to outworn shibboleths. Women actually began to be taken on the staff at the central office. In 1897, as has been noted above, a 'lady library assistant' was appointed, and a year later, following a decision that the Department itself should examine and grant certificates in cookery in training colleges, the need arose to appoint assistant examiners in the subject. The two women whose services were engaged for the purpose also made important recommendations to the Department as to the kind of training advisable in the colleges, and devoted what time they could to the inspection of domestic subjects in elementary schools.

These developments on the female side of the inspectorate probably owed their origin to the efforts of the Permanent Secretary, for with Acland's departure the impetus for reform from

---

[1] The Bryce Commission, significantly, was the first Royal Commission to which women members were appointed.

ministerial sources lost strength. Kekewich himself claimed that the Education Department was 'the first Government Office that ever employed women in responsible positions', and the first 'to recognise the latent efficiency and capacity of women, and to make a beginning in breaking down the absurd disabilities of sex'.[1] To Sir George almost certainly goes the credit for another innovation which, despite the somewhat clandestine manner of its introduction, was to have significant long-term consequences.

One of the main principles underlying the 1890 Code was the assumption by the state of the duty to care for the physical welfare of children. In pursuance of this duty, the Department prescribed that physical training should be made an integral part of the school curriculum. As a result, an increasing concern was felt for the health of children in general. Kekewich, seeing the need for expert guidance in this quarter, sought the attachment of medical advisers to his staff. Devonshire 'threw a douche of cold water on the proposal' but the ingenious Secretary managed to secure the services of an experienced doctor as a member of the ordinary inspecting staff. At first, the latter's duties were concerned with such questions in day-to-day school work as involved a medical issue, but with the growth of special schools the scope of his inspection rapidly expanded.

The last change of any note occurring in the inspectorate before the end of the century came about as a result of an inquiry into the distribution of the science and art grants. During the investigation, the committee learned that an anomalous situation had arisen over the inspection of drawing in elementary schools. It appeared that for some thirty years (1855–86) the Science and Art Department had controlled entirely this particular inspection. From 1886 the Education Department assumed responsibility for the examination of children in the lower standards, but the drawings of older pupils were still sent to South Kensington to be marked. Holding that all the instruction in an elementary school should be under the same administration and inspection, the committee recommended that the management of the drawing grant be handed over to the department in Whitehall. When shortly afterwards the proposal was implemented, the officers responsible for examining the subject were likewise transferred.

This move amounted to little more than the disposal of a minor

[1] Kekewich, *Education Department*, pp. 214, 215.

administrative inconsistency, anticipating the passage of the Board of Education Bill which was then being prepared, and affording, perhaps, some insurance against its rejection. Assuredly, the important reforms of the period had been the handiwork of two men: the Permanent Secretary, George Kekewich, and one of the Vice-Presidents, Arthur Acland. They had, between them, endeavoured to improve the inspectorate in five distinct respects. By admitting teachers to the higher ranks, they had given it a more democratic structure; by appointing women to perform general duties, they had given it a more representative character; by broadening the scope of its activities, they had given it a more comprehensive function; by creating the post of senior chief inspector, they had given it a more coherent organization; and by abandoning payment by results, they had given it a more educative role. Their achievements have tended to be overshadowed by those of Morant; yet without them the latter might well have failed to progress as far and as fast as he did.

Throughout the sixty years of its existence, the inspectorate had experienced many vicissitudes and undergone many alterations. In numbers alone it had increased from two to over 350. But it had grown in wisdom as well as in strength, at least in the wisdom with which it was utilized. Originally appointed as government watch-dogs over the expenditure of state funds, HM Inspectors had become financial assessors of supposed teaching ability. As such they had earned the opprobrium of the very people they had been designed to help. Then, as a more liberal spirit showed itself in Whitehall, a new interpretation of the inspectors' responsibilities evolved. Guardians of the public purse they remained, as they must probably always remain, but they also assumed much more the nature of missionaries, spreading the current pedagogical gospel wherever the need arose, and of maids-of-all-work, helping in innumerable ways to create the optimum conditions in which the educational system could flourish.

7

THE SCIENCE AND ART DEPARTMENT: SOUTH KENSINGTON IN EMBRYO

There is no necessary connection between Science and Art and . . . they owe their combination in this country to a merely administrative device.[1]

Technical education, in the sense that the term is used today, became necessary in England only after the Industrial Revolution had produced its full impact. Prior to this phenomenon, most skilled occupations were handicrafts learnt from an experienced exponent on a more or less individual basis; during it, the need for craftsmen was replaced by a demand for both a much smaller number of skilled engineers, and a much larger number of unskilled machine-minders. Except for a few trades, apprenticeship, the traditional method of technical training, lost its *raison d'être*. For the first half of the nineteenth century, the country was under neither economic nor social pressures to improve the quality of its workmen. There was an abundance of cheap labour and such skills as were required to keep the wheels of industry turning were of so low a standard that they could be easily acquired. Hence, state interference to raise standards of workmanship was regarded as superfluous; in any event it would have entailed higher taxes and increased costs of manufacture, apart from contravening the prevailing socio-economic doctrines of self-help and *laissez-faire*.

So far as the production of goods was concerned, therefore, manufacturers saw no reason to welcome, far less to solicit, state aid. But this complacency, or short-sightedness, did not extend to all industries or to all processes within a particular industry. Before an article can be produced it must be designed, and disturbing evidence was reaching these shores in the late 1820s that all was not well with the quality of British design. The first unmistakable signs appeared after Huskisson's lowering of the tariff barriers in 1824–5, when the influx of foreign goods, especially

[1] G. Balfour, *Educational Systems of Great Britain and Ireland*, 1903, p. 154.

French fancy silk goods which had hitherto been prohibited, demonstrated to our manufacturers how hopelessly inferior we were to the French in the matter of design. Falling sales and profits reflected the discrepancy, customers both at home and abroad showing their preference for foreign products. To counter this adverse trend English manufacturers began, at considerable expense, to import foreign designs.

But such a palliative could not cure the deep-seated cause of the malady, which seemed to lie in the fact that certain foreign countries were devoting much thought to the education of artists and artisans while England did virtually nothing. And, as industry appeared unable or unwilling to make the necessary effort to save itself, so the case for state intervention grew stronger. With the passing of the first Reform Bill, the need to act was reinforced by the will to act. The new House of Commons showed a refreshing readiness to investigate, to discuss and to take action upon a whole range of subjects, including that of instruction in the fine arts. Moreover, when in 1833 the state made the first grant for elementary schooling, many manufacturers expressed the view that it was equally the duty of the state to provide instruction for designers in order to improve our trade. These two influences were clearly at work when, in July 1835, William Ewart, M.P. for Liverpool, moved for the appointment of a select committee 'to enquire into the best means of extending a knowledge of the Fine Arts and of the Principles of Design among the people – especially the manufacturing population of the country; and also to inquire into the constitution, management and effects of Institutions connected with the Arts'.

Behind these terms of reference can be detected the hand of Ewart's friend, the artist Benjamin Haydon. Haydon had for some years been interested in securing an improvement in the teaching of fine art. Despairing of the contribution that the Royal Academy was prepared to make, he looked to the state for action. Early attempts at petitioning Parliament proved fruitless, but latterly his words reached more receptive ears. His main convert was Ewart, who was persuaded that the Academy was a stronghold of reaction and privilege and, as such, ripe for scrutiny, and who was already convinced that something must be done to provide artisans with a certain amount of artistic training. As a majority in the Commons shared his concern, the motion was carried.

6

In August 1836 the select committee published its final Report, which amounted to an outspoken attack on the deplorable condition of the fine and applied arts in Great Britain. It came to the conclusion that 'from the highest branches of poetical design down to the lowest connexion between design and manufactures, the Arts have received little encouragement in this country', and that there were very strong economic reasons for changing this negative attitude.[1] It accepted the judgment of witnesses who declared that Britain's continental rivals, especially the French, were far ahead in the matter of design, and it appeared to the Committee, seeking the cause of this superiority, that 'the great advantage which foreign manufacturing-artists possess over those of Great Britain consists in the greater extension of art throughout the mass of society abroad'.[2] This was particularly noticeable in France, where schools of design, superintended by the state, were diffused throughout the country, and the Committee felt that some such system should be introduced on this side of the Channel. 'Perhaps the Government would most judiciously interpose not only by creating a Normal School, but by applying to local institutions the species of assistance now extended to the building of school-houses.'[3]

On the other hand, assistance should not become a cloak for interference; a kind of benevolent yet disinterested patronage seemed the ideal solution. Government action 'should aim at the development and extension of art; but it should neither control its action, nor force its cultivation'.[4]

In fact, the government had, before the Report appeared, already anticipated one of its recommendations by deciding on the establishment of a Normal (or Training) School of Design. There was at that time, needless to say, no central educational authority in being to whom the duty of supervising the School – and any future provincial schools – could be assigned. However, the trend of the discussions within the committee, and the nature of the source from which the demand for such schools emanated, seemed to suggest that this was a subject intimately related to commerce and industry; accordingly, it was placed in the hands of the Board of Trade.

The decision rested on sound historical precedent, even if there was little to commend it on educational grounds. As far back as 1665 a Committee of Council for Trade had·been created, for the pur-

---

[1] *PP* 1836, IX, 3.   [2] *Ibid.* 4.   [3] *Ibid.* 5.   [4] *Ibid.*

pose, amongst other things, of restoring the former high standards of English workmanship. In the intervening period this function of improving the quality of manufactures had gradually faded into the background; now it was again brought into prominence. Unfortunately, the Board was ill-equipped to shoulder fresh responsibilities. New officials were appointed, but their duties were not defined, their activities were not co-ordinated, and no coherent policy was formulated for their guidance. These adverse circumstances account in large measure for the administrative mistakes and shortcomings that beset the Schools of Design in their early years.

In December 1836 C. Poulett Thomson, the President of the Board of Trade, called a meeting of certain Royal Academicians and others interested in art. They in turn appointed a Provisional Council of Management consisting of artists, representatives of industry, some Members of Parliament and various officers of the Board; either the minister or his deputy generally presided over this body when it was convened to do business. Rooms at Somerset House, which had formerly been occupied by the Royal Academy, were granted to the Council, and the Government School of Design opened in June the following year. Its purpose was declared to be 'to afford the manufacturers [i.e. industrial workers] an opportunity of acquiring a competent knowledge of the Fine Arts, as far as the same are connected with manufactures'. Thus the function of the School was to supply industrial designers, not to produce artists.

At about the same time as the government was establishing its metropolitan school, a number of provincial schools of design which had sprung up during the previous few years began to request financial assistance. At first, the Board of Trade was too much occupied with the venture in London to attend to their pleas, though it was fully aware that, for its policy to succeed, it must promote similar enterprises in the manufacturing towns. By 1841, it was in a position to do so, and in that year the government voted £10,000 to assist in the formation and maintenance of schools of design in industrial districts.[1] Predictably, the grant was made

---

[1] Between 1841 and 1852 seventeen of these schools were founded. In a number of towns, the Council was asked to establish the provincial school in connexion with the local Mechanics' Institutes which were flourishing at this period. This the Council declined to do. Partly as a result of this refusal the schools of design,

subject to inspection, and shortly afterwards the Director of the Central School (then William Dyce, R.A.) was empowered to act also as the Inspector of Provincial Schools.

Meanwhile, the executive body charged with the management of the Central School had undergone the first of several upheavals that were periodically to shake it during its brief existence. Ever since his appointment in 1838 Dyce had expressed misgivings about the Provisional Council, believing it to be too large, unwieldy and inefficient. He was given the opportunity to air his views officially when Gladstone became Vice-President of the Board of Trade in 1841. The latter, impressed by what he learned, approached his chief, Lord Ripon, suggesting that responsibility for the School should be transferred to the Committee of Council on Education. Had such a proposal been adopted at this early stage, many of the problems that bedevilled educational administration throughout the Victorian era would almost certainly have been avoided. Unhappily, it was rejected, not, as might be conjectured, because of ministerial opposition, not through any lack of enthusiasm or resolution on the part of the government, but by virtue of a minor point of constitutional law. The discovery was made that the grant of public money for the establishment of provincial schools had been voted to 'the Council of the School of Design'. Parliament, the argument went, had thereby given this body a statutory existence which the government could not remove without putting into motion the ponderous machinery of legislation.

Nevertheless, something had to be done about the Council. It could not be allowed to continue in its present form, since the representatives of the Board, who were legally responsible for the administration of the Schools, were liable to find themselves outvoted. To rectify this, the Board decided both to define more precisely the relationship between itself and the Council, and to reconstruct the latter. Henceforth, the School of Design would be placed 'under the management of a Director, subject to the control of a Council, and of a Council subject to the control of the Board of Trade'.[1] The reconstituted Council would consist of twenty-four members to be nominated by the Board.

---

many of which subsequently became schools of art, were isolated from other educational institutions. The isolation still persists in some degree.

[1] *Minute of the Council*, dated 15 May 1842.

Difficulties were experienced, too, in the immediate control of the School, the personnel of which was changed with bewildering frequency. On this aspect it is unnecessary to dwell, except to note those developments that affected the growth of the inspectorate. Up to 1843 the offices of Director of the Central School and Inspector of the Provincial Schools were combined. In that year they were separated when Dyce resigned as Director to become an 'Occasional Inspector of Provincial Schools'. Further alterations in the inspection of the schools occurred from time to time until July 1850 when 'Their Lordships of the Committee of Council appointed for the consideration of all matters relating to Trade and Foreign Plantations' were pleased to appoint Ambrose Poynter Inspector of Provincial Schools in the Government School of Design. Poynter thus enjoyed the distinction of being the first full-time inspector for higher education in this country, although neither he nor those attached to the subsequent Science and Art Department were accorded the title of 'Her Majesty's Inspector'.

Hopes that the School of Design would flourish under its new management were soon dispelled. Quarrels among the staff, insubordination on the part of the students, and unnecessary interference from the Council, all helped to diminish the School's reputation and value. 'The School of Design', protested *The Athenaeum*, in September 1847, 'has been turned into a school for scandal'. Inquiry followed inquiry until in 1848 the Board of Trade dissolved the Council and established a new executive body to control the School. Placed under the chairmanship of the Vice-President of the Board of Trade this 'Committee of Management', as it was called, consisted of three artist and five official (i.e. civil servant) members.

But the trials and tribulations of the School were by no means at an end. Perhaps the 'artistic temperament' of staff and students contributed to its difficulties; at all events the new regime functioned no more smoothly than its predecessors. During the autumn of 1848 the then Vice-President, Lord Granville, looked round for someone who might rescue the institution from its plight. His soundings led him to an assistant keeper at the Public Record Office, named Henry Cole, who in modern parlance would probably be described as a 'trouble shooter'. Cole was invited to submit proposals designed to restore the School's fortunes. His response was to create a climate of public opinion that would be favourable to the kind of radical reforms he considered necessary. No subscriber to half-measures, he founded a new periodical, the *Journal of Design*, in which he belaboured the authorities responsible, in his opinion, for past errors. The tenor of his argument was that the fault for the failure of the schools, both metropolitan and provincial, lay not with the industrialists, nor to any appreciable extent with the artists, but with the administrators, and above all, with the 'senile half-wits of the Board of Trade'.[1]

Cole's second line of attack was to seek a means for exerting parliamentary pressure. He found a sympathetic ally in Milner Gibson, a Liberal M.P. and a former Vice-President of the Board of Trade. Prompted by Cole, Milner Gibson called, in March 1849, for a select committee to consider the constitution and management of the Schools of Design. The case for a public inquiry was practically cast-iron, for the Schools, most of which had been in existence for a dozen years and which had received considerable subventions from the Exchequer, were in a parlous condition. The central school had been torn by internal dissensions, the provincial schools were on the verge of bankruptcy; in neither instance did they appear to be performing the task for which they had been established, namely, the training of industrial designers.

The duly appointed select committee decided that the root of the trouble lay in the confused relationship that prevailed between successive Councils or Committees of Management and the Board of Trade. It therefore recommended that the management of the Schools should be placed on a more definite footing, specifying that 'the supreme executive authority should be vested in the Board of Trade'. Acting upon this proposal, the Board in November 1849 abolished the short-lived Committee of Management replacing it by a new Committee composed of 'laymen' only and meeting under the President of the Board. Even this operation failed to resuscitate the languishing patients, and the Board eventually reached the conclusion that rule by committee itself might be largely responsible for their chronic condition.

The turning-point in their fortunes came in 1851 with the holding of the Great Exhibition. So far as the Schools of Design were concerned, the Exhibition had two important consequences: it demonstrated that Britain was falling a long way behind her rivals in the sphere of applied art, and it enhanced the reputation of

[1] Quoted in Q. Bell, *The Schools of Design*, 1963, p. 221.

Henry Cole who had been one of its foremost organizers. If Cole could be persuaded to undertake the management of the schools, there was some possibility that they might be revived and made to prosper. Accordingly, in October 1851, Lord Granville offered him the secretaryship of the School of Design. Cole accepted the post, attacking with characteristic energy and ruthlessness the formidable problem confronting him. On 15 January 1852 he wrote to Labouchere, the President of the Board of Trade:

In respect of the best way of reorganizing the management, my opinion is that a Department of the Board of Trade should be created . . . having a special secretary, through whom all the business should pass for the decision of the President or Vice-President. I submit, that, on the whole, this arrangement would best insure undivided responsibility and attention, and would work better than any special board consisting of several persons. If such a change were made, I would venture to suggest that the name of the 'School of Design', which is subject to misinterpretation, should be altered to one more nearly expressive of the objects in view. Such a name as the 'Department of Practical Art' would, I think, be well understood and appropriate.[1]

Both the Board and Treasury accepted this suggestion, and in February 1852 the Department of Practical Art came into existence. It was to be administered by one permanent whole-time official directly responsible to the Board of Trade. This 'General Superintendent' would be aided by an artist 'of high professional character, whose advice and assistance would be indispensable, but who could not be expected to give up all his time to the business of the department . . . '.[2] The Superintendent, it goes without saying, was to be Henry Cole; the position of art adviser was filled by Richard Redgrave, R.A., a professor at the School of Design.

Soon after their appointment, Cole and Redgrave outlined what they believed the three main functions of the new Department ought to be: to afford opportunities for general elementary instruction in drawing as a branch of national education as a whole, to provide advanced instruction in art, and to promote the application of the principles of technical art to the improvement of manufactures. They also laid down that the aim should be to make the

[1] H. Cole, *Fifty Years of Public Work*, 1884, vol. 1, p. 295.
[2] *Department of Practical Art Estimates 1852-3*. Letter from the Board of Trade to the Treasury dated 29 January 1852.

Department, as far as practicable, self-supporting in all its branches. The pursuit of this aim over the following decade was to have momentous consequences for elementary, as well as for technical, education.

Under the new dispensation, the Schools of Design, and indeed the Department as a whole, at long last began to prosper, so that within a comparatively short time the latter could justifiably boast of its achievements. Between 1852 and 1858 the seventeen ailing Schools of Design had grown into fifty-six flourishing Schools of Art, and the number of pupils had increased from 4,800 to 35,000. By 1866 there were 18,139 students in 102 schools of Art, 1,140 students in thirty-two night classes, and 80,084 children learning drawing in elementary schools.

How was it that Cole succeeded where others had failed? While full credit must be given to him for his personal contribution in terms of energy and inventiveness, it should be remembered that he enjoyed two enormous advantages over those who had preceded him: he was allowed virtually a free hand to put the Schools to rights, and he had the benefit of powerful economic and political forces working in his favour. He was fortunate, too, in that just as he took over the management of the School, its premises had to be evacuated. The old and thoroughly unsuitable quarters in Somerset House were exchanged for the more salubrious surroundings of Marlborough House. Cole was also wise enough to learn from the mistakes of the previous fifteen years. From the outset the Schools of Design had suffered from two crippling impediments: the first was administrative, the second doctrinal.[1] The former stemmed from the problem of trying to establish art schools in a country where basic elementary education was deficient, from the clumsy machinery that was devised to manage the schools, and from the temperamental nature of successive principals. Moreover, the whole enterprise had little chance of prospering given, on the one hand, officials who possessed only the vaguest idea of its purpose or of how to deal with the practical difficulties subsequently encountered, and, on the other, manufacturers whose ambivalent attitude was one of encouragement in theory combined with a disinclination to support the venture financially. The

[1] While the Schools, from their inception, were handicapped in many ways, one disability they did manage to avoid: an embroilment in religious controversy. Apparently the teaching of art, and later of science, carried no moral overtones.

doctrinal dilemma sprang from differences of opinion over what the ultimate purpose of the Schools should be. At one extreme, the exponents of 'High Art' led by Haydon, expected them to place the emphasis on 'art for art's sake', and to relegate the needs of industry to a minor place in the curriculum. Such a concept was acceptable neither to politicians nor to manufacturers. At the opposite extreme were those like Dyce who envisaged the schools developing into state-supported factories producing and selling their own wares in competition with industry and untainted by its materialism. This idea had even less chance of succeeding. In the end, a compromise had to be reached, in which the requirements of industry – for it was industry that paid the piper – would be paramount; and it was Cole who realized that, in a commercial society, the schools serving that society must themselves be commercial institutions if they were to entertain any prospect of success. Largely because of this, the Department's methods for many years afterwards 'smacked more of the world of commerce than of culture'.[1]

Several of the obstacles to the development of practical art education, such as the absence of efficient primary schooling and the suspicion if not the hostility of some industrialists, were also hindering the growth of technical and scientific instruction. But, just as the Great Exhibition acted as a catalyst in changing attitudes towards the one, so did it have a salutary effect upon the other. To the undiscerning eye the Exhibition was a tremendous triumph for Britain, demonstrating her to be the foremost industrial nation in the world; but to the far-sighted there were few grounds for complacency. For Britain's lead was fast diminishing, and the countries that were closing the gap were just those with well-organized systems of technical education, something that Britain so signally lacked. The writing was on the wall for government and industry alike to read.

Two events flowed almost immediately from the holding of the Exhibition. In the first place, it had made a profit of some £186,000 and the question arose as to how this surplus should be utilized. The Prince Consort, who was President of the Royal Commission for the Exhibition, proposed that it should be spent on the purchase of land upon which might be built institutions for

[1] E. J. R. Eaglesham, *The Foundations of Twentieth-century Education in England*, 1967, p. 21.

promoting the main objects of the Exhibition, namely the Union of Art and Industry. It so happened that on the market at that time were three large estates extending from Kensington Gore to the Brompton Road. With the aid of a Parliamentary grant of £150,000, these eighty-six acres of farmland were bought, and plans prepared for their development.

Meanwhile, another leading organizer of the Exhibition was endeavouring to direct public attention to the need for reforming the country's educational system. This was Lyon Playfair who by the age of thirty-three had already won a reputation for himself as a distinguished chemist. His influence increased considerably when he became what might be described as scientific consultant to Prince Albert. In 1852 Playfair travelled Europe to acquaint himself with the various systems of technical education to be found in the leading industrial countries. On his return he delivered a lecture, which received wide publicity, under the title 'Industrial Instruction on the Continent'. In all probability, it prompted the government to act. Later that same year, the following words appeared in the speech from the Throne at the opening of the new session of Parliament: 'The advancement of the Fine Arts and of Practical Science will be readily recognized by you as worthy of the Attention of a great and enlightened Nation. I have directed that a comprehensive scheme shall be laid before you, having in view the promotion of these Objects, towards which I invite your aid and co-operation.'

Soon after this announcement the short-lived Derby administration fell, but the Liberal government under Lord Aberdeen adopted this particular policy and swiftly implemented it. The Prince Consort took a personal interest and an active part in the exploratory discussions on the form that the scheme should take, Lord President Granville, Cole and Playfair all paying several visits to Windsor. In January 1853 Playfair informed Cole that a new Department was to be created,[1] in the naming of which the word 'Science' was to take precedence over 'Art', and in the administering of which Cole was made senior to Playfair, each being designated Joint-Secretary and both undertaking such inspectorial duties as might be necessary. By this ingenious formula, honour was evidently satisfied.

Action was taken at the official level on 16 March when the

[1] Described by W. H. G. Armytage as 'an unhealthy hybrid'.

Board of Trade wrote to the Treasury elaborating this basic plan, and justifying it. 'The time has now arrived when the consideration of the important question of supplying scientific and artistic instruction to the industrial classes of this country in a more systematic manner than has hitherto been possible, can no longer be postponed.'

It was Their Lordships' intention 'to extend a system of encouragement to local institutions for Practical Science, similar to that already commenced in the Department of Practical Art'. Endorsing the principle enunciated in 1841 and vigorously restated by Cole eleven years later, the letter emphasized that the motive power in the proposed Department would be 'local and voluntary – the system, in the main, self-supporting'. The Board felt also that the occasion presented a suitable opportunity for affiliating to the Department sundry public institutions that had some association with science or art, e.g. the Government School of Mines, the Museum of Practical Geology, the Geological Survey, the Museum of Irish Industry and the Royal Dublin Society.

Shortly afterwards, the government placed the scheme before Parliament, the announcement being made, for some obscure reason, in the course of a debate on a Charitable Trusts Bill, and not by the President of the Board of Trade but by Lord John Russell, then Minister without portfolio. While the proposals were generally welcomed, Ewart, whose interest in technical education was undiminished by the passage of time, questioned the wisdom of placing the Department under the superintendence of the Board of Trade. He did not understand 'why a commercial body who had already more to do than they were able to find time to perform, should be charged with the care of such matters', and he hoped they would be removed to some other department. Probably rather sooner than he expected, his hopes were to be realized.

Later the same year (1853) the newly-formed Department was investigated, along with other government offices, by a Committee of Inquiry consisting of Charles Trevelyan and Stafford Northcote. Their Report contained many details of the Department's *modus operandi*. Its aim was to create a system of education calculated to awaken a general interest in science and art, and to provide facilities for their study. To achieve this, it intended to foster the growth of schools of science and art throughout the country and to establish central institutions for the dual purpose of training masters for the local schools, and supplying more advanced instruction in special branches. Encouragement to local schools would be given in several ways: for example, by means of a well-organized scheme of direction and inspection; by the supply of good but inexpensive equipment and of properly educated masters; and by pecuniary assistance, chiefly in the form of masters' salaries. To operate this system, where the stress lay on self-help, only a small establishment at headquarters was deemed necessary. The Committee proposed that there should be, in addition to the two Joint-Secretaries-cum-Inspectors, a Registrar

whose duty it will be to render assistance in both Sections of the Department, to supply the place of either of the Secretaries in case of their absence, and to maintain harmony in the working of the system by communicating to the Secretary for one Section such information respecting the proceedings in the other Section as may obviate the risk either of collision, or of needless repetition of work.[1]

Redgrave's services as a part-time Art Superintendent were to be retained. The remainder of the staff would consist of six clerks, a storekeeper and sundry warehousemen, printers, messengers and attendants. In passing, the Committee noted that an Inspector of Drawing in elementary schools under the Education Department was shortly to be appointed. Since this officer was to be selected and employed by the Science and Art Department, the Committee felt that it was desirable that his salary should be charged upon the vote for that Department.

The Report was accepted by the Board of Trade and approved by the Treasury, but within two years it was found that the arrangement of having two Secretary/Inspectors was unsatisfactory. On the one hand, there was no real provision for the joint working of the Sections, on the other, the combining of duties in the same individual led on occasion to discontinuity of administrative procedure. Accordingly, in 1855, the two branches were amalgamated, Playfair becoming sole Secretary and Cole taking on the office of Inspector General.

Meanwhile, there occurred an event which was to prove of

[1] *Report of a Committee of Inquiry into the Department of Practical Science and Art*, 1853, p. 172.

some long-term significance, but which seemed of only minor importance at the time. In 1854, at the instigation of Harry Chester, one of its Vice-Presidents, the Society of Arts held in London a special loan exhibition of English and foreign educational aids. After it closed, many of the exhibits were left by their donors at the disposal of the promoters. The Society, unable to provide the necessary accommodation, presented the collection to the Science and Art Department, which displayed it in a part of the buildings newly-erected at South Kensington. Publishers and manufacturers were invited to contribute additional material, which they did in generous measure. Within a few years the nucleus of an educational library had been formed; figuring prominently in it were books on methods of instruction employed either at home or overseas. Subsequently, a reading room was opened and, to meet the needs of students, most of whom were attending science and art schools, a number of more advanced reference and text books were provided. Later still, reports and other works bearing on the history and progress of education both in this country and abroad were added, as were numerous English and foreign educational journals.

Thus, with much foresight and catholicity of outlook, the Department primarily concerned with technical education built up over a period of some fifteen years a library encompassing education in virtually all its aspects. It was justifiably proud of its achievement, as is shown in its Report for 1896, at which date the library was transferred to the Education Department.

The most important event of the year was the removal to . . . Whitehall, of the collection of books, numbering 5,868 volumes, known as the 'Educational Library' . . . which consists of works relating to the history, theory and practice of education, reports and memoirs on public instruction at home and abroad, educational periodicals and treatises. This collection appears to have been one of the earliest formed in any country, with the object of enabling teachers to become acquainted with treatises and reports bearing on their work.

A short time after the Department acquired the beginnings of a library, it severed its connection with the Board of Trade. By the Order in Council of 25 February 1856[1] authority was given for its transfer to the Education Department. The intention was that in

[1] See above, pp. 44–5.

future this Department should consist of two branches: one administering state aid to general or elementary education,[1] the other promoting, through financial and other assistance, technical or secondary education. Exactly why the government decided to make the change is not altogether clear. It may have occurred to them that 'it would be advantageous to the education of the working-classes if the State control of all their schools were centred in one body',[2] or, since there were regions where the activities of the two Departments overlapped, it may have been thought desirable that there should be a minister (or ministers) common to and in charge of both, who could, in Cole's words, 'render the working of any points of contact between primary and secondary education harmonious and consistent'.

Whatever the cause, the effect was hardly noticeable, and could scarcely have been the one intended. For, though this highly desirable marriage took place, the partners decided to go their separate ways from the first, even to the extent of living apart and employing their own distinct staffs and methods of housekeeping. Physically divorced, they drifted further apart in the years to come until, despite one brief attempt to bring them together, they ended up barely on speaking terms with each other.[3]

There were several outstanding differences between the two Departments that contributed towards their estrangement. For example, while the Whitehall Department generally consulted the Committee of Council on important questions of policy, the Science and Art Department was controlled by a Board composed only of the Lord President and Vice-President of that Committee, none of the remaining members being advised about the work of the South Kensington branch.[4] Again, the funds of the latter were

[1] This branch was called, in the Order in Council, the 'Educational Establishment of the Privy Council Office'; but it had always been known as the Education Department, and it continued to be referred to as such, although technically that term applied only to the departments combined.

[2] F. Ware, *Educational Foundations of Trade and Industry*, 1901, p. 32.

[3] Using a different metaphor, Professor Armytage likens the Science and Art Department after it emerged from the operation that delivered it (i.e. the Order in Council) to the 'Siamese twin of the Education Department, embarrassingly joined yet definitely separate'. W. H. G. Armytage, 'The Centenary of South Ken.', *British Journal of Educational Studies*, vol. v, no. 1, November 1956.

[4] Shortly after the union had been arranged, Playfair reported that Lord Granville 'did not see the point of juncture' between the two departments. This was odd considering that, in the Order in Council, Granville himself, as Lord President, had been designated 'the point of juncture'.

given a separate vote, and its Directory of Regulations was entirely distinct from the Whitehall Code. In addition, the Science and Art Department was much less subject to Parliamentary control than was the Education Department, for, unlike the latter, its regulations did not need to be submitted to both Houses for approval. Moreover, 'South Kensington' had wider responsibilities, geographically speaking, than 'Whitehall', since its area encompassed the whole of the British Isles, and even, for examination purposes, Britain's colonies and dependencies. Finally, the Education Department, at any rate during the period 1850–70, deliberately strove, in the interests of administrative simplicity, to restrict its functions to aiding the supply of elementary schooling to the generality of poor children only. The Science and Art Department, on the contrary, was constantly being required to take under its wing any society or establishment that had the remotest connexion with the two subjects in its title. To the motley collection of institutions it acquired in 1854 were added, over the next twenty years, many others, including the Navigation Schools of the Marine Department of the Board of Trade, the Royal Zoological Society of Ireland, the Meteorological Inquiry, the Solar Physics Committee and several museums. The administration of these numerous enterprises was not only demanding in the time and energy of officials who might have been more profitably employed, it also consumed a considerable part of the meagre allowance which the government placed at the Department's disposal.

At precisely the same time that the Education and the Science and Art Departments were being brought together by the exercise of the royal prerogative, they were being separated to satisfy the royal pleasure. Prince Albert's original scheme for the South Kensington estates envisaged the building of a vast and comprehensive teaching institution embracing the four great sections of the Exhibition, i.e. raw materials, machinery, manufactures and plastic art. While this grandiose conception remained very largely a dream, one fragment became a reality. Whatever else the land was used for, a home had to be found quickly for numerous objects which had been on display and which remained in London after the closing of the Exhibition. The south-eastern corner of the property was selected by the Prince Consort as a suitable plot for the proposed building, and a detachment of Royal Engineers was detailed to prepare the site. Commanding this small force of sappers was Lieutenant J. F. D. Donnelly, a young subaltern fresh from the Crimea. This officer was destined to spend the rest of his active service at South Kensington, where he exchanged the sword for the pen in a vigorous campaign for the spread of scientific and technical knowledge; he was, probably, the only example of a soldier who rose from the rank of captain to that of major-general while serving on the educational front.

The first building operations commenced in 1856 when an edifice of corrugated iron was erected. Into this supposedly temporary construction – which Londoners soon nicknamed the 'Brompton Boilers' – the collections of science and art exhibits were transferred. When, shortly afterwards, Marlborough House had to be vacated in order to make room for the Prince of Wales, there seemed little alternative but to move the evicted Department into the ramshackle structure where it remained ignominiously housed for the following fifty years.

By this date (1857) the Art Division of the Department, which had been given a flying start under Cole's dynamic leadership, was making rapid progress. Cole's methods were simple and direct. He fashioned the central School of Design into an institution which provided advanced instruction in art, and trained teachers for the benefit of the provincial schools. At the same time, he gradually withdrew the direct support which had been given to the latter, encouraging local committees to assume responsibility for the appointment and remuneration of teachers. He intended that the Department, instead of guaranteeing the salaries of drawing masters, should, *via* the committees, pay them on the results of their instruction. This ingenious idea seems to have originated in the summer of 1853, when Cole wrote to Lingen suggesting that, with a view to stimulating teachers into action rather than subsidizing them, some pecuniary value should be placed on the teaching of drawing. At all events, in 1854, the Director of Art divided art education into twenty-three subjects or stages, introducing examinations into each of them; and two years later the system of payment by results went into operation. As the figures given on an earlier page demonstrate, the response to the new policy was highly encouraging.

By comparison with this vigorous growth, the Science Division, at least until 1859, had little to show. When the combined Department had been formed some six years before, the Board of

Trade issued a statement of policy on the subject of science instruction. It made provision for the system of encouragement already operating for Schools of Practical Art to be extended to local institutions for Practical Science. A principle had been enunciated, but at first little attempt was made to apply it on a national scale. Though a number of Science schools were opened in various parts of the United Kingdom, most of them failed, and by 1859 the only places, apart from the Schools of Navigation, where science instruction was being given under the auspices of the Department were Aberdeen, Birmingham, Bristol and Wigan. Fewer than 400 students in all attended these courses, and the aid from the Department to science classes of every description for the six years 1853–9 amounted to a mere £898.

The truth had to be faced that science education was caught in a vicious circle. There were few science pupils because there were not enough science teachers; there were insufficient science teachers because there was no one to give them their basic scientific education. To break this circle a means had to be found for providing elementary instruction in science. Lyon Playfair, whose main interest lay in research, was not, perhaps, ideally suited to devise and administer a scheme appropriate to meeting this fundamental need. It was, therefore, a blessing in disguise when, following his marriage in 1857 to 'a lady of some fortune', he found he was no longer wholly dependent on his salary. Anxious to pursue his own studies, he obtained permission from the government to devote only half his time to the Department. Under the new arrangement, he relinquished the Secretaryship but stayed on as Inspector of Schools of Science. When the following year he was appointed to the Chair of Chemistry at Edinburgh, he quitted the civil service altogether. The way was now clear for Henry Cole to assume overall responsibility for the Department and to repeat in the case of science instruction the successful rescue operation he had already conducted in respect of art.

8

THE SCIENCE AND ART
DEPARTMENT: COLE'S KINGDOM

The characteristic British procedure in administration is to drift, lapse or muddle into a method or system that will serve, with a disposition to stereotype it as soon as it runs fairly well.[1]

Predictably, Henry Cole succeeded Playfair as Secretary of the Department, and the vacant Inspectorship of Science was filled by Captain Donnelly, who had impressed with his energy and resource during the building operations at South Kensington. His administrative ability could only be surmised, but if the worst happened and the appointment proved a failure there would be no difficulty in dispensing with his services. As the army had only seconded, not released, him, he could be returned to regimental duty should the need arise. In fact, the choice proved highly successful.

Donnelly's first assignment was to formulate, with Cole's guidance, a plan on which the science division might be based. A memorandum outlining its main features was submitted to the Lord President (the Marquess of Salisbury) and the Vice-President (C. B. Adderley) in March 1859. The Secretary, in his diary, recalled the meeting. 'Two hours talking about science. Lord Salisbury became impatient that science instruction had not advanced like art, and said if we could not find how to teach his carpenters at Hatfield some science useful to them he would abolish the name "Science" from the title of the Department.'[2] Adderley, who was likewise disturbed at the lack of progress, threatened to reduce the Science and Art Department grant to zero unless some speedy action was taken.

With very little delay, therefore, the memorandum was translated into an administrative minute. The new system, like that already in operation on the art side, was one of payment by results. It was designed 'to assist the industrial classes of this country in supplying themselves with instruction in the rudiments of

[1] G. A. Christian, *English Education From Within*, 1922, p. 197.
[2] Cole, *Fifty Years*, p. 310.

Geometry, Mechanical Drawing, Building Construction, Physics, Chemistry and Natural History'.[1] Any person who passed the Department's examinations and was duly certificated could become a science teacher, to be paid by the central office in proportion to the examination successes obtained by his pupils. Thus, in the space of a half-a-dozen years the Department took the decisive steps towards 'turning itself into a vast examining organism, with ramifications in many directions'.[2]

By the close of 1859 the Science Division was a going concern, and Donnelly prepared a review of its work and an outline of future plans. A copy of this document was sent to Robert Lowe, the Vice-President, who returned it, according to Cole, 'as a reprieved convict did the Prayer Book to the Chaplain, with thanks, having no further use for it'. In fact, Lowe did find it, or at least the ideas it embodied, of considerable further use, for when, in 1861, he was searching for some means to increase the efficiency of elementary teaching and decrease the load on the Whitehall Department, he remembered Cole's patent remedy and asked him if he would prepare a scheme for payment by results in writing, reading and arithmetic.

It was, however, one thing to offer grants and quite another to persuade people to make the necessary effort to qualify for them. In the same year, therefore, that the science minute was adopted, an 'Organizing Master' was appointed to publicize the Department's activities. The man chosen for the role of educational propagandist was T. C. Buckmaster, an able scientist who was also much interested in art. For many years he toured the country, demonstrating the national need for skilled artisans, explaining the regulations under which grants could be obtained, and persuading numerous individuals to establish classes. The dimensions of his success may be gauged by reference to the growth of science instruction over the relevant period:

	1851	1862	1867	1872
Schools	–	70	212	948
Classes	38	140	560	2,803
Pupils	1,330	2,543	10,230	36,783

[1] *Minute of the Science and Art Department*, dated 10 June 1859. The syllabus of the science curriculum was widened from time to time; by 1873, for example, it included twenty-three different subjects.

[2] R. J. Montgomery, *Examinations. An Account of their Evolution as Administrative Devices in England*, 1965, p. 85.

One hastens to add that behind these figures lay influences other than those of Buckmaster, who was not a lone prophet crying in the wilderness. In the year he was appointed Darwin's *Origin of Species* was published, and shortly afterwards appeared Spencer's *Treatise on Education*. These books, particularly, contributed to the spreading of the idea that science should play a more important part in English education. Nevertheless, Buckmaster's impact on the immediate situation was profound, so much so, indeed, that in many places he came to personify the Science and Art Department.

In common with other government offices, the Department was investigated, either directly or indirectly, by numerous committees and commissions during the second half of the nineteenth century. Because of the nominal tie established in 1856, whenever the Whitehall Department formed the subject of an inquiry, so usually did South Kensington. In fact, the latter received the more frequent attention, owing to the increased interest shown in scientific and technical education during the mid-Victorian years.

In 1865 it came under the simultaneous scrutiny of two committees of inquiry. One was the Commons' select committee under Sir John Pakington which had been deputed to report on the transactions of the Committee of Council. As such, it may have come as something of a surprise (unless the terms of reference had been intentionally circumscribed) for the committee to discover that technically it was not empowered to investigate the Science and Art Department. If Members of Parliament imagined that the Committee of Council exercised the same jurisdiction over 'South Kensington' as it did over 'Whitehall', they were speedily undeceived. Lowe testified that the Committee had 'nothing to do with Science and Art', and Granville that the members of that Committee, apart from the Lord President and Vice-President, had never been consulted on the Science and Art Department's business. This was conducted by a Board which consisted of the two ministers, the Secretary and Assistant Secretary of the Department, and the Inspector of Art. It was 'entirely a consultative body and entirely in the hands of the Lord President'.[1] It generally met once a week, and always at South Kensington.

The select committee broke up before it could come to any agreed conclusions, but the chairman wrote a Draft Report in

[1] *Report of the Select Committee on Education*, 1865, q.823.

which he revealed his disquiet at the lack of system manifest in the oversight of state-assisted education. To repair this deficiency, he proposed the appointment of 'a Minister of Public Instruction . . . who should be entrusted with the care and superintendence of all matters relating to science and art and popular education in every part of the country'. Appeals of this kind for a minister armed with substantial powers to co-ordinate educational policy were to be made with depressing frequency over the ensuing thirty years.

The second committee of inquiry instituted in 1865 was undertaken by the Treasury and was designed to settle the appropriate establishment for the Science and Art Department. Reporting, the committee found that

The Department . . . differs in one important point from most other branches of the public service. Its duties cannot with advantage be wholly discharged by salaried officers. Recourse must constantly be had to persons who have qualified themselves by the independent exercise of their profession, and by their possessing the public confidence to assist the department as referees, inspectors and examiners.[1] The fixed establishment ought therefore to be confined to the smallest possible number of officers, who . . . should give up their whole time to the public service, and should be appointed and promoted solely with reference to their aptitude for the administrative duties of the department; and the services of a professional and technical character should be entrusted to persons selected and paid for the occasion . . . The practice of the department during its expansion has been more and more in this direction, and the arrangement may now be accepted as a result which has been fully confirmed by experience.

These principles underlying the staffing at South Kensington – that the permanent officials should be as few as possible, and that they should be supplemented by temporary, part-time specialist officers – were maintained for almost as long as the Department retained a distinct identity. It was possible to adopt them because the system of payment by results, which was the only one the Department chose to operate, was both comparatively easy to administer and reasonably simple to understand.[2] Question papers

[1] Many distinguished scientists – including Thomas Huxley – offered their services as examiners or lecturers – and, what was more important for the Department's success, they publicized its activities.

[2] As the Department's Report for 1871 laconically explained, 'If a teacher produces nothing, he gets no pay . . . The object of the State is to have results; the machinery for producing them is immaterial.'

were annually despatched to numerous outlying centres, where the examinations, invigilated by paid local secretaries and voluntary helpers, were held. The scripts were returned to South Kensington for marking, after which schedules of results and grants earned were published.

As the numbers of candidates grew, so did the problems of ensuring that the examinations were conducted with scrupulous honesty. Many members of the local committees being inexperienced, mistakes or irregularities occurred from time to time. What seemed to be required was that the small staff of administrators in the central office should be supplemented by a larger force of occasional inspectors distributed throughout the country and charged with the duty of ensuring that the examination regulations were complied with at all stages.

The Department found the ideal and, as it happened, the only source for the recruitment of this supervisory body from among the commissioned ranks of Her Majesty's armed forces. For some years Royal Engineer officers had been employed at headquarters in various capacities. A Captain H. C. Owen was appointed a full-time inspector in 1854; Captain Fowke, called in to design and construct the iron building, had stayed on to help Cole draw up the plan of development for the Science Division; and Captain Donnelly became Inspector for Science in 1859. Soldiers had also been found helpful in less exalted positions. In 1857 the then Vice-President informed the Treasury that he proposed to employ

a sufficient number of Royal Engineers, who, being artisans, are specially qualified to assist in the general arrangements and safe custody of the Museums and Schools. This is a useful and economical arrangement both for the department and for the corps of Royal Engineers. The department . . . obtains very competent and disciplined services, which may be dispensed with readily without entailing permanent claims, and the men, when their official duties are over, are taught Drawing, Photography, &c., by the department, which are of great use in their military duties.

This letter summarized the arguments that were later to be advanced in support of employing Royal Engineer officers as supervisors of the annual examinations. They were inexpensive,[1] they

---

[1] They were paid a guinea a day for their services, plus travelling expenses and a graded personal allowance.

were knowledgeable,[1] and they could be discharged without difficulty at any time.[2] They were, moreover, readily at hand, stationed throughout the kingdom as they normally tended to be.

Conscious of these advantages, Cole wrote to the military authorities in December 1867 asking for permission to employ army officers in a purely civilian capacity.

It would be impossible, except at great public expense, to send down to all parts of the country qualified persons, and retain them there for this purpose alone. If officers who are accustomed to examinations, and acquainted with official routine, would undertake to visit schools in their district, this difficulty would be met; and as the examinations are entirely in the evening, there is no reason to suppose it would interfere with their other duties.[3]

War Office consent obtained, the experiment was introduced the following year. It proved so successful and convenient that it became a regular feature of the Department's administrative machinery. Engineer officers continued to act as local inspectors for a whole generation. They made preliminary inspections of schools, and then assisted the local committees during the examination period, seeing that the rules were properly carried out and securing uniformity of procedure. By all accounts they performed their duties with efficiency and diligence.

The use of these officers, taken in conjunction with the limited role assigned to the inspectorate under the system of payment by results, enabled the Department to restrict, within extremely narrow limits, the number of permanent inspectors required. In 1870 there were only two full-time inspectors; and in spite of the increasing work involved in checking and collating the examination results, in assessing and allocating the grants, and in visiting the schools, the headquarters staff was kept remarkably small. By 1880 it had grown to no more than four.

---

[1] Officers of the Royal Engineers were, at that period, 'one of the few bodies of men in the country with an organised scientific training'. *Report of the Board of Education for the Year 1913–14* [Cd. 7934], p. 24.

[2] In a Memorandum on the Corps of Royal Engineers as Civil Servants of the Crown, Cole had suggested that 'Royal Engineer Officers furnish a ready means of trying experiments in administration. New actions can be tried without creating a new office for life, or entailing the cost of retirement and superannuation on the State'. Cole, *Fifty Years*, vol. 2, p. 325.

[3] *Report of the Department of Science and Art for 1868*. Appendix A.

There was, however, at least one major weakness in the inspectorial arrangements, as Donnelly noted in his Report for 1870.

The inspection of Science classes as well by the regular inspectors of the Department, as by the Royal Engineer officers employed as occasional inspectors . . . is primarily to check and supervise administrative details, and in this it is thoroughly successful and effective at a very small cost . . . There is another branch of inspection which this system does not fully meet, – I mean in the way of giving advice and assistance as to teaching. Strictly speaking, this is no part of a system of payment on results . . . But it would undoubtedly be a very good thing if men of eminence in the various branches of science which are taught could from time to time visit the schools, and each in his own special line give assistance and advice to teachers.[1]

This particular shortcoming – that the inspector's duty was far more administrative than educational in character – was not wholly confined to the Science and Art Department. Both the Education Department, through choice, and the Charity Commissioners, from necessity, were similarly defective.

Despite the progress made during the 'sixties in terms of examinations sat and grants earned, the state of English technical education was still causing some concern. And, in the light of the current series of international exhibitions, not without reason. In 1851, out of a hundred different departments in which goods were displayed, Britain had been awarded the palm of excellence in nearly all; but at the Paris Exhibition of 1867, where there were ninety departments, she excelled her competitors in only ten. Lyon Playfair, who had been a juror in Paris, attributed Britain's relative decline to deficiencies in her educational system. On his return, he wrote to the chairman of the Schools Inquiry Commission,[2] Lord Taunton, stating that 'the one cause of this inferiority [of British exhibits] upon which there was most unanimity is that France, Prussia, Austria, Belgium and Switzerland possess good systems of industrial education for the masters and managers of factories and workshops, and that England possesses none'.

Asked to inquire whether this allegation was justified, the Com-

[1] *Report of the Department of Science and Art for 1870*, p. 55. HMIs were somewhat contemptuous of the South Kensington inspectorate: 'Science and art were considered pastimes for retired officers, who had exchanged the sword for an HB pencil, and all sorts of majors and captains used to be mixed up with the study thereof.' Sneyd-Kynnersley, *HMI. Some Passages*, p. 112.

[2] See pp. 221ff.

missioners circulated Playfair's letter to a number of manufacturers, who were requested to comment on it. Their replies
endorsed the views expressed therein.

The Government's reaction to these criticisms was prompt and
sensible. It recognized that the country stood in two-fold need:
there was the general need to reconstruct the entire system of
national education in so far as it was assisted or supervised by the
State, and there was the particular need to improve technical and
scientific instruction in both quality and amount.

Towards the close of 1867 plans were prepared to meet the first
requirement. Lord Robert Montagu, the then Vice-President,
invited Cole to submit to the government his views on the administration of public education. The Secretary's reply closed
with the following cogent plea:

I consider that elementary education, secondary or technical instruction,
the management of public libraries, galleries and museums and all the
votes for education, science and art, should be concentrated in the
administration of them, so far as the expenditure of public funds at
least is concerned, under the sole authority of the same Minister of the
Crown.

The Minister of Public Instruction ought not, I think, to be the Lord
President of the Council. The work is ample enough to engage the sole
attention of a Minister who, I venture to say, ought to rank as a Secretary of State. He would sit in either House, according to the circumstances of the Cabinet. There should be an Under Secretary also in
Parliament.

In my opinion, the present work at the Privy Council Office, with
all the calls for charters, health, cattle plague, quarantine, etc. made
upon the attention of the Lord President, make it impossible for that
high functionary to devote sufficient time to numerous questions involved in public instruction, viewed comprehensively.

To enlarge elementary education, making it truly national, to reform
educational charities, to increase technical instruction throughout the
United Kingdom; to reorganize the British Museum, the National
Gallery, the National Portrait Gallery, etc., so as to make them work
efficiently and harmoniously together are functions which ought not, I
conceive, to be treated as of secondary importance to any others.[1]

These bold submissions may well have furnished one reason for
the government's *volte-face* over the proposal to appoint a Secretary

---

[1] 'Notes on Public Education', dated 28 November 1867. Cole, *Fifty Years*,
p. 350.

of State for Education with wide-ranging responsibilities. Unfortunately, the grand design was abandoned and the reforms that Cole had suggested were shelved; all eventually came to be adopted, but only piece-meal and at intervals over the next hundred years.

However, the government, aware perhaps that their ambitious scheme might fail to materialize, took out an insurance policy. On the very day (24 March 1868) that the Duke of Marlborough introduced his Education Bill, a select committee was appointed, under the chairmanship of Bernhard Samuelson, a noted iron-master, to inquire into 'the provisions for giving instruction in theoretical and applied science to the industrial classes'.

Most of the evidence taken before this committee came from Science and Art Department officials and from industrialists. Cole described the Department's administrative structure, at the apex of which stood the Board. The executive part of this body consisted of the Lord President and the Vice-President, or either of them separately; and these ministers were advised by four senior officials who always attended its meetings, viz. the Secretary; Norman Macleod, the Assistant Secretary; Captain Donnelly, the Official Inspector for Science; and Richard Redgrave, the Inspector General for Art. Cole, when giving his opinion on the Board's value, stated that he could not imagine 'any organization more comprehensive, or more complete or more instantaneous in action . . . [or] better adapted for its purpose'; and, with understandable pride in the instrument he had helped to create, he added that 'the organization of South Kensington ensures the highest amount of Parliamentary responsibility and the greatest promptitude of action'. Quite possibly, the administrative machinery was as efficient as Cole claimed; less free from criticism were the long-term effects of its operation.

The committee also discovered that, apart from the ministerial link, there was only one point at which the central authorities for elementary and technical education met. Lingen pointed out that some schools coming under the Education Department offered instruction in drawing, and therefore were eligible to receive grants from, and were liable to inspection by, South Kensington.

On the wider issue, manufacturers called as witnesses were almost unanimous in laying the blame for Britain's failure to maintain her commercial superiority on deficiencies in her educational system.[1] To some extent the state itself was culpable, for it showed great unwillingness to spend money on purely technical instruction. Government policy on this matter was stated in a memorandum drawn up by Donnelly the previous year (1867).

Real technical education – the teaching of a trade or art itself on scientific principles – necessarily entails workshops for practice. It would be scarcely possible to devise a more effectual blow to the manufacturers of a place than for the State to establish a real technical school for their trade, with its workshop, under no constraint to pay its expenses, underselling them and interfering with their market.[2]

Illogical the argument may have been, for the schools need not have produced articles for sale. Yet it could sound convincing enough to those who feared the insidious encroachment of state capitalism.

But employers themselves were part-authors of their predicament, since most of them were, not unnaturally, reluctant to have technical processes passed on to potential competitors.

When the members of the Committee came to make their Report, they, too, reached the conclusion that the growing success of foreign producers could be attributed at least in some degree to a failure in Britain's scientific and technical instruction. They found that three main factors – defective education at the elementary stage, neglect of science at the secondary stage, and a dire shortage of science teachers – were responsible for this failure. Ways of supplying these deficiencies were recommended.

Parliament had scarcely had time to digest the Report when the Gladstone administration, having come under heavy pressure from several eminent scientists, appointed a weighty Royal Commission to examine the related questions of scientific instruction and the advancement of science. This Commission, under the chairmanship of the Duke of Devonshire, sat for five years (1870–75), and issued no fewer than eight Reports.

While it deliberated, two events affecting the functions and

---

[1] One writer has recently argued that Playfair's evidence concerning Britain's technological failure – evidence which carried much weight – was based on a misconception. In the case cited, the situation he described was produced not by weaknesses in England's educational system, but by her patent laws. West, *Education and the State*, p. 107.

[2] *PP* 1867–8, XV, 449. Not until 1901 did the Department make grants for teaching practical subjects; before that date grants were restricted to instruction in the *principles* of science.

functioning of the Science and Art Department took place. Although the 1870 Elementary Education Act contained not a single reference to the Department, that statute made a considerable impact on it. For the school boards, anxious at one and the same time to offer nourishing educational fare and to hold down the education rate, sought ways in which their schools might earn additional grants from central funds. 'In the Science and Art Department they found a willing milch-cow; providing the requisite technical subjects were taught, life-giving grants would flow.'[1] In this manner the Department became involved in the work of schools for which the Whitehall Office was legally responsible, and from these unpretentious origins emerged that first enterprising (if presumptuous) attempt to provide secondary education for all – the higher grade school.[2]

The other significant occurrence was the retirement, in May 1873, of Sir Henry Cole, as he now was, from his position of Secretary of the Department and General Superintendent of the South Kensington Museum.[3] He had served his country well, first by rescuing the Schools of Design from their unhappy predicaments, then by laying the foundations for a national system of scientific and technical instruction. As the progenitor of payment by results, he would have been surprised and hurt by the verdict passed upon that system by most historians. Cole would, in fact, have been proud to take the credit for it. For him, it was the only instrument for improving technical instruction of which the ruling classes would approve and to which students and teachers would respond; it was the ideal combination of stick and carrot, and, above all, it achieved the immediate purpose for which it was devised.

Cole's departure was the occasion for a major reorganization of the Department. The dangers of rivalry and conflict between, and the wastefulness of duplicated effort by, that Department and its counterpart in Whitehall led the government to decide in favour of their amalgamation. Accordingly, in June 1874, Sir Francis Sandford, then Secretary of the Education Department, was made

[1] W. H. G. Armytage, 'J. F. D. Donnelly: Pioneer in vocational education', *The Vocational Aspect of Secondary and Further Education*, no. 4, May 1950, vol. 2, p. 10.

[2] South Kensington grants went also to some endowed grammar schools which came under the jurisdiction of the Charity Commission.

[3] It was, perhaps, inevitable that Sir Henry, during the last years of his reign, should have been affectionately nicknamed 'Old King Cole'.

permanent head of the Science and Art Department also. Other changes followed. Macleod, formerly the Assistant Secretary and Accounting Officer at South Kensington, became Controlling Officer there and an assistant secretary of the Education Department. Donnelly, who had shortly before been raised to the rank of major by his military superiors, was given the title of 'Director of Science' by his civilian superiors, and Directors of the Art Division and of the Museums Division were appointed at the same time. As a result of these new dispositions, the Permanent Secretary of the Whitehall Office began attending the Board meetings at South Kensington. But it is doubtful if Sandford had much time – even supposing he had the inclination – to superintend the business of the Science and Art Department, fully occupied as he was elsewhere with the plenteous repercussions of the 1870 Act. In all probability the three Directors were circumscribed very little in their authority.

Meanwhile, the Devonshire Commissioners were making steady, if ponderous, progress in their investigation into the facilities for, and the development of, scientific instruction both in this country and abroad. Of the eight Reports they produced, two have particular relevance to this study of the growth of central authorities for education in England. In the Second Report (1872), elementary schools under the Education Department and science classes under South Kensington figured prominently among the matters considered, and they provided the Commissioners with much food for thought. Professor Huxley, who was himself a member of the Commission, scathingly attacked the existing system when he came to give evidence. He had been led to understand that such scientific instruction as was available in the kingdom had been introduced in the teeth of fierce opposition from the Education Department, and he protested that separating the teaching of science from education was 'like cutting education in half'.

It is a wonderful state of affairs, and the result is that practical antagonism, which I believe does not exist now, but which for a number of years, I am told, did exist, when one half of the department of the state which had charge of education was opposed to that which the other half was doing.[1]

[1] *Reports of the Royal Commission on Scientific Instruction and the Advancement of Science* [C.536], 1872–5, vol. 1, q.354. Sneyd-Kynnersley refers to the uneasy relations between the two departments. 'At that time [1872] elementary education pure and simple was controlled from Whitehall. Science and art were

Impressed by withering criticisms such as these, the Commissioners recommended that 'the instruction in elementary science classes under the Science and Art Department, be so arranged as to work in complete harmony with the general system of public elementary education'; but at the same time they considered it 'important that the Education Department and the Department charged with Instruction in Science shall continue to be co-ordinate'.[1] It rather looked as if the Commissioners wanted the best of both worlds. They sought to integrate the work of the departments without integrating the departments themselves, fearing perhaps that if South Kensington lost its identity it would also lose much of its influence. At all events, the action taken in 1874, when a common Secretary was placed over the two departments, each of which remained a distinct entity, suggests that the government was equally impressed by both arguments.

Science inspection formed another major issue upon which the Commissioners expressed grave concern. They learnt that there were only two permanent inspectors of local schools of science and art, and that each was responsible for inspecting both kinds of establishment. 'It is obvious', the Report declared, 'that their supervision must be inadequate to provide any important check against irregularities, or to greatly influence the methods and means of instruction.' Nor did the employment of Royal Engineers as temporary local inspectors meet the basic need, for their only duty was to see that the regulations of the Department were complied with; they had no responsibility for improving teaching techniques. Although the Commissioners made no specific recommendation on the subject, the implications of their remarks were unambiguous; inspection as practised in the Department had been weighed in the balance and found wanting.

In their Eighth Report (1875) the Commissioners dealt with 'the Central Organization which is best calculated to enable the Government to determine its action in all Questions affecting Science'. They found not only that the science work of the government was carried on by many different departments, but that there was 'nothing to prevent analagous, if not actually identical, in-

---

the care of another establishment, which we knew as "South Kensington". The Montague and Capulet retainers never met; only they bit their thumbs when the other house was mentioned. . . . In the later 'seventies we began to clash . . .' Sneyd-Kynnersley, *HMI. Some passages*, p. 112.

[1] [C.536] *Second Report*, 1872, vol. i, xxviii.

vestigations being made in each of these, or to secure to one Department an adequate knowledge of the results obtained, and the circumstances under which they were obtained, by another'. They were led inexorably to the conviction that 'the Creation of a Special Ministry dealing with Science and with Education is a Necessity of the Public Service'. Such a ministry would be occupied 'with all questions relating to Science and General Education, so far as these come under the notice of the Government', and its political head 'should not be distracted by any immediate Responsibility for affairs which have no connection with Science, Education or Art'.[1]

Despite a pressing need for vigorous action, most of the Devonshire Commission's recommendations were pigeon-holed, including those advocating the establishment of a comprehensive Ministry of Science and Education.[2]

At the same time that one Royal Commission was examining the Science and Art Department as an element in the national system of education, another was examining it as an element in the home civil service. From the evidence supplied to the Playfair Commission, a number of striking facts concerning the Department's establishment emerged. As in the case of the Whitehall Office, none of the staff officers at South Kensington was appointed by open competition, although the Treasury was beginning to query the continued use of the method of direct nomination. The examiners at South Kensington resembled their Whitehall counterparts in two other respects; they were selected on account of their administrative ability, not for their educational knowledge, and they did no actual examining, but simply saw that the rules of the Department were properly carried out. The same might be said of the science and art inspectors, whose functions were mainly administrative, and whose duties were to ensure that the Departmental regulations were strictly observed throughout the country. These officers were obliged to examine science and art indiscriminately, and one witness who had been originally appointed as an art inspector confessed that he did not feel qualified to examine a science school. Finally, the Department was remarkable for this

---

[1] *Ibid. Eighth Report*, 1875, p. 45.
[2] A step in this direction was finally taken in the late 1950s when the then Lord President of the Council added to his many responsibilities that of Minister of Science. In 1964 his duties as such were assumed by the Secretary of State for Education when the Department of Education and Science was formed.

reason: that, in relation to the amount of work performed, it was probably the smallest-staffed government department. Employing as few permanent officials as possible, it called on temporary staff to supply the additional assistance which seasonal pressures made necessary.

Many of these features continued to typify South Kensington for the remainder of its independent existence. Indeed, one of the Science and Art Department's most remarkable characteristics was its resistance to change over the years – whether in terms of policy or organization or size of establishment. Up to a point, this constancy was due to the inertia displayed by successive administrations, but, as has been shown in earlier chapters, parliamentary disapproval or governmental indifference presented no insuperable barrier to a determined minister or secretary bent on extending his department's activities. The cause more probably lay in a combination of two influences: the pull of tradition, and continuity of control. At its inception the Department had formulated certain principles that would govern its actions. It remained true to those principles long after they had served their purpose, long after they had become a hindrance rather than a help to further development. One does not have to look far to see why this occurred. Geographically isolated from the centre of government in Whitehall, the Department was rarely, if ever, under the close and constant supervision of a minister, with the result that it was left very much to its own devices. Inevitably, power became concentrated in its administrative head. For all but eight of its forty-eight years two men only governed the Department's destinies; the first of these had laid down its original policies, the second was the protégé of the first. Small wonder that South Kensington's outlook was orthodox, if not conservative. In some ways the institution was a modest embodiment of the 'arrested state' as conceived by Plato.

Certainly, not everyone was convinced that the Department was meeting the challenge of the times with an adequate, or even an appropriate, response. Private individuals, acting singly or collectively, took up the gauntlet which they felt the state was unable or unwilling to accept. In 1877 the city companies of London formed a committee to prepare a plan for technical education. The outcome was the foundation in 1880 of the City and Guilds of London Institute for the Advancement of Technical Education. Its purpose was to 'provide and encourage education adapted to the requirements of all classes of persons engaged, or preparing to engage, in manufacturing or other industries'.[1] Several other kinds of establishment for continuative education sprang up about this time, notably the polytechnics. In 1880 the best known of them moved to Regent Street, where Quintin Hogg, its founder, sought to instruct artisans and clerks in the principles and, to some extent, the practice of their occupations.

But this haphazard growth of various forms of technical education itself gave cause for anxiety over and above that occasioned by increasingly successful foreign competition. Conscious of the twin needs to learn from others and to put our own educational house in order, A. J. Mundella, soon after becoming Vice-President, persuaded the government to appoint a Royal Commission 'to inquire into the instruction of the industrial classes of certain foreign countries in technical and other subjects, for the purpose of comparison with that of the corresponding classes in this country; and into the influence of such instruction on manufacturing and other industries at home and abroad'. Under the chairmanship of Bernhard Samuelson, the Royal Commission on Technical Instruction began its work in July 1881 and produced its Final Report some three years later.

While the Commissioners deliberated, the Department pursued its policy of payment by results with commendable efficiency, showing a stoical refusal to be deflected from its self-chosen course by any change either in the climatic conditions or in the nature of its objective. Progress was steady rather than spectacular; innovations were few and far between. However, Mundella's term of office did witness the beginning of one fresh enterprise. The Vice-President was keen to establish a Normal School of Science – similar to that which had long before been created for Art – which would serve both as a training ground for teachers of science and as an institution for scientific research. Donnelly, who, together with Huxley and several other eminent scientists, had been pressing for some years for such a project, was asked to draw up a memorandum for submission to the Treasury. No objection was raised to the proposal, provided it did not involve the Exchequer in any additional expenditure. Undeterred by this lack of financial support, the Department went ahead with its plan.

[1] *Second Report of the Royal Commission on Technical Instruction*, 1884, vol. 1, p. 401.

7

9

THE SCIENCE AND ART DEPARTMENT: COMMANDING OFFICER, MAJOR-GENERAL SIR JOHN DONNELLY, K.C.B.

> I am the very pattern of a modern Major-Gineral;
> I've information vegetable, animal, and mineral; . . .
> I'm very well acquainted too with matters mathematical
> I understand equations, both the simple and quadratical . . .
> I'm very good at integral and differential calculus,
> I know the scientific names of beings animalculous . . .
>
> — W. S. Gilbert.

Donnelly's services, both past and present, to the Science and Art Department were rewarded in December 1881. On Norman Macleod's retirement, Donnelly – now a colonel – was appointed an assistant secretary of the Education Department and Chief Executive Officer at South Kensington, in addition to retaining the position of Director of the Science Division there. The Department over which he ruled was small in numbers and symmetrical in structure. Its administrative staff was divided into two main branches. Common to both were an inspectorate and a clerical section. Save in one small particular, the establishments of the Science and the Art Divisions were identical. Each possessed a Director, an assistant director, an official examiner and at least one assistant examiner; the only difference between them was that 'Science' enjoyed the services of a second assistant examiner, whereas 'Art' had to make do with those of an examination clerk.[1]

---

[1] The Duke of Devonshire was later (1899) to comment: 'The Department has a character distinct and differing from anything which exists in the State, and, I think, differing from anything which exists in any other country . . . Its internal arrangements are also of a peculiar character, having, as it has, directors of science and art who possess no executive authority, and whose functions and responsibilities I have always found it rather difficult to understand'. *Hansard*, 4th ser., LXVIII, cols. 676–7. By that date, in spite of a considerable growth in the Department's activities, there had been an addition of only one to the staff at headquarters.

Both Divisions could call upon the services of four inspectors of schools, and numerous 'occasional' and 'acting' inspectors. (Occasional inspectors were employed, as the necessity arose, to supplement the technical knowledge of the permanent inspectors in either of the two 'faculties'; acting inspectors, who generally held commissions in the Royal Engineers, assisted the permanent inspectors in the purely administrative portion of their work.) Clerical duties for the Department as a whole were discharged by a staff of forty-three clerks of various grades.

At this date the responsibilities of the inspectors were still largely administrative. Professional examiners set and marked the examination papers on the results of which grants were given, so that the inspectors' main function was to see that the schools were properly conducted according to the rules laid down by the Department. But, in addition, they were required to report generally on the efficiency of the teaching, to hold local inquiries, and to re-examine where any suspicion of unfairness in the conduct of an examination arose. Moreover, unlike the Whitehall Department, South Kensington was not averse to appointing as inspectors men who possessed relevant knowledge and practical experience; for example, all four serving in 1882 had received professional training and were expert practitioners in their respective fields.

Since their formation, both the Science and the Art Divisions had made heartening progress. On the science side especially, expansion, expressed in quantitative terms, was remarkable:

	SCIENCE		
Year	Number of schools	Number of classes	Students
1862	70	140	2,543
1872	948	2,803	36,783
1882	1,403	4,881	68,581

	ART		
	Year	Number of schools	Students
Schools of Art	1872	122	22,854
	1882	169	33,729
Art Classes	1872	538	17,256
	1882	545	21,215
Elementary Day Schools	1872	1,773	194,549
	1882	4,808	809,352

However, the Technical Instruction Commission, reporting finally in May 1884, was not over-impressed by statistics such as these; they tended to obscure certain fundamental defects in the national provision for technical education. The Commissioners maintained that the latter was not the province of artisans and mechanics only, as the regulations of the Department indicated; and they believed that technical education, by encompassing such subjects as languages, mathematics, history and geography, should have a wider connotation than it then possessed; they were of the opinion also that more practical instruction ought to be given in both elementary and secondary schools; and, anticipating Bryce, they argued that the best preparation for technical study was a sound secondary education.

The Commissioners' recommendations followed naturally from their findings. Persuaded that the different grades of technical schools should be co-ordinated one with another and with schools in the elementary and secondary sectors, they proposed that there should be one central authority for technical education. To assert the belief that the country needed such an authority for *all* forms of public instruction did not fall within the Commissioners' terms of reference, but such a conviction was clearly implied. They also advocated the establishment of secondary and technical schools wherever there were deficiencies, and in particular they suggested that school boards or local authorities should be empowered to establish, conduct, and contribute towards the maintenance of classes under the Science and Art Department.

In contrast to earlier inquiries, the labours of the Samuelson Commission bore fruit, partly because its arguments were supported by another Royal Commission. Between 1883 and 1886 Britain suffered a severe slump in trade; it was of sufficiently serious proportions to justify the appointment of a Commission to analyse its causes. In their final Report, published in 1886, the Commissioners attributed a portion of the blame for the depression to the nation's backwardness in education. A minority report, signed by four members, was more explicit, stressing the importance of an adequate system of technical education, and asserting that 'we shall only be able to hold our ground by a continual advance in intellectual training, scientific knowledge and true artistic taste on the part of both employers and workmen'.

Two attempts at legislation in 1887 and 1888 proved abortive, but a third achieved success in 1889. The Technical Instruction Act empowered any county or borough council or urban sanitary authority to levy a penny rate for technical instruction.[1] It also designated the Science and Art Department as the central authority[2] which would decide, in the case of schools and institutions, or between schools and local authorities, on questions concerning the distribution of grants, the sufficiency of provision, and the composition of governing bodies.[3] Moreover, the Act having failed to define with any precision, or even clarity, the term 'technical instruction', responsibility for determining more exactly the statute's scope and limits was entrusted to the Department. In the event, the latter interpreted its functions so broadly that the opinion was commonly held that its grants might be used for the teaching of every school subject, the Classics alone excepted.

Having followed the fortunes of the Technical Instruction Commission to the point at which their efforts were crowned with some success, we must briefly retrace our steps to consider two other events which took place in the year its final report was issued. At the end of August 1884, the Select Committee on Education, Science, and Art (Administration) published its findings on the matter of ministerial responsibility for the education votes. After a modicum of desultory questioning of ministers and officials, the Committee expressed itself satisfied with the degree of co-ordination then prevailing between the central authorities for elementary and technical education. Its members saw 'no reason to disturb the existing arrangements as to the supervision of the Science and Art Department'. These 'arrangements' mainly consisted of the Board meetings which were held at South Kensington generally once, but sometimes twice, a week. Over the years there had been

---

[1] The Act was placed on a sound administrative basis by the Local Government Act of 1888, which created viable local authorities; and on a sound financial basis by the Local Taxation (Customs and Excise) Act of 1890, by which certain sums of money were allocated to local authorities either to relieve the rates or to subsidize technical education. Ultimately, many authorities chose to follow the latter alternative.

[2] It would be more accurate to say that the Department was made *one* of the central authorities for technical education. In the same year that the Technical Instruction Bill became law, the Board of Agriculture was created. As part of its functions it undertook the inspection of any non-elementary schools providing technical instruction connected with agriculture.

[3] This was contrary to the Cross Commission's recommendations. The majority advised that the Education Department, not the Science and Art Department, should supervise technical instruction.

little change in the Board's composition and function. It comprised the executive officers of the Department, and was presided over either by the Lord President or by the Vice-President; occasionally both ministers attended. In this connexion, Lord Carlingford stated that 'according to the usage of the Department, the President of the Council takes a larger part in the affairs of South Kensington and its branches in Dublin and Edinburgh than in the affairs of primary education'.[1] Mundella, on the same point, said that the Science and Art Department occupied him one day a week, and the Education Department proper five days a week. The Board itself was a consultative body only, the political heads being responsible for all its decisions and entitled to over-rule the officials if there was a difference of opinion. Nevertheless, it was, according to Carlingford, a 'most convenient institution', for it saved a vast amount of correspondence between South Kensington and Whitehall, and it disposed of business much more rapidly and efficiently than could be accomplished by written communications.

Apart from the ministerial connexion, there were, or had been, two other points of contact between the Departments. Inspection provided the first; HM Inspectors and South Kensington Inspectors rendering one another assistance in examinations.[2] The second was that both Departments had the same Permanent Secretary. However, this was something of a broken reed, since, a few months before the Committee reported, it had been thought 'unnecessary that the secretary at Whitehall should, as a rule, attend those [Board] meetings unless some question affecting primary schools happened to be on the business of the day, in which case he might do so'.[3] Thus, the only real link remaining between South Kensington and Whitehall was that afforded by their being subject to the same political chiefs; this was, almost by definition, quite incapable of providing the necessary continuity or

[1] Although in 1885 the Scottish Department of Education received a Secretary of its own, the Science and Art Department continued to function for Scotland until 1897 (and for Ireland until 1900).

[2] Describing the mutual aid provided, one HMI wrote: 'They used to examine in drawing, and they conducted examinations in May and December with a code of regulations of their own composing . . . and, when, as occasionally happened, we were appealed to for help in superintending their examinations at the training colleges, we danced in fetters of red-tape'. Sneyd-Kynnersley, *HMI. Some Passages*, pp. 112–3.

[3] *Report from the Select Committee on Education, Science and Art (Administration)*, 1884, q.649 (Carlingford).

of ensuring that the work of the two authorities was dove-tailed into a coherent and consistent whole.

Doubtless the combining of the departments presented difficulties, but that they were not insuperable was demonstrated when Morant became Permanent Secretary. The experiment of 1873–84, when Sandford administered both offices, failed because the will to make it succeed was lacking. Examined superficially, the reasons for reverting to the earlier arrangement appeared convincing enough.

The business of the two Education Departments in addition to the business connected with the Endowed Schools Branch of the Charity Commission and of the Scottish Endowed Schools Commission, is now so extensive as to fully engage his [the Secretary of the Education Department] whole time, and is as much as can be attended to by any one person. The supervision therefore which he would be able to give to the Science and Art Department affords no sufficient control over it. While on the other hand, the imposition of this supervision and responsibility on him necessarily more or less delays the transaction of business, reduces the direct responsibility of the controlling officer at South Kensington and impairs his authority over the Staff of that large and increasing establishment.[1]

Yet, in 1899, by which time the work in each department had grown appreciably, Kekewich could assure Devonshire that neither he (Kekewich) nor Abney (the Secretary of the Science and Art Department) thought that any difficulty or friction was likely to arise from the proposed amalgamation of the departments, *provided that arrangements were made for devolving the work upon subordinate supervising officers.*[2] Here – in the wise delegation of authority – lay the key to the problem, a key that ministers and officials had ignored or overlooked during the crucial decade when Sandford was overlord.

Be that as it may, when the latter retired, the decision was made to appoint Donnelly Secretary and permanent head of the Science and Art Department, exclusively responsible for its general efficiency. At the same time, it was arranged that all questions in which the action of that Department encroached upon the business

[1] PRO Ed. 24/8. Letter, dated 24 April 1884, from the Secretary of the Education Department to the Secretary of the Treasury.
[2] PRO Ed. 24/61. Letter, dated 8 June 1899. (Italics supplied.)

of the Education Department should be first submitted to the Secretary in Whitehall.

Opinions differ as to the wisdom of the separation. On the one hand, there is the view that it was 'undoubtedly a great mistake', and showed 'how far the Government still was from any idea of a national system of education. The quite unnecessary rivalry, which was thus created between these two branches, led to much extravagance and much waste of energy'.[1] On the other, there is the judgment that 'Donnelly's formal assumption of the post of permanent head at South Kensington signalised a decade of rapid advancement in vocational education. Freed from Whitehall, South Kensington took over where the Education Department finished, till it rapidly assumed a large measure of control of an expanding network of state secondary schools which were almost independent of the Education Department.'[2] It is possible to reconcile these widely divergent assessments. The dichotomy led to competition and rivalry, both of which up to a point redounded to the benefit of education; beyond that point, however, the competition became wasteful and the rivalry bred mutual hostility. In the short term the disunity proved fruitful, in the long run it turned out to be counter-productive.

At all events, during the last decade of the nineteenth century three well defined trends affecting the South Kensington Department became discernible. The first was a striking increase in the Department's influence, in terms both of the volume of work it undertook and of the broadening of its activities; the second was the gradual abandonment of payment by results; the third was a growing concern at the chaotic state of educational administration, both central and local. These trends were by no means unrelated. The Department's efforts to aid technical and secondary education achieved considerable success, but at the cost of creating formidable administrative problems for itself. Examinations, in particular, presented immense difficulties, both in the setting and marking of the papers and in the actual supervision of the examination itself. In 1890, for example, over and above the conducting of some 14,000 practical tests, there were 190,000 science, and 107,000 art, scripts to be marked. By 1892 these numbers had risen to an alarming 214,000 and 123,700 respectively. Since these nation-

[1] F. Ware, *Educational Foundations of Trade and Industry*, 1901, p. 33.
[2] Armytage, *VASFE* May 1950, p. 13.

wide examinations were invariably held at the same time each year, there arose the distinct threat that the supply of competent examiners would be exhausted and that South Kensington would be drowned in a sea of scripts.

Hence, as in the case of Whitehall, so at South Kensington, the *administrative* argument for modifying the system of payment by results became overwhelming. There was, besides, a strong *educational* case to be made for substituting inspection for examination, and the accession of Arthur Acland to the Vice-Presidency in 1892 signalled the likelihood that both virtue and necessity would triumph. The following year, with a view both to improving the supervision of science instruction and to promoting further co-operation with local authorities, Acland secured the appointment of a small group of highly qualified and experienced inspectors.[1] These additions enabled the Department to dispense with the services of several 'acting' inspectors, and to divide the country into districts, each the responsibility of one inspector. It was hoped that the permanent inspectors, now numbering seventeen, would be looked upon as 'advisers' in all matters connected with science and art instruction.

Thus, when the Code of 1894–5 announced that grants to Organized Science Schools would be paid on the results of inspection as well as of examination, the necessary personnel were ready in the field with their duties fully explained to them. They were responsible for the inspection of technical schools, schools of art, those secondary schools in receipt of South Kensington grants, science and art classes and manual instruction in elementary schools, evening classes (though not evening continuation classes), and pupil teacher centres. If they were adequately to carry out these responsibilities, it was clear that the district inspectors would require some assistance. Accordingly, in 1894 Acland appointed a number of First and Second Class Sub-Inspectors who would be allocated to the various districts and work under the direction of the inspectors in charge; the intention being ultimately to appoint eighty of these officers, so replacing almost man-for-man the Royal Engineers hitherto employed.

The outcome of this growth and reorganization was the de-

---

[1] Though thirteen in number, these inspectors became known as Acland's 'Twelve Apostles' on account of the evangelistic zeal with which they performed their duties.

velopment of an inspectorial hierarchy at South Kensington somewhat analagous to that already in existence at Whitehall. After a
large number of sub-inspectors had been transferred to the Education Department in 1898 to inspect drawing in elementary
schools, the remaining sub-inspectors were re-named Junior Inspectors. At the turn of the century the Science and Art Department inspectorate consisted of a Senior Chief Inspector, four
Chief Inspectors (in charge of divisions), fifteen Inspectors (in
charge of districts), and seventeen Junior Inspectors.

But, and here emerges the third trend, the success and expansion
of the Department were themselves major factors in its downfall.
Its multifarious activities were now causing great confusion in the
organization of education, both as between secondary and technical
education and as between elementary and higher education. On
the one hand, it was 'sponsoring a kind of one-eyed secondary
education without an Act [which] made for artificial distortion';[1]
on the other, its operations penetrated the system of elementary
education at several places. Indeed, 'it was the very nature of
South Kensington's infiltration into all spheres of vocational education that prompted the constitution of another Royal Commission under James Bryce'.[2]

During their survey of the variegated patchwork of statutory
instruments, financial regulations and government agencies that
constituted the central machinery for the administration of 'public'
secondary education, the Bryce Commissioners made an intensive
and impartial study of the Science and Art Department. They
found that, so far as there then existed any central authority for
technical education, the Department performed that function.
They discovered, too, that its relationship with secondary education in general was only vaguely defined, and depended primarily
on the aid which it gave to the establishment and maintenance of science and art schools and classes, day or evening. But
its activities were limited in that it could 'take cognizance only of
certain subjects out of the number of those which are comprehended in Secondary Education'.[3] They learnt, moreover, that
while the Education Department and the school boards stood in

[1] J. S. Maclure, *Educational Documents. England and Wales. 1816–1963*,
1965, p. 9.
[2] Armytage, *VASFE* May 1950, p. 16.
[3] *Report of the Royal Commission on Secondary Education* [C.7862], vol. 1, p. 64.

organic and precise relation to each other, there was in the case of
the Science and Art Department no such clear and regulated connexion between the centre and locality.

Examining next the degree of liaison to be found among the
various central authorities dealing with secondary education, the
Commissioners were informed that the sole link connecting South
Kensington and Whitehall was a personal one, residing in the
circumstance that the Vice-President of the Committee of Council
was the minister in charge of both departments. But not even that
somewhat unstable bond attached the Science and Art Department
to the Charity Commission, the only point of juncture between
them being the recently created Joint Departmental Committee –
and this was a consultative, not an executive, body.

These several discoveries naturally led the Commissioners to
consider the desirability or otherwise of merging the Science and
Art Department with one or both of the other authorities. Not
unexpectedly, Major-General Donnelly fought to preserve the
independence of the organization which he had done so much to
develop and to which he had devoted almost the whole of his adult
life. He contended that it would prove no service to education to
join South Kensington, which had avoided sectarian squabbles and
thrived as a result, to the Education Department, which had been
hampered by such controversies. In any case, the existing situation was by no means unsatisfactory. Admittedly the two departments were separate, but it was, he argued, a physical separation
only; otherwise there was full consultation on matters of common
concern.

However, Donnelly's *cri de cœur* fell on unreceptive ears. The
Commissioners readily acknowledged the Science and Art Department's contribution to educational progress: 'It has encouraged
studies which our traditional methods of education had completely ignored; fostered institutions that without it could never
have lived; created an interest and an attitude of mind which has
been a real culture to multitudes of our English people.'[1] Particularly commendable was the way in which its outlook had
broadened in recent years. 'In defining technical instruction, the
Department has kept in view the varying needs of different
localities, and has been liberal rather than strict in its interpretation.'

[1] *Ibid.* p. 101.

Nevertheless, the arguments in favour of integrating the work of the Department with that of the other authorities were too many and too strong to be gainsaid. Witness after witness adversely criticized the Department, or the lack of co-ordination between Departments, or both. One – the Clerk of the Manchester School Board appearing as the representative of the Association of School Boards – complained that, in dealing with schools, the Science and Art Department was much more independent of legislative control than the Education Department, and so tended to harass them by too frequent changes of regulations about which the boards were not previously informed. Other witnesses maintained that there was overlapping and confusion right across the educational map, that is, both at the centre, between the Whitehall and South Kensington Departments as well as the Charity Commission, and at the circumference, where these Departments impinged upon the local authorities and the schools.

Confronted with such testimony, the Commissioners felt bound to ask whether the Science and Art Department ought not to be combined with other educational departments. Convincing reasons had certainly been advanced in support of this proposition. Union or incorporation was urged alike on grounds of efficiency, both as regards the inspection of schools,[1] the methods of instruction, and the distribution and range of subjects; of economy, both as regards imperial and local funds; and for the sake of unity of spirit and aim in education; and of harmony of relations in all sections of work between the central and local authorities.[2]

In their summing up, the Commissioners pronounced heavily in favour of amalgamation. They felt that the objections to the Science and Art Department's continued existence as an autonomous body were very great indeed.

Its defects are not those of administration, but they are, as it were, inherent in its constitution. It is too centralized and too specialized, too

[1] See the evidence of J. G. Fitch, a former HM Inspector of Training Colleges. 'It seems to me that there is a great waste of power in attempting to deal separately with that part of elementary education which happens to fall under the head of Art, and a similar difficulty is found with Science. In so far as the science is purely elementary, it is judged by the ordinary inspector of schools, but if science grants are claimed, there comes in a new inspector, and there is a new scale of grants.' *Ibid.* vol.3, q.9085.

[2] *Ibid.* vol.1, p. 101. Elsewhere the Commissioners gently chided the central and local authorities for frequently subsidizing in kindly ignorance the same schools.

little able to adapt itself to the changes it has been a main factor in effecting, while also too irresponsible in its modes and times of adaptation. It was not originally intended to be, in the strict sense of the term, a department of education, i.e., its functions were not those of the creation, the control, the inspection and the development of schools; but it was designed to encourage the study of subjects which the ordinary curricula of schools did not recognize, and which seemed to be mainly outside their province. Hence it was not so much education it had in view as instruction in special subjects, especially those that promised to be of most use for our arts and industries; and its examinations were, alike as regards forms and time, more adapted to adults than to school boys.[1]

But, the Report continued, the course of events had made it what it was not meant to be: an education department,

supplementing in some respects, duplicating in others, the Department properly so-called. And now, in order to meet the new conditions, it needs to be more liberal in its recognition of literary subjects, to feel that they are essential to education, and not alien to science; to have regard to schools as wholes, and not simply to sections or subjects, to judge scholars as it judges schools, and test more by inspection and less by examination.[2]

Besides, the nation required 'less of the disturbance which comes to education from the multitude of authorities which have to do with it, and more of the feeling of responsibility to a single head'. In short, unity in administration was dependent upon the creation of a united department.

More compelling even than the educational and administrative considerations were those of a financial nature. Two phenomena appeared to characterize the prevailing situation: the variety of the sources, national and local, whence money could be drawn for scientific and technical education, and the multitude of bodies through which and by which it could be spent. To achieve economy and efficiency, a single central authority must be established, in which the whole grant would be concentrated, which would spend increasingly through the local authorities, and which would be equipped to regulate and harmonize policies at district level.

Finally, when the Commissioners came to discuss the contri-

---

[1] *Ibid.* pp. 101–2. [2] *Ibid.* p. 102.

butions of, and the relations between, the Science and Art Department and the Charity Commission, they became quite lyrical.

While the Charity Commission represents the endowments which are our inherited educational wealth, South Kensington represents in great part the taxation which is our current educational income. The one thus conserves the accumulations of the past, but the other distributes and regulates the resources of the present. And the correlates of the means they possess are the schools, or the departments in schools, they respectively control, the one mainly the older schools with their classical traditions, the other chiefly the more modern schools or departments, with their more practical aims, with the result that the one influences largely, though by no means solely, the more literary learning, the other the newer and more scientific.

And these are so many reasons for the co-ordination of these two offices. The accumulated and current wealth of the nation ought not to be, as here, divided in idea and use, but so combined as to bring about a more excellent result . . . It would be more statesmanlike to help inexperienced local authorities by concordant advice from the centre, instead of perplexing them by counsels which are always independent and often inconsistent. Thus the Charity Commission and the Science and Art Department would, were they co-ordinated, form an office capable of fulfilling the functions of husbanding educational resources and making it easier to harmonise educational ideals.[1]

After such an indictment and such a verdict, the judgment was almost a foregone conclusion. The Commissioners thought that the Department ought to be absorbed into a reconstructed and enlarged Education Office, those of its functions which related to secondary education being transferred to a proposed secondary branch within the office, and those which touched upon elementary schools being discharged by the officials in the Education Department who already dealt with such establishments.

The government's acceptance, in principle, of the Bryce Commission's recommendations, reinforced by the mounting pressure of informed public opinion, meant that the Science and Art Department's days were numbered. It cannot be pretended that the manner of their passing presented a very edifying picture. Just as (indeed, partly because) the last years of the Whitehall Office were disfigured by a series of unhappy incidents, so were the closing stages in the life of the South Kensington branch.

To begin with, the Bryce Report had inadvertently opened the

[1] *Ibid.* p. 103.

flood-gates of criticism. Angry voices, all complaining of the Department's baleful influence, began to be raised from several quarters. Technical schools were chafing under the restrictions imposed upon them. They demanded that the South Kensington grants which were given for separate subjects should be replaced by Treasury block grants which responsible local bodies would distribute. The expanding county councils brought the accusation that the technical instruction which directly emanated from these grants was illiberal. School boards were irritated by having to comply with two sets of regulations and by being required to receive two types of inspectors into their schools. Members of Parliament expressed disapproval at the manner in which the Museums Division administered the institutions under its control, and secured the appointment of a select committee to investigate its activities. The National Union of Teachers directed its fire at the Secretary of the Department who was cast as the villain of the piece. In his presidential address to the NUT annual conference of 1898, Dr Macnamara, a former Chairman of the Secondary and Technical Education Committee of the Union's Executive, declared to loud applause: 'With regard to the question of the central authority we have had enough of that *opéra bouffe* education administrator, Major-General Sir John Donnelly, K.C.B., and his attempt to bolster up a deservedly tottering institution by making the Science and Art Department the central authority for Secondary Education must be resisted to the bitter end.'[1]

The teachers did not have to endure their *bête noire* for long. On 3 July 1899 Donnelly, having reached his sixty-fifth birthday, was obliged to retire. It is almost certainly no accident that his departure and the passing of the Board of Education Bill occurred in the same year – almost in the same month. Influenced by sentiment or guided by prudence, perhaps, the government waited until the veteran commander was compelled to relinquish his baton before they requisitioned his army. And this was only justice, for to have done so sooner would have been to mete out shabby treatment to a man who had given such long, honourable and distinguished service in the causes of education and science.[2] For

[1] Reported in *The Schoolmaster*, 16 April 1898.
[2] Donnelly, who died only three years after his retirement, did not live to see the machinery he had so patiently constructed systematically dismantled by Robert Morant.

just as Cole to all intents and purposes *was* the Science and Art Department between its inception and 1873, so the latter half of its history is largely Donnelly's biography. In the case of the Science Division, at least, there was no one else who could take the credit or shoulder the blame for its work over the preceding forty years. Opinions differ as to the value of Donnelly's contribution to technical, scientific and secondary education. Made as it was through the agency of payment by results, that contribution is belittled by some who, in condemning the system, stigmatize the product as necessarily mis-shaped and inadequate. Others take the view that, given that the system was inescapable, Donnelly made it work so effectively that the Department, far from achieving too little, succeeded too well and had to be restrained. Probably the truth lies somewhere in between these two extremes; precisely where is of no great moment. For, as one of his colleagues tersely – and rightly – observed: 'Whatever the defects of the educational policy pursued, the study of science grew immensely under Donnelly's direction'.[1] Still more important,

there was also, diffused throughout the country, a growing feeling that liberal education should, in its widest sense, be not only a vocational education for the liberal professions; but should consist of a ripened acquaintance with the underlying principles of the natural world, and a realisation that it was necessary to educate up to life, and not away from it.[2]

It was this legacy, predominantly posthumous though it may have been, for which Donnelly should be remembered.

Although the Board of Education Act might at first glance appear to have directly precipitated the amalgamation of the Science and Art Department and the Education Department, in reality the act of union occurred prior to the statute and independently of it. On 12 June 1899 the Duke of Devonshire wrote to Kekewich: 'I hope the Board of Education Bill will pass but even if it should not we shall want [a Departmental] Committee to consider the arrangements to be made on Sir John Donnelly's retirement, whose office we should not in any case fill up.'[3] Some decisions affecting the senior executives had already been taken, and these were submitted to the Treasury on 16 June. Their substance was that,

[1] *Dictionary of National Biography*, article on Donnelly.
[2] Armytage, *VASFE*, May 1950, p. 20.   [3] PRO Ed. 24/61.

following Sir John's departure, Kekewich would become Secretary of the Science and Art Department, while continuing to hold the position of Secretary of the Education Department; Mr. W. Tucker, one of the Assistant Secretaries at Whitehall, would be appointed to the new post of Principal Assistant Secretary of the Education Department; and Captain Abney, the Director of Science at South Kensington, would hold a corresponding position in the Science and Art Department. Each Principal Assistant Secretary would undertake the general supervision of his own Department and both would act under the direction of the Permanent Secretary. It looked like 1874 all over again; but there was this difference – the day after Donnelly left South Kensington a departmental committee was set up to consider and report what changes in staff and organization were necessary 'in order to . . . bring those Departments into closer relation to each other'.[1] This time there would be no turning back; the marriage was to be permanent.

It can hardly be claimed to have made a very auspicious start. In his memoirs, Kekewich has much to say about the early days of his dual appointment. He was compelled to visit South Kensington frequently since 'neither Department could be left to shift for itself for days together',[2] and when he arrived he found no warm welcome awaiting him. 'The staff, speaking generally (for there were exceptions), consistently opposed me, not openly or violently, but with a sort of quiet sustained determination and policy of attrition.'[3] Sir George attributed this hostility to their resentment at the importation from Whitehall of a man who was neither an artist nor a scientist, but an organizer and administrator.

Matters got worse rather than better, until Gorst (inspired by some South Kensington officials) delivered the final insult by forbidding Kekewich to carry out his declared intention of investigating the Science and Art Department's administration, although it certainly appeared to be in need of an overhaul. Consequently, as Kekewich bitterly complained, 'from that time my authority over the Science and Art Department was gone'.[4] If South Kensington, which had seldom been on good terms with Whitehall, and which felt deeply aggrieved by its loss of independence, was

[1] Education Department Minute of 4 July 1899.
[2] Kekewich, *Education Department*, p. 219.   [3] *Ibid.* p. 220.
[4] *Ibid.* p. 224.

demanding a sacrificial victim as the price of ending its campaign of passive resistance and non-co-operation, then it succeeded rather too well. For this incident in all probability caused the final break between Kekewich and Gorst, who turned elsewhere for advice. Morant was conveniently on hand to proffer it. Before long the Science and Art Department discovered it had got rid of King Log only to be visited by King Stork.

So the Department's career ended in much the same way as it had begun – in controversy and confusion. But neither of these phases was typical of South Kensington's essential character. Over the intervening years it had made a significant contribution to the spread of technical and scientific education, and its achievements were the more impressive considering the lack of support it received from successive governments and the opposition it often encountered from industry. Between 1854 and 1899 the Department had increased, not so much in size as in influence;[1] and it was precisely the strength and nature of this influence that compelled the state to direct the Department's activities into the mainstream of educational advance.

'South Kensington' was essentially the handiwork of two men. Civil servant Henry Cole had revived the ailing infant to such good effect that, by the time he retired, his foster-child had grown into a lusty and energetic organism. Professional soldier John Donnelly took over its guardianship and stamped his own personality upon it. Indeed, the most notable feature of the Department is that its virtues and defects closely resemble those which one sometimes associates with the average British army officer, particularly in the Crimean War period: resolute but conservative; generous but authoritarian; reliable but unimaginative; unswerving and often unthinking in his devotion to what he conceived to be his duty; scrupulously fair to the point of being insensitive; given more to action than to philosophical speculation; impervious to criticism and hostile to outside interference; possessed of an implicit, even blind, faith in the efficacy of 'Queen's Regulations and Army Council Instructions' as instruments for maintaining standards and achieving orderly progress; bravely fighting the battles of the present war with the weapons and tactics of the last.

The Department had competently conducted the thankless

---

[1] See note pp. 279–80.

operations of invading uncharted territory, establishing lines of communication and introducing law and order; but now that the preliminary campaign had been completed, it was time for another, better adapted, controlling agency to assume responsibility for future development.

10

THE CHARITY COMMISSION:
FROM BROUGHAM TO TAUNTON

We are confronted by the paradox that a temporary commission has in many cases proved to be the precursor of a permanent office and the creator of a new department of English government.[1]

The third of the principal central authorities for education – the Charity Commission – could claim a longer and more illustrious ancestry than either of the others. The Education Department started life as a temporary derivative of the Privy Council. The Science and Art Department had an even lowlier birth; conceived at the Board of Trade, seventeen years were to pass before it was finally delivered, and then only after much surgical attention. Whereas the Charity Commission (the central authority for secondary education so far as one existed in the nineteenth century) could trace its origins back to the mediaeval courts of justice.

From earliest times the state had assumed some measure of control over charities, including those of an educational character.[2] This control was designed to protect the charities against waste and loss, and to preserve them for the objects to which they had been dedicated, and it was exercised in return for the privileges of permanence and perpetuity which charities enjoyed. Such protection was provided through various agencies, the oldest and most frequently employed being that of the Courts of Chancery.

By the beginning of the nineteenth century it had become clear that the latter were ill-designed both to afford the necessary degree of protection and to exercise an adequate measure of control. Their unsuitability was apparent before, during and after the legal proceedings which recourse to the Courts involved. In the first place, the wheels of Chancery could be set in motion only by the Attorney-General acting on information received, or by a private

---

[1] J. Redlich and F. Hurst, *Local Government in England*, 1903, vol. 2, p. 319.
[2] A 'charity' has been defined for legal and legislative purposes, as 'any legitimate dedication of property upon a trust, whether express or implied, capable of permanent duration for the benefit . . . of the public . . .'. *Report of the Charity Commissioners*, 1881, App. A.

individual willing to be the plaintiff. Since there were few people who could afford the time and expense involved, and even fewer who were prepared to lay themselves open to the execration of those brought to account, it was hardly surprising that abuses were seldom uncovered. Assuming, however, that some public-spirited person furnished the evidence, then the cost and delay of the litigation[1] – arising largely from the temptation it offered lawyers to prolong the proceedings at the expense of the charity itself – were found to be such as to make the treatment more damaging than the disease. Finally, supposing that the due processes of the law had been completed, there was a very real possibility that, in the case of educational charities, the new dispensation would prove little better than the old; for the Court of Chancery dealt with all forms of endowments and made schemes for many different eleemosynary purposes, so that when it encountered educational endowments it made schemes for schools, and, having virtually no relevant experience, it sometimes devised extremely odd schemes. In any event, the Court's jurisdiction was limited to rectifying technical abuses only: that is, the employment of charitable property in ways other than those intended by the founder, or, in the case of failure of a trust, to prescribing new uses *cy-près*.[2]

Such disadvantages might not have been serious had the number of endowments been small and their value inconsiderable. But this was far from being the case, as was demonstrated in 1786 with the publication of the 'Gilbert Return'. In taking up the cause of Poor Law reform, a Member of Parliament, Thomas Gilbert, had attempted to make a survey of English charities. The results of his investigation, faulty and incomplete though they were, provided some indication of the extent and worth of the country's charitable trusts, and more than an indication that these stood in dire need of more honest, efficient and intelligent administration.

[1] The expression 'in Chancery' refers to the difficulty experienced in extricating oneself from the coils of this court of law. Chancery proceedings were so leisurely that Bewdley Grammar School was closed for twenty years while its case was argued, and so costly that several schools went bankrupt as a result of becoming involved in lawsuits.

[2] In circumstances where it had become impossible to carry out literally the wishes of the founder, the Court of Chancery would presume that the testator had a general charitable intention and would direct that the income of the endowment should be applied to some other charitable purpose as near as possible (*cy-près*) to the testator's declared intention. 'Unattainable' trusts could therefore be revised; but the Courts possessed no power to modify 'useless' trusts.

Gilbert's Return, which was reprinted in 1810 and again in 1816, supplied useful ammunition for those reformers who were bent on the eradication of human and financial waste alike. In 1812, as the result of a motion proposed by William Wilberforce, legislation was passed requiring trustees to register with the Clerk of the Peace for the county, the capital, income and objects of charities, and the names of both the trustees and of the person holding the instrument of endowment. Since, however, no penalty was imposed for non-registration, compliance depended on the conscientiousness of those affected. In an attempt to ensure the observance of the founder's wishes, the Act[1] also placed the endowed schools unambiguously under the control of the Court of Chancery; but, again owing to inherent weaknesses in the statute, this provision remained a dead-letter. Reformers realized that effective legislation was highly improbable without the holding of an official investigation which would reveal the size and seriousness of the problem; although they were also aware that, given the complexion of Parliament at that period, the fulfilment of even this preliminary requirement seemed unlikely. Fortunately, the times produced the man.

On Samuel Whitbread's death in 1815, Henry Brougham had assumed the leadership of the small group of men who were profoundly disturbed by the state of English education. As a lawyer, Brougham was horrified by the negligence with which charitable trusts were being administered; as an advocate of popular education, he believed that, if these trusts were properly handled, they would go far to supplying existing educational deficiencies. On 28 May 1816 he called for the appointment of a select committee to inquire into 'the Education of the Lower Orders in the Metropolis'. So unobjectionable was this suggestion, that it encountered little opposition; but the members who indulgently and unsuspectingly approved it might well have hesitated could they have foreseen the consequences of their action.

Within a few weeks the committee produced its Report. Contained among the conclusions was this apparently innocuous observation:

Although your Committee have not been instructed to examine the state of Education beyond the Metropolis, they have, in addition to what has appeared in Evidence, received communications, which show

[1] 52 Geo. III, c. 102. Charitable Donations Registration Act.

the necessity of Parliament as speedily as possible instituting an inquiry into the management of Charitable Donations and other Funds for the Instruction of the Poor in this Country, and into the state of their Education generally, especially in the larger Towns . . .[1]

It was the cloud no bigger than a man's hand. Not that Brougham was hoping at this stage to do anything more than rectify some of the more flagrant abuses in the administration of charities. There was no intention of devising means whereby obsolescent trusts might be revised or inappropriate trusts altered to meet changed circumstances, nor any thought of creating a permanent body to supervise endowments.

The Committee's request for a further investigation was granted, and by 1818 its members were declaring that their earlier opinions upon the neglect and abuse of charitable funds connected with education had been amply confirmed. Brougham was now convinced that a more powerful and flexible instrument than a select committee was necessary to expose every instance of mismanagement of such funds. He therefore introduced a Bill for the appointment of a Parliamentary Commission to inquire into the administration of educational charities in England and Wales, as a prelude to legislation on them. Opposition in the Commons was substantial, but the measure survived relatively undamaged. Brougham had briefed himself well. He struck the right note by confidently asserting that a system of national education could be financed out of existing endowments provided they were properly used, and that only a very small part of the expense would ultimately fall on the public. And he came armed with a massive dossier containing the replies from several thousand clergymen he had circularized requesting information. From these 'there emerged a damning story of vast endowments bequeathed by the pious of the past six centuries but the income from which had been largely alienated, squandered or even embezzled by careless, self-seeking or positively dishonest Trustees'.[2]

But in the Lords it was a different matter, for many of these trustees had friends in high places; indeed, they were often to be

[1] *PP* 1816, IV, 3.
[2] S. Maccoby, *English Radicalism 1786–1832*, 1955, p. 343. For a contemporary account of the deplorable condition of the endowed schools – an account which could scarcely have failed to strengthen the reformers' case – see N. Carlisle, *A Concise Description of the Endowed Grammar Schools in England and Wales*, 1818.

found in high places themselves. By the time the Bill reached the Upper House a hostile force of prelates, law lords, and representatives of vested interests had been assembled to cripple it. As a result of their assault, the Bill was mutilated almost beyond recognition. Originally, it had provided for the appointment of eight Commissioners whom it named; a quorum was fixed at two so that they could traverse the country in pairs, thus allowing simultaneous investigation by four boards. The Act vested the appointment of the Commissioners in the Crown, which permitted the abuse of patronage; and it raised the quorum to three so that only two boards could operate at any one moment. At the same time the Commissioners' powers were drastically restricted. In the Bill they were authorized to inquire into the administration of all charities and to require the attendance of witnesses and the production of evidence. Under the statute they had to confine themselves to educational charities, and even within this narrower field there were limitations imposed. To the list of exempted institutions,[1] were added not only Harrow, Rugby and Charterhouse, but all schools which were already under the care of special visitors, and since the latter were appointed by the trustees, the safeguard they were intended to provide was often illusory; in fact, some of the worst examples of corruption were to be found in the institutions so 'protected'. Moreover, the Commissioners were deprived of the power to compel testimony; in other words, they could make inquiries only with the consent of the examinee. And the government delivered what appeared to be the *coup de grâce* by refusing to appoint as Commissioners most of those recommended by Brougham's select committee; instead, the carrying out of the Act was placed in the hands of those who had strenuously opposed it.

Brougham could hardly be blamed for thinking that little worthwhile would result from the deliberations of such an emasculated body. Equally, he could hardly have anticipated that the government, in the following year, would introduce its own Charitable Foundations Bill which, in repealing the recent legislation, substituted for it a measure that more nearly conformed to Brougham's original intentions. The Commissioners' terms of reference were widened to include non-educational charities, and the size of the Commission was increased to twenty members, any two of whom

---

[1] These were Oxford, Cambridge, Eton, Winchester and Westminster.

could act as a board, thus expediting its work. Furthermore, in spite of Brougham's gloomy forebodings, the Commissioners showed a high sense of responsibility in the performance of their duties. They may have been slow and unsystematic, but at least they were conscientious and thorough.[1]

This Parliamentary Commission was not, let it be understood, an executive or punitive instrument; it was designed to compile an inventory, not to correct abuses. The Commissioners were virtually impotent unless the maladministration were so deplorable that they felt entitled to notify the Attorney-General so that he could take legal proceedings. Otherwise, their only strength lay in their moral influence and in the salutary effect their published reports might have upon dishonest, careless or incompetent trustees.

By 1834, when the Commission's second term of office expired, the great majority of English charities, some 27,000 in number, had been investigated. In view of the unexpected length of time taken to conduct the inquiries to date, of the cost involved, and of the need to determine what action should be taken on the reports, the government decided to appoint a select committee to review the position.

The first essential was to speed the completion of the survey. This, the Committee estimated, could be achieved within three years, provided that the number of Commissioners was greatly increased and that they were allowed to act individually instead of in pairs. But beyond the immediate matter of settling unfinished business lay the question of ensuring the future sound management of the endowments so painstakingly examined. The committee's suggestion was that 'the superintendence and, in certain cases, the administration of all property devoted to charitable uses should be entrusted to a permanent Board of three Commissioners, or some other independent authority, on whom should be imposed the duty of superintendence and control over the administration of all property devoted to charitable uses . . .'[2]

---

[1] This Commission was the first of many that studied various aspects of education in the nineteenth century. They, and the numerous select committees that were also appointed to investigate educational problems, played an important part as instruments for guiding the actions of the government departments concerned, and for supplying ideas generally on the role of the state in a changing society.

[2] *PP* 1835, VII, p. 638.

Specifically, the Commissioners' powers would include the right to scrutinize accounts, to dismiss incompetent trustees (or, where necessary, masters of endowed schools), and to authorize 'such arrangements as shall appear calculated to promote the object of the Founder; and in cases in which that object is useless or un-attainable, to suggest such other appropriation as may appear desirable'.[1]

While the Committee's recommendation for a non-political administrative body was hardly revolutionary – the Poor Law Commission provided a recent precedent – it proved too radical for Parliament to stomach.[2] Perhaps members took alarm at the proposal to equip the Board with really effective powers of control and direction. Thus, although the concept of revising 'unat-tainable' trusts was unobjectionable (that, after all, was the point of the *cy-près* formula), to suggest the amendment of 'useless' trusts was to introduce novel, even dangerous, possibilities. This would entail both disregarding the founder's wishes (however absurd or malicious they might be), which in the context of the age amounted almost to sacrilege, and interfering with 'private' property, which was viewed with even greater repugnance.

So nothing was done to exploit the valuable mine of information which the Commissioners had brought to light. Brougham made several spirited but fruitless attempts to spur the government into action. In July 1835 he brought in a Bill providing for the creation of a Government Board, consisting of three Ministers of State, who 'should have a constant, and . . . a perfectly effectual control over estates held in trust for charities, so as to prevent their mismanagement and abuse'. Unable to win support, Brougham withdrew his Bill; he re-introduced it in a modified form two years later, with an equal lack of success.

Yet Brougham could be consoled with the knowledge that not all his efforts to secure the better administration of endowments had been in vain. Acting on the advice of the select committee, the government re-constituted the Charitable Trusts Commission,

---

[1] *Ibid.* p. 639.

[2] Incidentally, the Commissioners of Inquiry into the operation of the Poor Law had themselves lately delivered the opinion 'that if the funds now destined to the purpose of education, many of which are applied in a manner unsuited to the present wants of society, were wisely and economically employed, they would be sufficient to give all the assistance which can be prudently afforded by the State'. *PP* 1834, XXVII, 205.

increasing the membership, improving its procedure and placing it under the chairmanship of Brougham himself. It was ordered to complete its inquiries within two years.

The Commissioners finished their assignment in good time, although the final report did not appear until 1840. Viewed cumulatively, the labours of the successive Commissions had resulted in a financial and social survey of monumental dimensions, consisting of no fewer than thirty-two reports which, with the accompanying evidence, filled thirty-eight closely-printed folio volumes. Unfortunately, so massive a work tended to defeat its own object, 'for the practical effect was that no person ventured even to look into it'.[1] However, this drawback was partly rectified a few years afterwards when an analytical digest was compiled, containing the reports, summaries of the evidence and the essential information on each of the 28,880 charities investigated.

The Commissioners reckoned that the capital resources of these endowments amounted, in aggregate, to over £6 million; nearly half-a-million acres of land were found to be held in trust, much of it situated in the immediate vicinity of large towns and therefore likely to appreciate in value. On these assets they calculated that the annual interest earned totalled almost £$1\frac{1}{4}$ millions, and of this some £312,000 (about 26 per cent) was devoted to educational purposes.[2] All this wealth represented an imposing tribute to the philanthropy of bygone days, and, given certain conditions, held out the prospect of extensive benefits in the years ahead.

To their Final Report the Commissioners attached a short abstract of their findings and a number of recommendations. Although they had in the course of their inquiries come across numerous cases of inefficient and inept administration, they had found gratifyingly few instances of fraudulent conversion.[3] They

[1] Lord Chancellor Cranworth speaking in the House of Lords on 3 May 1853. (*Hansard*, 3rd ser., CXXVI, col. 1010.) In terms of the magnitude of the undertaking, the only comparable survey in English history up to that time had been the Domesday Inquest. Nearest to it in respect of the kind of information elicited was that conducted by Henry VIII's commissioners prior to the dissolution of the monasteries.

[2] Since the Commissioners unwittingly overlooked some 4,000 charities, the actual total of endowment income was even higher.

[3] Evidence that private individuals were not the only trustees who were failing adequately to carry out their responsibilities is provided by another Commission that was concurrently investigating institutions of local government. The members of this body discovered many examples of mismanagement, by Corporations, of educational endowments. Thus: 'from various causes, some-

also discovered that many charities could not be managed efficiently because of the absence of any machinery for the making of speedy and inexpensive decisions on what were often only minor points of law. The Commissioners' proposed solution to all these difficulties was the creation of a permanent supervisory board exercising both administrative and quasi-judicial powers. On the problem posed by those trusts that seemed to be useless or harmful, though not necessarily unworkable, the Commissioners, endorsing the recommendation of the select committee of 1835, thought that 'it would be of great advantage if there were some competent authority to direct the application of charities of this description to the purposes of education, or to some other substantial benefit of the poor . . .'.[1]

Members of Parliament were now in possession of a formidable array of facts concerning charitable endowments and were, if not constitutionally, at least morally, bound to take some corrective action. Ultimately, this they did, but only after a lapse of thirteen years, the prompting of another Royal Commission, and the failure of no fewer than ten attempts at legislation. Each successive year, from 1844 to 1852 inclusive, a Bill of one kind or another dealing with the administration of charities was presented to one House or the other by one government or another; but for one reason or another – pressure of business, party manœuvring, refusal to disturb vested interests, or just sheer indolence – these came to nothing.[2]

Nevertheless, this otherwise sterile period did produce one measure which indicated that Parliament was not entirely in-

---

times from the improper selection of the master, . . . sometimes from making the education exclusively classical, the schools have become in a great measure useless to the inhabitants, and much valuable property given for the purposes of education is thus wasted'. *First Report of the Royal Commission on Municipal Corporations*, 1835, p. 48.

[1] *Final Report of the Commissioners for Inquiring concerning Charities*, 1837, vol. 32, pt. 1, p. 5.

[2] A Bill was introduced in 1841 conferring on the Committee of Council a limited administrative authority over the regulation of small educational endowments. It was rejected, according to Kay-Shuttleworth, because the actions of the Committee were filling the religious bodies with apprehension and both Houses of Parliament with suspicion. (*Report of the Schools Inquiry Commission*, 1868, vol. 5, q. 17,429). But in 1844 the passing of a minor Act (7 & 8 Vict. c. 37) did enable trustees of endowed schools to accept a grant on the conditions laid down by the Committee of Council notwithstanding any clause to the contrary in their trust deeds.

different to the necessity for adapting educational endowments to the requirements of the time. Owing to the application of the *cy-près* rule, and more particularly to Lord Eldon's judgment in the Leeds Grammar School case of 1805, it had become the established doctrine of the Court of Chancery that, when a school was founded to teach Greek or Latin, the school authorities could not be required to teach anything else on the funds of the foundation, however unsuitable that instruction might be in terms of the pupils' abilities or society's needs. This rigid adherence to antiquated trust deeds provoked the industrial and commercial classes into pressing for the reform of the endowed schools, and led eventually to the Grammar Schools Act of 1840, whereby the Courts of Equity were empowered, in certain circumstances, to broaden the narrow classical curriculum of individual institutions. Strictly limited in its scope, the statute had little practical effect; but at least it constituted a move in the right direction.

In the long run, moreover, those frequent and ineffectual legislative endeavours were not wholly futile, since they led, in 1849, to the appointment of a fresh Commission which was instructed to inquire 'into those cases [of charity malpractice] which were investigated, and reported upon, by the Charity Commissioners, but not certified to the Attorney-General'.[1]

In their Report, the Chichester Commissioners, having reiterated the recommendations of both the Brougham inquisitors and the 1835 select committee, subjected Parliament to a mild rebuke for not implementing them, declaring that the need for some 'permanent and vigilant control' over charitable trusts, so far from diminishing, had increased with the passage of time. They found that there were many charities of which the income had been irretrievably lost from the want of some proper authority to watch over the trusts; many others had been abused and diverted from their proper objects because 'persons locally acquainted with the circumstances have declined to incur the pecuniary responsibility or odium of instituting legal proceedings'. There were, moreover, numerous charities where the maladministration was wholly attributable to ignorance on the part of the trustees, who 'under competent advice and direction, would be quite willing to correct what is irregular or defective'. In the Commissioners' opinion, the answer to these several difficulties lay in the creation of 'some

---

[1] See *Hansard*, 3rd ser., CXXVI, cols. 1009–1010, Lord Cranworth's speech.

public and permanent authority, who should be charged with the duty of supervising the administration of all these Charitable Trusts'.[1]

At long last, in April 1853, the Aberdeen administration brought in a Charitable Trusts Bill that passed successfully, if not unscathed, through all its stages to become law. So far as its central purpose was concerned, the Bill followed the pattern set by its nine discarded predecessors in providing for the establishment of a body that would exercise a general superintendence over all charitable trusts in England and Wales. Probably at Kay-Shuttleworth's prompting, the government's original intention was that, as many of these charities related to education, this body should be the Committee of Council on Education equipped with such legal assistance as proved necessary for dealing with any difficult question of law that might arise. Unfortunately, the Bill, on reaching the Lords, was referred to a select committee which came to the conclusion that 'it would be better that the question of general superintendence and administration of charities should be altogether separated from any political question, and from interests of any party'.[2]

Faced with the likelihood of yet another legislative miscarriage, the government accepted the amendment, with the result that the Charity Commission as constituted under the Act was kept apart from the other state departments responsible for educational administration.[3] It remained largely isolated from them for the remainder of the century.

The Charitable Trusts Act of 1853, when it finally received the Queen's assent, turned out to be a mild, not to say timid, remedy for the maladies affecting the endowed charities, and far less drastic than that proposed by the successive investigating bodies previously mentioned. Apparently, Parliament's tardy recognition of the necessity for social reform was still being tempered by a deeper, though perhaps not disinterested, respect for the liberty of the individual and for the rule of law. In short, the Act established a Board of Charity Commissioners who were authorized 'from time to time, as they in their discretion may see fit, to

[1] *PP* 1850, XX, 18.

[2] *Hansard*, 3rd ser., cxxix, col. 1154 (Lord John Russell).

[3] The Charity Commissioners were directed to submit their annual reports to the Home Secretary, although they looked to the Lord Chancellor as the minister who would be responsible for amending the law under which they worked.

examine and inquire into all or any Charities in England and Wales, and the nature and objects, administration, management, and results thereof, and the value, condition, management and application of the estates, funds, property, and income belonging thereto'.

They were also empowered to apply through the Attorney-General to the Court of Chancery in case of malversation, or where it appeared to them that a new scheme for the management of the charity was necessary, provided it could be carried out within the established case-law on charities. Where, however, they considered that some greater change was necessary than the courts would sanction, they were authorized to make a new scheme for the better management of the charity, and for a change in the disposal of its funds; the scheme, when framed, had to be laid before Parliament, where, after passing through all the stages of a Bill, it would become law.

The Board was to consist of four members, three of whom were to receive payment; of these, two had to be barristers of not less than twelve years' standing, and the Chief Commissioner was bound to be a barrister. The fourth Commissioner would be unpaid, so providing for representation of the Commission in the House of Commons.[1] Associated with the Board were two Inspectors.

To the untutored eye, the Commissioners' powers must have appeared formidable, but not many years were to pass before they were seen to be limited in all vital particulars. Thus, the Commissioners could demand information only from trustees, not from third parties. More important, though, was the total inadequacy of the provisions relating to the formulating and sanctioning of new schemes. The Commissioners found, on the one hand, that proceedings in Chancery for this purpose were still extremely costly and dilatory, and, on the other, that, where they themselves prepared a scheme and laid it before Parliament, they experienced the greatest difficulty in obtaining the assent of both Houses to it. The reasons for this difficulty were not hard to find and should have been anticipated: no minister was made responsible for such

---

[1] This office was not annexed by law to any particular minister or member of the House, appointments to it being made by the government of the day. After 1856 the custom was for the place to be filled by the Vice-President of the Committee of Council by virtue of his connexion with education.

schemes and few members were interested in conducting them through their various stages or in defending them against attack. As a result, the slightest opposition was sufficient to prevent their enactment.

Not surprisingly, the Commissioners fretted under these restrictions and showed their dissatisfaction in one annual report after another. By 1860 Parliament had come to realize that the time was at hand either to extend the authority of the Commission or to abolish it altogether. In that year Robert Lowe introduced a measure which, had it been carried through in its entirety, would have achieved, at long last, the aims of the 1835 Report. On this occasion it was the Commons that forced the insertion of an amendment which rendered the ensuing statute less effective than it might have been.

Nevertheless, the second Charitable Trusts Act was a distinct improvement on the first. By it, the Commissioners were vested with certain judicial powers, enabling them to make orders for establishing schemes and for appointing or dismissing trustees. An important limitation, however, was placed on the Commissioners' jurisdiction. Their scheme-making powers were restricted to those charities having an income of £50 per annum or less; for the remainder, the consent of a majority of the trustees was necessary. The practical effect was that while the overwhelming majority (over 80 per cent) of endowments came under the Commission's quasi-judicial authority, this number represented only a small fraction (some 15 per cent) of the total amount of charity income. So far as the substantial endowments were concerned – and these included many schools – the Commissioners' powers were limited to those they were permitted to exercise under the earlier Act, entailing one or other of the laborious procedures mentioned above.

Even so, the 1860 Act made the Charity Commission a much more productive instrument than it had previously been. It could offer the smaller charities all the benefits of judicial action with few of its disadvantages. Possibly, the Commissioners' endeavours were less beneficial as regards educational endowments than they were in respect of those of a non-educational kind. Some thirty-five years later, the then Chief Commissioner recalled these early experimental days: 'From 1860 they [the Commissioners] had to make the best educational schemes they could. They were not equipped educationally, and, although they did their best, the schemes, I imagine, were not very successful from an educational point of view'.[1] Furthermore, neither the Commissioners nor the Courts could deal with schools in relation one to another; they had to be considered as separate entities.

When, therefore, the Newcastle Commissioners were appointed in 1858 to inquire into the state of popular education in England, it was fitting that they should make an intensive survey of educational endowments and a thorough examination of their management and the purposes to which they were put. On the evidence they obtained from both witnesses and their own investigators, the Commissioners reached a series of interesting and important conclusions. They found generally that 'the Educational Charities possess powers of promoting education among all classes of people which are at present undeveloped and which better organization, more active supervision, and greater freedom of progressive improvement and adaptation to the changing exigencies of the times would call into action'. They did not know, nor was there any means of ascertaining, the current aggregate revenue of these charities, for, although the law required annual returns of each charity to be submitted to the Charity Commission, the latter experienced difficulty in enforcing this regulation. Consequently, it was hardly surprising that the Newcastle Commissioners were unable to say what proportion of these charities belonged to popular, as distinct from 'higher or middle' education.[2] But, in any case, they were reasonably certain that a large proportion of these various charities 'are not turned to good account at present . . . It is not so much positive abuse that now calls for remedy, as inefficiency, languor, and inadequacy of the results to the pecuniary means of the foundations'. They learnt, too, that educational trusts, like many other charities, were scattered unevenly over the country, being most plentiful in the places which were populous and wealthy in the sixteenth and seventeenth centuries, and least numerous in the new urban areas.

Endowed schools, being charities, were liable to inspection by

---

[1] *Report of the Royal Commission on Secondary Education* [C.7862], vol. 3, q. 11,446 (Longley).

[2] The Commissioners added that they did not propose 'to divert from the higher or middle education any endowments which are now usefully serving that purpose'. Significantly, perhaps, they did not make a similar declaration in the case of elementary education.

8.

the Charity Commission; but as the members of that body themselves pointed out, such inspection was occasional, not periodic,
and instituted only when called for by special circumstances. In
consequence, many schools had never been officially inspected at
all. Moreover, however desirable in theory regular inspections
might be, in practice they were unattainable, simply because the
Commission's staff contained only five inspectors for charities of
every description. Nor were these five particularly qualified to
make an educational, as distinct from an administrative and
financial, inspection, since three were barristers, one was a
solicitor, and the fifth lacked any previous professional experience.
There was, it seemed, little that the Charity Commissioners could
do to improve the situation, as they had no voice in the selection
and dismissal of their inspectors, and the appointing authority,
namely the government, had never consulted them on the subject.

The Newcastle Commissioners paid a handsome tribute to the
useful progress that the Charity Commission had made in rectifying faults in the administration of charitable trusts. But, so far
as educational endowments were concerned, they felt that, compared with the other central authority responsible for popular
education, it suffered from at least three serious defects. It was,
in the first place, 'an authority less recognized and looked up to
by the nation, and less powerful in dealing with local interests than
the Privy Council'. Secondly, it was not, 'like the Education
Committee of the Privy Council, a body constituted with a special
view to the management of places of education', and the Commissioners considered that 'no body but one so constituted can do
what is requisite in the case of places of education so peculiarly
in need of active and experienced supervision as the endowed
schools'. Lastly, the Charity Commission had, practically speaking, no effective power of initiation.[1]

Turning to the Court of Chancery, the Commissioners acknowledged that this court performed a necessary function in
framing new schemes for charities, in order to prevent them from
becoming 'by lapse of time and change of circumstances, obsolete
and useless, or even noxious to the interests which it was the object

[1] The Charity Commission by this date (1861) appears to have given up in
despair any attempt to frame its own schemes and to obtain parliamentary
approval of them.

of the donors to promote'. On the other hand, schemes framed by the Court – and, indeed, those sanctioned by statute – were seldom suited to the requirements of educational institutions. Furthermore, the Court could interpose only in extreme cases, and then only when it had been activated by the Attorney-General or by private applicants.

Finally, the Newcastle Commissioners considered the problem of what action should be taken in respect of those charities which, by reason of the passing years, had become redundant, outdated or incongruous. Assistant Commissioner Cumin had been employed in tracing the extent and nature of these wasted assets. He found numerous examples of charities where the conditions which had called them into being no longer existed, such as endowments for providing archery butts, or for repairing wells, and he thought that in cases like these it seemed 'reasonable to say that they should be applied to education, instead of being left to be dealt with by the Court of Chancery, according to the doctrine of *cy-près*'. The Commissioners concurred with this view, arguing that the need for speedy and decisive action in respect of such bequests rendered it all the more essential that a powerful government department be made responsible for dealing with them, 'because local interests are likely to be more unreasonable and tenacious in their opposition'.

Summarizing their conclusions, the Commissioners declared:

1. That the educational charities are capable of being turned to better account;
2. That of the charities not at present applicable to education some might, under proper authority, be lawfully and advantageously applied to that purpose.[1]

In order to achieve these objects, and because there was 'an obvious convenience, and there will probably be a saving of expense, in placing our whole system of public education, so far as it is connected with Government, in the same official hands', they recommended:

1. That ... the Charity Commission be converted into a department of the Privy Council; that the Committee of Council on Education become the Committee of Council on Education and Charities; and that the Privy Council be invested with the power, to be exercised

[1] *Report of the Newcastle Commission*, vol. I, pp. 539–40.

through the Committee, of making ordinances for the improvement of educational charities, and for the conversion to the purposes of education, wholly or in part, of charities which are noxious or useless as at present applied . . .

2. That all endowed schools now subject to inspection by the Charity Commission become subject to inspection by the Privy Council, and that the middle and elementary schools be annually visited and examined by the Privy Council Inspectors, and their accounts audited on the spot.[1]

These were bold and imaginative proposals, as the Commissioners themselves were aware: 'The measure here suggested no doubt is extensive, but the objects to be gained are also great, both as regards the promotion of what is good and the suppression of what is evil.'[2]

Time passed. The government did nothing; or rather it very speedily implemented a part of that section of the Newcastle Report which recommended payment by results, but it seemed strangely disinclined to adopt those proposals relating to educational charities. Questions began to be asked in Parliament, and the reasons for this reluctance began to emerge. In February 1863 Earl Granville, the Lord President, replied to an inquiry about the government's intentions. He thought there was much to be said for and against the Newcastle plan, but he doubted very much 'whether Parliament would agree to the main principle of that plan, which would transfer to the Committee of the Privy Council powers which would render them a quasi-judicial body – powers which hitherto had been exercised only by the Court of Chancery'.[3]

He added that the Charity Commissioners 'had now the advantage of the presence of the Vice-President of the Council, who formed a sort of link between them and Parliament'. Moreover, to talk of new legislation was premature, since a Bill had recently

[1] *Ibid.* pp. 540–1. The modern secondary school examination system began about this time. In 1857 the Bath and West of England Society for the Encouragement of Agriculture, Arts, Manufactures and Commerce formed a committee to organize a local examination for middle-class school boys. As it had no desire to make this examination a permanent part of the Society's activities, the committee suggested to the Committee of Council that the Education Department 'might be interested in extending its powers'. The offer was 'hastily brushed aside' by Lingen (Montgomery, *op. cit.* p. 47). The local committee, and subsequently the secondary schools in general, turned instead to Oxford and Cambridge who agreed to shoulder the responsibility.

[2] *Report of the Newcastle Commission*, vol. I, p. 537.

[3] *Hansard*, 3rd ser., CLXIX, col. 184.

been passed increasing the jurisdiction of the Charity Commissioners, and assigning to them powers which until then had been exercised by the Court of Chancery. Sufficient time had not elapsed to test the working of that measure, but it appeared to be progressing satisfactorily.

Four months later in the Commons, Vice-President Lowe was even less encouraging. Speaking as one of the Board of Charity Commissioners, he had no hesitation in saying 'that a more efficient tribunal does not exist'; and he could make that assertion without any breach of good taste because he had 'no part in their decisions, being merely the medium of communication between them and the House of Commons'. He could not understand why, when the Charity Commissioners had effected, and were effecting, vast improvements, the powers they possessed – and were using with so much discretion – should be taken from them. He thought further that it would be 'most objectionable to arm any political Department with such powers. That would be placing in its hands an immense amount of local influence, and it would be quite impossible to escape the suspicion of partiality and corruption'.[1]

And there the matter was allowed to rest. Doubtless Granville was correct in believing that Parliament would have refused to accept the Newcastle recommendations, but the government did not even put that assumption to the test. Perhaps if the Education Department had been held in higher esteem at that time and had been conducted by men who commanded widespread respect as educationists, the story might have been different. At all events, this opportunity, like others before and after it, was allowed to slip by; the Charity Commission and the Education Department were kept at arm's length from each other, and the country had to wait another forty years before they were brought together in roughly the way that the Newcastle Commission had proposed.

While Parliament fumbled uncertainly with the problems posed by the endowed schools as a whole, a small group among them were managing to secure for themselves a privileged position both within the hierarchy of educational institutions and in their relation to the state. It may be recalled that a number of the so-called public schools had received exceptionally favoured treatment in 1818 by obtaining exemption from the Brougham inquiry commission. By the middle of the century it could hardly have been claimed

[1] *Hansard*, 3rd ser., CLXXI, col. 723.

that they had justified their unrestricted freedom from public control; truer to say that they had fully earned the severe criticism to which they were subjected at this time. Not that their detractors wished to achieve anything more than a broadening of the curriculum and an improvement in the teaching therein; almost no one advocated any form of long-term government intervention. Eventually, in 1861, the Palmerston administration agreed that the nine 'great' public schools constituted an appropriate subject for parliamentary inquiry and it appointed a Royal Commission under Lord Clarendon to conduct the investigation. This Commission, manned by some of the most enthusiastic supporters of the schools, recommended several useful reforms concerning their management and curricula, and these were subsequently carried into effect under legislation enacted in 1868; but, predictably, it avoided offering any suggestion that the nine establishments be brought even indirectly under permanent statutory supervision.[1] For an explanation of parliamentary refusal to integrate them into the evolving publicly-superintended system, it is probably unnecessary to look further than that given some years afterwards by W. E. Forster. Questioned as to why these schools should be treated differently from other endowed schools, he replied that he saw no reason, except that 'a very considerable number of the Members of both Houses have been educated in them'.[2]

But if Parliament studiously avoided exercising any control over the public schools, it was experiencing increasing difficulty in evading its responsibility for the bulk of the endowed schools, and particularly in determining in what manner and to what extent that responsibility should be discharged. Few questioned the need for these schools to be placed under some kind of state supervision, but there were widespread doubts as to whether the Charity Commission provided the most suitable agency for that purpose, and growing anxiety over the continued separation of the Commission from the government department primarily concerned with educational matters.

For, in spite of legislative, judicial and administrative activity, the endowed schools remained in a state of stagnation. Admit-

[1] To encourage the development of the schools as expensive boarding establishments, the Commissioners also authorized the governing bodies to disregard the founders' provisions concerning 'poor scholars'.

[2] Report from the Select Committee on Education, Science and Art (Administration), 1884, q. 495.

tedly, Wilmot's Grammar Schools Act had allowed for a modification of the purely classical curriculum in particular schools, but this statute had only a very restricted application. Similarly, the schools were not greatly affected by the establishment of the Charity Commission; for, although educational endowments came under its jurisdiction just as did other trusts, it had no authority to undertake a major reform. The Commissioners could devise schemes *cy-près* for schools, but only in exceptional circumstances; and they could deal with schools solely on an individual, not on a collective, basis. Given existing conditions, it was unrealistic to expect that the schools would put their own houses in order, or to imagine that the Charity Commission as then constituted could develop into a central authority competent both to undertake their reform and to superintend them subsequently.

It was at this point that the middle classes began to press for a thorough-going inquiry into the endowed schools. Rejecting the elementary schools as socially and educationally inferior, and recognizing that the public schools were too few in number and too élitist to provide an adequate or realistic alternative, they saw in the free grammar schools the ideal vehicle for achieving the ambitions they entertained for their children. So that when it was observed that the state had interfered, apparently to good effect, in the sphere of popular education, and was interfering, potentially to good effect, in the sphere of upper-class education, there seemed every reason to persuade it to intervene in the sphere of middle-class education. In 1864, therefore, at the request of Sir John Pakington, the government was prevailed upon to appoint a third Royal Commission, its brief being to inquire into the education given in those schools which had not been included in either the Newcastle or Clarendon Commissions and 'to consider and report what Measures (if any) are required for the Improvement of such Education, having especial Regard to all Endowments applicable or which can rightly be made applicable thereto'.

The Schools Inquiry Commission, often referred to as the Taunton Commission after its chairman, had to plough a long furrow, for there were no fewer than 782 endowed schools to visit and assess; small wonder that over three years elapsed before its investigations were completed and its Report published.

But in the interval a remarkable development occurred which to some extent anticipated and even prejudged the Commission's findings. Late in 1867, the third Derby administration, in the persons of the Duke of Marlborough (the Lord President) and Lord Robert Montagu (the Vice-President), decided, for reasons not altogether self-evident, to integrate the three main central authorities for education and to place them under a Secretary of State.[1] In October and November three memoranda were prepared, dealing respectively with the Education Department, the Department of Science and Art, and the Charity Commission, and at the same time Henry Cole was asked to express his opinions on educational administration.[2]

The third memorandum was drawn up by the Vice-President himself, and indicated that the government was on the point of carrying out a major educational reform along the lines of that eventually adopted in 1899. In it Montagu argued that the proper distribution of charitable endowments was basic to the 'due advancement of what is understood by *popular education*', and must, in fact, 'present the first object for consideration in any practical and comprehensive educational scheme'.[3] This being so, the administration of educational endowments needed to be under the control of an educational – not a quasi-judicial – department. In any case, the objections to the Charity Commission, as then constituted, were many and grave; apart from anything else its Parliamentary position was quite exceptional as regards both its representation in the legislature and its privity with the Committee of Council.

The Vice-President then proposed that the jurisdiction of the Commissioners should 'merge and pass to' the Education Department. However, the latter as it stood was ill-equipped to discharge even its existing responsibilities, far less was it able to shoulder additional ones. A fundamental re-organization of the Department was essential.

In brief, the plan came to this: the Charity Commission should be converted into a Department of the Privy Council; the Com-

---

[1] These proposals were produced in the same year that the second Reform Bill became law, and the possibility arises that they formed part of the Conservative policy of 'dishing the Whigs'. It is worthy of note that at the very time he was opposing Russell's resolution calling for a Minister of Education possessing wide powers, the Lord President was preparing a Bill along just those lines.

[2] See above, p. 175.

[3] PRO Ed. 24/54. Memorandum by the Vice-President on the Privy Council Committee of Education. October 1867, pp. 4, 5. (Italics supplied.)

mittee of Council on Education should become the Committee of Council on Education and Charities; and a permanent Board or Council of Education should be established acting under, and subject to the complete control of, the Lord President. Among the many reasons given for making these alterations were two of some significance: 'That the change will render the Council of Education the central and only Department for all educational purposes (for example, the Poor Law Board Schools &c); . . . That it will lend additional weight to a Department of State over which it has been stated a Cabinet Minister should preside'.[1]

Then followed a series of specific recommendations regarding the composition of the projected Council or Board, which would consist of five members, to be, in the first instance, the three Charity Commissioners, together with Ralph Lingen, and Henry Cole who 'would take the Science and Art Department and Technical Education'.[2]

Lord Montagu closed his memorandum by intimating that the suggestions contained therein would

tend to render a comprehensive Government Bill complete, and perhaps popular. They are not capable of being treated separately. Any Bill short of being comprehensive will only appear to be an effort to 'prop' up a bad system. There is no use increasing either the number of schools, teachers or school-children, while the central authority is known to be unable to control them.[3]

Unhappily, the entire project came to nothing. The Lord President introduced his Bill in March 1868 but failed to carry it through even the Upper House before a general election returned a Liberal administration. The change in government need not, by itself, have proved fatal to the project, had not other events conspired against it. For in December 1867 Russell, now aged seventy-five, decided to retire from the leadership of the Liberal Party, to be succeeded by Gladstone, who was opposed on principle to the creation of new departments of state powerful enough to secure Cabinet representation. In the following February, Derby resigned the premiership owing to ill health, to be followed as leader of

[1] *Ibid.* p. 11.
[2] This Board was designed to operate on the same lines as the Board of Admiralty; that is, the members would act on an individual, not a collective, basis, each one having charge of the work of his own department. The political head would take sole responsibility for policy decisions.
[3] *Ibid.* pp. 17–18.

the Conservatives by Disraeli, who was equally hostile, though for different reasons, to the formation of an 'all-purpose' Ministry of Education. To complete the catalogue of coincidences: on 2 December 1867 the Taunton Commissioners signed their Report recommending an entirely different central authority for the control of charitable endowments from that proposed by the Newcastle Commission and adopted by the Derby administration. One of the members of the Taunton Commission was W. E. Forster, shortly to become the next Vice-President of the Committee of Council.

And so this opportunity for radical reform went begging, with the result that the administrative unification of the country's educational system was again postponed – as it happened, for over a generation. But more serious even than the delay was the fact that during that period each element in the fragmented system developed upon its own separate lines which were not only educationally but also socially distinct. A century later, the effects of that division have been by no means entirely eradicated.

To understand the reasoning behind the Report of the Schools Inquiry Commission, it is necessary to remember that throughout the Victorian era 'education was envisaged in terms of social class . . .'.[1] In crude terms, the lower classes received their instruction in the elementary sector, the upper classes would receive their education in the public schools sector, while the middle classes could receive their schooling in the endowed schools sector.[2] But, however convenient this formula might seem to be in theory, its practical application presented difficulties, for its success depended on there being a sufficiency of schools of each type. What the Taunton Commissioners found when they came to look at the provision for middle-class schooling was that the schools which might purvey this particular brand of education were both deficient in quantity and unsatisfactory in quality.

Some 782 endowed schools, or roughly a quarter of all such schools in England and Wales, were supposedly offering education beyond the elementary stage and were therefore of particular concern to the Commission. Of this number, only 209 could be considered genuine classical schools, while 340 taught neither Greek

[1] *Report of the Consultative Committee on Secondary Education*, 1938, p. 32.
[2] One Lord President – the Duke of Marlborough – bluntly referred to the Taunton Commissioners' Report as the 'Report of the Middle Class Schools Commission'. (*Hansard*, 3rd ser., CXCI, col. 119).

nor Latin, nor any other subject, very effectively. Indeed, most of the schools in this category provided an education little wider than that given in the average elementary school.

There were similar variations so far as the schools' resources were concerned. Endowments ranged from Christ's Hospital, enjoying an annual income of £42,000, to poverty-stricken establishments receiving less than £10. The majority could hardly be described as affluent, only 229 schools possessing a yearly income of £100 or more. Likewise, the distribution of the schools left much to be desired: of the 512 towns with a population of over 2,000, as many as 208 were without secondary schools.

For these defects the Commissioners found the state largely to blame.

There is no public inspection to investigate the educational condition of a school by direct examination of the scholars, no public board to give advice on educational difficulties, ... not a single payment from the central government to the support of a secondary school ... In any of these senses there is no public school and no public education for the middle and upper classes ... [The State] might give tests, stimulus, advice, dignity; it withholds them all, and leaves the endowed schools to the cramping assistance of judicial decisions, which may be quite right as regards the interpretation of the founders' words, and quite wrong as regards the wise administration of the schools they founded.[1]

The Commissioners saw little evidence to indicate that the existing machinery was providing the desired mixture of control and encouragement, and no prospect that it could ever do so in its present form. On the one hand, there were serious objections to the jurisdiction of the Court of Chancery which acted slowly, expensively and merely in a legal capacity. On the other hand, the Charity Commission suffered from a number of fundamental weaknesses. It could not act spontaneously but only on local initiative; it required the consent of the majority of trustees if the charity amounted to over £50 a year; it lacked the means to examine scholars; it was unable to conduct an effective audit of charitable accounts; it was too deliberate in its procedure and too limited in its operations; it employed inspectors who were unsuited to the task of advising on the schools they visited; and it possessed neither the powers, nor the officers, nor yet the comprehensive view which the situation demanded.

[1] *Report of the Schools Inquiry Commission*, vol. 1, pp. 107–8.

Turning from the present to the future, the Taunton Commissioners expressed the opinion that the problem of reform could be solved only if certain conditions were met. First, the heterogeneous collection of endowed schools must be considered as a whole, not simply as isolated units. Secondly, little could be achieved unless the law on charities were revised. Without there being available some readier means to alter trusts than special Acts of Parliament, it was hopeless to attempt to reform the schools or to convert numerous ill-applied charities to educational purposes.[1] Thirdly, some form of inspection was necessary to prevent waste, to secure efficiency, and to prepare the way to improvement.

Regrettably, when the Commissioners came to make their recommendations, they showed little of the insight that had been so prominent a feature of their diagnosis, studiously avoiding the solution advanced by the most distinguished educationist of the period. Kay-Shuttleworth, in his evidence, proposed the creation of a

department of public charities corresponding to or identical with the Committee of the Privy Council, which now administers the education grants ... Thus a relation might be established between the elementary, the grammar schools, and the Universities. They might form a series of institutions, with means of transition from the lowest to the highest; thus establishing for the greatest capacities of all ranks an equality of privileges which, for political and social purposes, is of national importance.[2]

But the members of the Taunton Commission had no desire to construct an educational ladder that all children might have the opportunity of climbing. Their intention was to provide a system of secondary education which would be a predominantly middle-class preserve. The very last thing they wanted was that the endowed schools should be brought under the superintendence of the Committee of Council, for in that eventuality they might ultimately be made part of an integrated system. They planned instead to separate the classes 'so as not to educate the lower above their station or embarrass the higher with low company'.[3]

---

[1] In fifteen years the Charity Commissioners had succeeded in carrying only eighteen Bills through Parliament, and of these a mere nine related to schools.

[2] *Ibid.* vol. 5, qq. 17,568, 17,457.

[3] H. Perkin, *The Origins of Modern English Society 1780–1880*, 1969, p. 301.

When, therefore, the Commissioners framed their proposals, no mention was made of a combined, multi-purpose central authority superintending all forms of education which derived any part of their income from public funds. Secondary education was treated as an entirely distinct type of education which required its own separate authority. This, they thought, might be a re-constituted Charity Commission which would include at least one member appointed for his educational knowledge, and one Member of Parliament who could explain the Commission's actions to the Commons. To this strengthened body would be confided the duties of approving or rejecting all schemes for the re-settlement of educational trusts, of providing for the inspection of endowed schools, of inquiring into all charities which might be referred to it as useless, or mischievous or obsolete, and of deciding whether or not they ought to be converted to educational purposes; to it also would be granted the power to abolish free places or closed scholarships for poor or local boys, even when this meant ignoring the founders' wishes or contravening the trust deeds of the grammar schools affected. Parliament, or in certain cases the Privy Council, would remain the supreme arbiter on the question of whether or not a scheme should become operative.

Aware, perhaps, that the proposed Charity Commission would still be inadequate and unsatisfactory as an *education* authority, the Report recommended that a second central authority be established with powers to frame rules for examinations, to appoint examiners for schools, and to control the entry of teachers into the profession at the secondary level. Completing the administrative framework were plans for the creation of provincial authorities, each of which would be responsible for the management, curricula and inspection of the secondary schools within its 'province'.

11

THE CHARITY COMMISSION:
THE RULE OF THE TRIUMVIRATE

To every class we have a school assign'd
Rules for all ranks and food for every mind.

– George Crabbe

Shortly after the publication of the Taunton Report, the government hurried through an interim Endowed Schools Bill with the object of preventing the creation of new vested interests which might hamper either the operation of subsequent legislation or the remodelling of any scheme. Work was then begun on drafting a measure based on the Commissioners' recommendations. There was no attempt to carry into effect the whole of their complex plan, for neither the government nor the other parties involved were prepared to allow the state to gain continuous control over the endowed secondary schools, even to the limited extent envisaged by the Commission. Thus, the proposals relating to provincial authorities were rejected, those concerning inspection held in abeyance, and those dealing with the central authority considerably modified.

As originally conceived, the Endowed Schools Bill of 1869 was arranged in two parts, one being of a 'temporary', the other of a 'permanent', nature. In the event, only the temporary section became law. The second part, dealing with the creation of a state examination system under the control of an Educational Council, was detached from the rest of the Bill in Committee, to linger on as the Endowed Schools (No. 2) Bill. It encountered violent opposition both from Members of Parliament, who denounced it as an unwarrantable interference with the liberty of the subject, and from the public schools, the supporters of which were against state intervention of any description. It never reached the statute book, although it did provoke the establishment of the Head-masters' Conference the following year.

The first part, however, received Parliament's unenthusiastic approval to become the Endowed Schools Act, 1869. According to the preamble, the purpose of the measure was to promote the greater efficiency of educational endowments and to carry into effect the main designs of the founders by putting a liberal education within the reach of children of all classes. This object was to be achieved through the medium of three Commissioners who would have power,

in such manner as may render any educational endowment most conducive to the advancement of the education of boys and girls, or either of them, to alter, and add to any existing, and to make new trusts . . . in lieu of any existing trusts . . . which affect such endowment, and the education promoted thereby, including the consolidation of two or more such endowments, or the division of one endowment into two or more endowments.[1]

To repair past neglect in the supply of girls' secondary education, the Act laid down that in framing schemes provision should be made for extending to girls the benefits of endowments.

The initiative, then, to formulate schemes passed to the Commissioners who need not wait for the trustees to make application. But the Act broke even more strikingly with precedent by empowering the Commissioners, with the co-operation of local governing bodies, to take over for educational purposes certain obsolete trusts 'which have failed altogether or have become insignificant in comparison with the magnitude of the endowment'.[2] Thus, in specified circumstances, the Commissioners were permitted to disregard the hallowed and hitherto almost inviolable doctrine of cy-près.

Taken together, these were extensive powers.

It is scarcely too much to say that the Endowed Schools Commissioners could do what they liked with regard to any educational endowment[3] subject to certain savings for endowments which were undeniably attached to the Church of England, provided they paid due regard . . . to the educational interests of any particular class of persons whose privileges were abolished.[4]

---

[1] Endowed Schools Act, 1869, Section 9. Exempted from the Act's operation were endowments less than fifty years old, and, it is hardly necessary to add, the nine great public schools.

[2] *Ibid.* Section 30.

[3] It has been facetiously suggested – and not without good cause – that the Endowed Schools Commission could turn a boys' school in Northumberland into a girls' school in Cornwall.

[4] R. Barker (ed.), *Owen's Education Acts Manual*, 1936, p. 425. Prior to the Act, the doctrine of the Court of Chancery had been that an educational foun-

For this reason, and perhaps because the government contemplated that the reformation of the endowed schools could be completed without undue delay, the Act laid down that the Commissioners' powers should expire at the end of 1873.[1] For this reason, too, elaborate safeguards were built into the Act for the protection of interested parties. Following an inquiry and consultation, the Commissioners could frame a scheme. They then had to submit it to the Committee of Council on Education, who passed judgment on it. The scheme, if approved, was then published and placed before Parliament where it had to lie on the table of both Houses for forty days; then, provided no Address to the Queen to disallow the scheme was presented during that time, it was lawful for Her Majesty to ratify it. In addition, those opposed to a scheme might appeal to the Judicial Committee of the Privy Council.

In common with all other educational statutes, the Endowed Schools Act was a compromise; in adopting it Parliament had steered a middle course between the ambitious Taunton designs and the *status quo*. Its effectiveness as a measure of educational reform would depend on the energy, skill and vision of the men chosen to put it into effect. The government played its part by appointing as Commissioners individuals who would not be afraid or reluctant to wield the formidable powers with which they had been armed. Selected as Chief Commissioner was Lord Lyttelton, who was a keen supporter of both educational and charity reform; indeed, he declined the position when it was first offered on the ground that he was already too deeply committed to be impartial. The remaining Commissioners were Canon H. G. Robinson, formerly Principal of York Training College, and Arthur Hobhouse. The latter, a Queen's Counsel, had been appointed a Charity Commissioner in 1866, and was known to be a strong advocate of the reform of the law governing charitable endowments. He retained

---

dation must be regarded as belonging to the Church of England in the absence of evidence to the contrary. Section 19, however, refused to treat an endowment as attached to the Anglican Church, unless express documentary evidence that it was so attached could be produced.

[1] After the terminal date the responsibility for administering educational endowments would revert to the Charity Commission. This body continued to function side by side with the new Commission, the considerable powers it possessed under the Charitable Trusts Acts, so far as they concerned educational endowments, being held in abeyance while the Endowed Schools Commissioners remained in existence.

his seat on the Board of the Charity Commissioners, thus constituting a link between the two authorities.[1] Working in close
association with these three, was the Secretary to the Commission.
Between 1869 and 1872 this office was held by H. J. Roby, who
had previously been the Secretary to the Taunton Commission;
as such he had become a firm believer in the need to improve
radically the endowed schools, most of which were found to be in
'an indescribable state of inefficiency and maladministration'.[2] As
might be expected in view of the authority vested in it and the
personnel involved, the Endowed Schools Commission had a brief,
stormy, but highly productive existence. Inevitably, perhaps, in
view of its reforming zeal, it roused more opposition than it gained
support.

One of the reasons for its unpopularity lay in the fact that its
relationship with elementary, as distinct from secondary, endowed
schools was ill-defined. Whatever the preamble to the Act might
say, the Commissioners considered that their overriding responsibility lay towards secondary education. Yet it was impossible to
draw a sharp line between elementary and secondary endowments,
and one of the Commission's most difficult tasks was to determine
in which category a trust belonged. For example, numerous
schools, which had been founded as grammar schools, had declined
to the elementary level. In many such cases, the Commissioners
endeavoured to reverse the process by applying the endowment to
the award of scholarships tenable at a grammar school, much to
the resentment of local inhabitants who accused the Commission
of showing undue favouritism towards secondary education.
Moreover, when the Commissioners laid down the rule that academic attainment, or the payment of fees, or both these together,
should form the sole criteria for admission to grammar schools, it
was tantamount to handing them over to the middle class, for the
application of such a principle meant that all but a few working-
class children would be denied entry, even though the school in
question had been established specifically or principally *for the
poor*, as vast numbers of educational foundations had been. It was
this aspect of the Commission's work which gave rise to the charge

---

[1] The Endowed Schools Commissioners came to be regarded as such powerful
potentates that they were known variously as the 'Three Kings at Whitehall'
and the 'Triumvirate'.
[2] *Dictionary of National Biography*, article on Roby.

that the legislation of 1869 amounted to 'legalized embezzlement'. The whole issue was confused rather than clarified by the Elementary Education Act of the following year. Section 75 recognized that endowments for elementary education required treatment distinct from that applied to other educational trusts, and in respect of such endowments it vested separate scheme-making powers in the Education Department. But while the jurisdiction for the various educational trusts was divided in this way, no rules were laid down as to the respective limits of the two authorities, and the Commissioners aroused considerable indignation for the way they chose to interpret the 1870 Act. Yet another source of discontent sprang from the decisions they made regarding the reconstitution of governing bodies, both the Anglicans and the Dissenters accusing the Commissioners of showing preference to the other side.

In view of all this controversy, and because the task of reforming secondary education was still very far from completion, the government in 1873 appointed a select committee to inquire into the working of the Endowed Schools Act.

Giving evidence before this body, the various members of the Commission described its machinery and the progress it had made. Apart from the three Commissioners and the Secretary, the Commission's staff consisted of one occasional and six regular Assistant Commissioners, and a small number of clerks. For convenience, the country had been divided into three districts which were visited for the most part by the Assistant Commissioners, who conducted inquiries and exchanged views with interested parties in the locality before reporting to their superiors in London. On the basis of this information the Commissioners prepared a draft scheme which was published and circulated. After three months, and in the light of any representations made in the meantime, they could then frame a definitive scheme which in turn had to be submitted to the Education Department. At this point a serious difficulty arose. Once the scheme had been presented to the Department, no one had any authority to alter it in the slightest particular. The Department, which was seldom consulted about the formulation of a scheme, could only approve or reject, but not amend, it.[1] Nor had the Department any right to interfere

---

[1] Cumin, at that time an Assistant Secretary in the Education Office, was the official who, with the aid of one clerk, transacted the business that came before

with, or give instructions about, any scheme until it had reached the Whitehall Office. Moreover, even a minute error in a scheme could not be corrected except by Act of Parliament or by drafting a fresh scheme, which involved a delay of about twelve months.

Another weakness the working of the statute disclosed lay in the fact that the Commissioners had no power to inspect the schools after schemes for their improvement had been sanctioned. Both the Endowed Schools, and the Charity Commissioners had tried to secure some degree of educational efficiency by inserting in their schemes a provision that there should be an annual examination of the scholars carried out by an independent party who would report to the governors on the school's instruction and discipline. A copy of the document was to be forwarded to the Commissioners. Since, however, the latter possessed neither the staff to examine the reports, nor the means of remedying any defects revealed by them, the stipulation proved largely ineffective.

As to achievements, the Commissioners could report but moderate progress. The making of schemes was turning out to be a much more complicated and gradual process than Parliament had envisaged. By 1872 only twenty-four schemes had actually passed into law, with thirty-four framed and submitted to the Education Department for approval, and eighty-four draft schemes published. Schemes for a further 214 schools were under discussion. These figures were not unimpressive; but there remained an enormous gap between the 142 schemes and draft schemes already completed and the total number of endowed schools, the majority of which were in need of re-organization.

From the select committee, the Endowed Schools Commissioners received two somewhat muted cheers. They were congratulated on their general performance to date, but admonished for being too outspoken and over-enthusiastic in particular instances. With certain modifications, their powers should, the committee recommended, be continued beyond the date on which they were due to expire. For this to happen, legislation was required, and it soon became obvious that the Lords were unwilling to renew the Commission's mandate for an extended period. In the end, Salisbury,

---

the Department in connexion with the Endowed Schools Act. In his experience, the Commissioners only twice consulted the Department on any question.

the leader of the Tory peers, agreed not to oppose the amending Bill, on condition that the Commissioners' powers be reviewed after a year's elapse.

Before the extra time had run its course, however, the Conservatives were back in office, and this time there was to be no reprieve. The Commission had made too many enemies, and these were resolved at most to destroy, at least to shackle, it. It was resented by lawyers who disliked the quasi-judicial authority it exercised. It was feared by Anglicans who believed that it was aiding and abetting the secularization of endowments. It was distrusted by Nonconformists who were uneasy about the matter of religious instruction in schools. It was unpopular with the public schools who saw in it a possible threat to their freedom. It was disliked by many endowed schools, the staffs of which were concerned lest their comfortable existence should be disturbed. It was resented by the Conservatives because its handling of moribund and misapplied trusts had been so effective. It was attacked by the champions of the labouring classes who complained that it had expropriated the revenue from a considerable number of endowments intended for the poor, and had ensured that secondary schools would be preponderantly middle-class institutions. Finally, it was blamed for the administrative difficulties and legal confusion that were said to have arisen from the circumstance that, since every endowed school was also a charitable trust, both it and the Charity Commission exercised concurrent jurisdiction over the same property.

At all events, the Disraeli administration was resolved to check the Commission's activities and to reverse, where possible, its decisions. In the summer of 1874 a Bill was introduced which had as its object not only the extinction of the Endowed Schools Commission, but also the denationalization of schemes made under its authority. So unashamedly partisan and reactionary were the proposals that even *The Times* felt constrained to comment: 'It is difficult to find a precedent for it – a bill proposing the wholesale redelivery to one religious body, of schools which, founded for national purposes and endowed with national property, have been set free for the use and education of all Englishmen.'[1] Indeed, the Tory backbenchers themselves jibbed at translating the scheme into law, and the government had to be content with a statute that

[1] *The Times*, 22 July 1874.

merely slowed down the rate of progress, instead of one that put the clock back.

In essence, the Endowed Schools Act, 1874, simply transferred for a period of five years the powers and duties of the Endowed Schools Commission to the Charity Commission – a body that could be relied upon to control its enthusiasm.[1] At the same time, the Crown was authorized to enlarge the Charity Commission by the appointment of two more paid Commissioners and an additional secretary. The responsibilities of the new Commissioners – unlike those of the men they replaced – were not confined to the purposes of the Endowed Schools Acts. They possessed the same authority and performed the same functions as the original members of the Board. But there was one significant difference between the two types of Commissioner: whereas those appointed under the Charitable Trusts Acts held their commissions 'during good behaviour', those appointed under the 1874 Act held office on the same tenure as the Parliamentary Commissioner, that is, 'during Her Majesty's pleasure'. The government, having rid itself of two thorns in the flesh in the shape of Lyttelton and Roby (who had succeeded Hobhouse on the Commission), were determined not to risk being saddled with another set of executive officers whose removal might present awkward problems.[2]

One unforeseen difficulty arose over the ambiguous part that the Vice-President of the Committee of Council was expected to play under the new legislation. This minister now found himself discharging a dual responsibility with regard to the endowed schools. As the fourth Charity Commissioner he was, at least in theory, a party to the framing of schemes; as Vice-President he was bound by law to approve or disapprove those same schemes. When the point was raised in the Commons, Lord Sandon, who was then Vice-President, gave a pledge that he himself would no longer act in his capacity as a Charity Commissioner. From then onwards, successive ministers debarred themselves, by a sort of self-denying ordinance, from sitting on the Board, their only function being,

[1] The powers were from time to time renewed through the agency of the Expiring Laws Continuance Acts.
[2] By Section 1 of the Act, the Endowed Schools Commissioners were relieved of their duties. Roby eventually became a Member of Parliament; but Lyttelton, who suffered from fits of melancholia, grew so depressed over the abolition of the 1869 Commission that he committed suicide within a few months of his dismissal.

so far as the Commission was concerned, to represent it in Parliament 'merely as a mouth-piece . . . answering questions on information given to [them]'.[1] Thus the primary purpose behind placing one of the Ministers of Education in a position where he could influence the preparation of schemes was entirely nullified.

And so after a short, vigorous and turbulent career, during which it had produced no fewer than 317 completed schemes, the Endowed Schools Commission's contract was summarily terminated. Because its policies were controversial to a degree, the contribution it made to educational development has been the subject of some debate and much disagreement. Few, however, would quarrel with the tribute paid some dozen years after its demise by Henry Longley, when the future Chief Commissioner was acknowledging the debt that the Charity Commissioners owed to the Endowed Schools Commissioners.

They were the pioneers who led the van of the movement; . . . they accumulated a vast amount of experience of which we have had the benefit . . . There can be no doubt that they cleared the way for us, and if we have had any success, it is in very large measure due to them; and further, it is due to the fact that they have collected and transmitted to us a staff which, for efficiency and ability, I should think has never been equalled in any public office.[2]

The Triumvirate had carried out their novel and exacting duties with singular speed, competence and ruthlessness – indeed these were the qualities that proved their downfall – and they laid a firm foundation on which their successors could build. There was, all the same, a murkier side to their activities, for, in following too closely the Taunton recommendations, they pursued a policy which often resulted in the exclusion from the endowed schools they restored just those pupils for whom the schools were intended, thereby creating, or at the very least reinforcing, a grave educational injustice.

---

[1] *Second Report of the Royal Commission on Civil Establishments* [C.5545], 1888, q. 16,375 (Longley).
[2] *Report from the Select Committee on the Endowed Schools Acts*, 1886, q. 6242. Longley paid a special compliment to the Assistant Commissioners whom the Endowed Schools Commission had appointed. What method of selection was employed is not altogether clear. In Lyttelton's words: 'We did not select them at all; they were, so to say, ready to our hand if we were fortunate enough to obtain them'. One of the Assistant Commissioners was HMI Fitch, who was seconded from the Education Department.

It has been contended that the revival of the grammar schools was conditional upon the financial support of, and their acquisition by, the middle classes. Others have argued that this reform – by seriously impeding the introduction of secondary education for the majority of children – was bought at too high a price.

Whatever the pros and cons of this particular debate, there is no doubt that the late 'sixties and early 'seventies marked a decisive period in the development of education in this country. During it, what was possibly the last aristocratic government in English history created a closed system of schools for the governing class. During it, too, what was arguably England's first middle-class government answered Matthew Arnold's eloquent plea and laid the basis for a system of efficient secondary education for the middle class by delivering the endowed schools from the hands of 'private desultory enterprise'.

The working class might also be presumed to have had its educational needs and rights. But the horizons of its members perforce were limited, and as yet they possessed neither the political power nor the economic strength to press, nor yet the literacy to formulate, their claims.

12

THE CHARITY COMMISSION: THE ENDOWED SCHOOLS DEPARTMENT

> Lawyers, I suppose, were children once.
> — Charles Lamb

The Endowed Schools Act of 1874 came into operation on 31 December of that year. For purposes of administration a new department was created within the Charity Commission to handle educational endowments. It was staffed by the officers of the defunct Endowed Schools Commission who – apart from Lyttelton and Roby – were all retained in their several posts.

After some initial confusion, caused by the circumstance that for more than a year the two offices had to remain housed in buildings at a considerable distance from each other, the Charity Commission settled down to continue the work so energetically begun by the Commission it had superseded, or to be more accurate, absorbed. It was not long, however, before the Commissioners became conscious of the same flaw in the system that had troubled the Triumvirate: namely, the absence of any effective inspectorial machinery. Every year that passed lessened the value of the facts and opinions recorded by the Schools Inquiry Commission, yet schemes which were based on those facts, and which prescribed in some detail the subjects to be taught, continued to be framed. There was obviously a valid case for the Charity Commissioners having the power to inspect a school *before* they addressed themselves to the task of laying down a curriculum for it; and there was almost as strong a case to be made for enabling them to conduct inquiries about the working of the schemes *after* they were introduced. Between 1877 and 1888, when the Commissioners took the law into their own hands, the need for such guidance and control became a recurring theme running through one Annual Report after another. Thus in 1877:

We should have wished . . . to have given some precise information as to the educational results of the altered administration of Endowed Grammar Schools and to have been able to describe the character of the instruction given in the schools, the methods employed in teaching, and the qualifications of teachers. We feel that the whole country has an interest in knowing how far the result of these endowments is commensurate with their extent and importance, but we have not at our disposal the means of obtaining information of that kind, for which a process of examination by means of a staff of qualified inspectors would be necessary. It may therefore deserve to be considered, when the work of reorganisation under the Endowed Schools Acts is more nearly completed, whether some general system of examination and supervision may not be desirable so as to ensure the continued efficiency of the reformed foundations.

And again in 1881:

In the absence of any organised system of inspection of Endowed Schools, we are not in a position to make any general statement as to the extent to which the directions [i.e. schemes] in question may fail to be carried into active operation; but judging from the occasional opportunities of observation afforded to us in the course of our ordinary business under the Charitable Trusts Acts, we are led to believe that in many instances they are disregarded, and we know of no means by which security can be taken for their due execution, except by the creation of some such system of periodical inspection of Endowed Schools as we have already advocated in previous reports.

And the Commissioners went on to point out that many of the schemes made under the first Endowed Schools Act already required alteration, owing to a change in the 'circumstances of the locality or value of the endowment or other causes'. But the insistent appeals went unanswered, partly because the Charity Commissioners were in their turn becoming increasingly unpopular. For this, their defective constitutional position was largely to blame. Governments were understandably reluctant to place additional authority in technically irresponsible hands.

In any case, so far as charitable trusts were concerned, Parliament's attention was concentrated at this time on a more pressing problem than that of providing for the regular inspection of endowed schools. As early as 1865, the Charity Commission had reported on the unsatisfactory state of the parochial charities of the City of London. On the one hand, their annual income had risen out of all proportion to the size of the population; on the other, many of the endowments were archaic, not to say grotesque.[1]

[1] Some of the more interesting examples included bequests for sermons celebrating the defeat of the Spanish Armada and the failure of the Gunpowder Plot,

Little was done to reform these charities until 1878, when Liberal members finally persuaded the Home Secretary, Richard Cross, to appoint a Royal Commission to inquire into the matter.

Presenting their Report three years later, the Commissioners recommended that, in the case of non-ecclesiastical endowments, once the individual parishes had ear-marked a sufficient portion of the funds for spending in accordance with the founders' wishes, the surplus should go into a pool for the general good of the inhabitants.

Such half-hearted proposals failed to satisfy many of the more radical reformers. These included James Bryce, who prepared a Bill which was designed to free the great bulk of City endowments from both parochial control and the restrictions imposed by donors. The City interests fought back, even attempting to use charity income to finance their campaign, but in the end Bryce had his way.

Briefly stated, the objects of the Parochial Charities Act of 1883 were to extend the 'beneficial area' of City endowments from that of the mediaeval capital to that of the modern metropolis, and to adapt those endowments to current needs. Temporarily enlarged for the purpose,[1] the Charity Commission was required to assess the charitable trusts of the 107 parishes affected. The latter would be relieved of their responsibilities for endowments, the income from which would thenceforth be devoted to a variety of estimable causes, including the promotion of the education of the poorer classes in London through the agency of secondary, technical or art education.

The twin processes of calculating the resources and pronouncing on their disposal took longer than expected, and it was 1889 before the Commission's master plan was produced. Under it education received exceptionally favourable treatment. Not only was more

---

for the tolling of the bell at St Sepulchre's before executions at Newgate, for the ransoming of Christian captives from Barbary pirates, for killing ladybirds on Cornhill, for maintaining an oil lamp at the corner of Billingsgate 'forever', and for the purchase of faggots for burning heretics.

[1] One of the two additional Commissioners appointed to handle the extra work was Sir Francis Sandford who vacated the Secretaryship of the Education Department in 1884. The other was James Anstie, Q.C., a Nonconformist barrister. This was the first of two appointments to the Charity Commission of men with radical leanings made by A. J. Mundella, who was determined that the Commission should make vigorous progress in its reformation of the endowed schools.

than £160,000 to be spent on the provision of polytechnics and similar establishments, but the former were to receive over £20,000 a year *in perpetuity*,[1] and an additional £5,000 was to be paid annually to another group of technical institutions. These recommendations, although they did not receive universal acclaim, were ultimately adopted. By the terms of the Act, the administration of the funds passed out of the Charity Commission's hands into those of a specially constituted body: the City Parochial Foundation.

Meanwhile, the Charity Commission had entered troubled, not to say stormy, waters; and it was Bryce who accurately diagnosed the reason. Speaking in the Commons in June 1883 on the occasion of Sir John Lubbock's motion calling for a separate Ministry of Education, he argued that the Commission was unpopular because it was, 'so to speak hidden away in a dark corner. It was not amenable to public opinion; and there were no means of ascertaining what it did, or what it did not do, or what were the grounds of its action'. He asserted that 'the only way in which they could deal with the Charity Commission was to place it under a responsible Department, whose Head sat in the House of Commons'.

As a result of the debate, of which this speech formed a part, a select committee was appointed to consider the question of ministerial responsibility for the administration of the votes for education, science and art. In due course it investigated the triangular relationship involving the Charity Commission, the endowed schools and colleges, and the Education Department.

Douglas Richmond, one of the Charity Commissioners, described some of the points of contact existing between the Commission and the schools for which it was responsible: 'Having informed ourselves as fully as we can about the endowment, we then approach the question, What educational work shall we design for it in the future?; and in that matter we have the assistance of skilled Assistant Commissioners . . .'[2] After the scheme had been approved, however, the Commission had no specific authority to supervise its implementation. There was, nevertheless, a loophole in the law which might enable the Commissioners

---

[1] In view of the complaints the Commissioners themselves had made about, and the difficulties they had experienced with, the inflexibility of testamentary dispositions, this bequest is scarcely credible.

[2] *Report from the Select Committee on Education, Science and Art (Administration)*, 1884, q. 1552.

to perform this function without their having to seek additional powers; for the Endowed Schools Acts authorized them, once having made a scheme, to make amendments to it, and they were already entitled to investigate a school with a view to making *or remaking* schemes. Thus they had the power to send down an Assistant Commissioner to every one of the (reformed) endowed schools whenever they liked, under the pretext that they wanted to amend the scheme. Such a stratagem was scarcely ideal, but it was better than nothing.

If witnesses were agreed that the Commission's control over the progress of a scheme once it had been ratified could be improved, they were of like mind in holding that the connexion between the Commission and the Education Department was less than satisfactory. For, although the latter was responsible for approving schemes, it had very little, if anything, to do with their formulation. The Department, in reality, acted more as a check on the Commission than in the capacity of an educational adviser to it. And the fact that the Vice-President was one of the Commissioners had no practical value so far as their treatment of educational endowments was concerned. For, as Forster had discovered, the minister's position as an official member of the Charity Commission was highly anomalous.

I quickly found out [that it] was an office I had better not attempt to fulfil, because I found I had no ministerial power there, and that, therefore, if I took part in the [proceedings] my vote went for no more than those of anybody else, and therefore, I thought I had better leave the Charity Commission schemes to come solely upon their authority to the House of Commons, and I found that the other members of the Commission quite accepted that . . .[1]

The Vice-President was, nevertheless, the minister in the Commons who answered questions arising out of the Commission's activities, a state of affairs which caused the chairman of the select committee to wonder how the Vice-President could be responsible as a minister in Parliament 'for work of which he knows nothing'.

Just as the Commission was ill-informed about the success or otherwise of the schemes after they had been approved, so also was the Department. Mundella deplored a situation in which the Department, although legally responsible for the sanctioning of

[1] *Ibid.* q. 399. In any case, the Vice-President was the Fourth Commissioner by custom, not by right.

educational schemes, received reports on their progress from neither the Charity Commission nor the schools themselves. He considered that all endowed schools ought to be subject to an annual inspection conducted by the Department's inspectorate.

To this suggestion the select committee gave its support, recommending

that when schemes for Endowed Schools, whether in England or in Scotland, have come into operation, the Minister of Education should have full authority to call on the Governing Bodies to furnish him with such reports and information as he may require, and to direct any inquiries or inspection to be made which he may deem necessary.[1]

Somewhat daringly, the committee proposed that the Minister should also be entitled to request the public schools (and, incidentally, the grant-aided universities) to submit reports; but its members could not bring themselves to advise that his powers should extend to ordering an inspection of these schools. Nothing, unfortunately, was done to implement any of these recommendations.

1884, the year in which this Committee reported, marked the end of what might be called the (reconstituted) Charity Commissioners' 'honeymoon period'. Such was the relief felt by many people at being freed from the incubus of the Endowed Schools Commissioners that their successors, initially, were seen in a particularly favourable light. But by the early 1880s there were ominous signs of a reaction against them and of mounting opposition to their policies.

The first heavy salvo was fired in 1884 with the publication of the Second Report of the Technical Instruction Commission. This roundly declared that

the transfer of the functions of the Endowed Schools Commissioners to the Charity Commissioners has not had the effect of increasing the rate of progress in the reorganization of our secondary schools. We consider it to be essential that steps should be taken to ensure that this work shall be carried on with greater vigour in the future than it has been hitherto.[2]

Such a criticism hardly squared with the satisfaction expressed by the Commissioners themselves some three years previously,

---

[1] *Ibid*, p. iv.   [2] *PP* 1884, XXIX, 516.

when they reported that 'the fusion [in 1874] of the two Commissions before existing, has greatly facilitated public business by removing the possibility of friction or conflict of jurisdiction that might not improbably arise between the two Departments having cognisance of the same subject matter', adding that the concentration under one roof of the records of the relevant endowments had 'materially obviated delay and difficulty in the transaction of business'.[1]

However, the main attack launched against the Commissioners during the 'eighties was directed more at their *mode* than at their *rate* of procedure. An indication of the widespread and sustained uneasiness felt about this aspect is provided by the fact that in the space of eleven years (1884–95) the Commission was subject to no fewer than seven investigations. The first of these – a select committee inquiring into the operation of the Charitable Trusts Acts – reported that the unpopularity of the Commissioners was chiefly a result of their management of business appertaining to the endowed schools. Former Commissioner Hobhouse explained it in this way:

In the case of the educational endowments, it was their duty to go about the country and overhaul all the endowments in turn, and a great many people did not want to be overhauled, and there was a great deal of objection . . . [In addition,] they were administering a new law very often without compass or rudder, with very little to guide them in the Act, and they had to make what in effect were new rules, and of course there was a great deal of dissatisfaction . . .[2]

Much of the dissatisfaction had arisen, the Committee found, from the Commissioners 'declining to appropriate funds to the direct support of elementary schools', and from their refusal 'to maintain or institute any system of indiscriminate gratuitous [secondary] education'.[3] Accordingly, the Committee recommended that the working of the Endowed Schools Acts should as soon as possible form the subject of a special inquiry.

And so yet another select committee was appointed, which throughout 1886 and 1887 listened to all the familiar and by now tedious arguments for and against the Charity Commission's policies. Not surprisingly, there was little new to say. The Com-

---

[1] *29th Report of the Charity Commissioners*, 1881, p. 15.
[2] *Report from the Select Committee on the Charitable Trusts Acts*, 1884, q. 2938.
[3] *Ibid.* p. ix.

mittee learnt, perhaps with some misgivings, that of the seven Commissioners who constituted the executive board, all but one were barristers-at-law, including the two members appointed under the Endowed Schools Act of 1874. In the 'Endowed Schools Department'[1] itself there were seven Assistant Commissioners. One of these was engaged as Acting Secretary, another as draftsman; the remaining five were employed in conducting local visits, inquiries and correspondence. All seven were barristers as well. It was also the Commission's policy that every one of the higher division clerks should have been trained as either a barrister or a solicitor.

But the shortcomings and dangers arising from entrusting the reform of secondary education to lawyers agitated the minds of politicians less than the question of the Commission's accountability. One of its members explained why the Commission stood in a special relationship to the Legislature: '[Its] work is not like the work of an ordinary political department. It is work not only administrative, but, in a very large measure, judicial; and it is work which Parliament has seen fit therefore to separate to a certain extent, from distinct political control.'[2]

Yet another perennial problem was that of the inspection of schools after they had been reformed. D. R. Fearon, the Acting Secretary to the Endowed Schools Department, pointed out that 'when once the scheme had been approved . . . and the files are closed, and all persons who were concerned are duly notified, the Endowed Schools Department has nothing more to do with the scheme'.[3] This, however, was a matter not of choice but of necessity. 'The powers of the Assistant Commissioners appointed under the Endowed Schools Acts . . . are limited to the purposes of those Acts, which extend only to the making of schemes; and . . . they are not empowered to inquire into the working of schemes under those Acts . . .'[4]

---

[1] It later (1888) transpired that there was no such thing as the 'Endowed Schools Department'. Although reference was often made to such a Department, it did not 'strictly in reality' exist. It was, according to one Assistant Commissioner, 'an expression for a convenient division of labour'; it had 'reference to the business and not to the people'. *Second Report of the Royal Commission on Civil Establishments* [C. 5545], qq. 16,526, 16,531.

[2] *Report from the Select Committee on the Endowed Schools Acts*, 1886, q. 6232 (Longley).

[3] *Ibid.* q. 368.   [4] *Ibid.* q. 6371 (Longley).

In 1887 the select committee issued its Report which gave a cautious endorsement to the Charity Commissioners' policy over the preceding thirteen years. Although their progress had been less rapid than was hoped, they had nevertheless succeeded in reconstituting some 800 endowments, yielding a total income of about £400,000, and the schools affected now contained twice as many pupils as before their reorganization. But to this commendation the Committee added a rider warning the Commission that, when endowments belonging to the poor were converted into scholarships and exhibitions, everything possible should be done to guard their 'paramount interests'; an injunction that ought not to have been necessary, but obviously was. On the burning issue of the responsibility of the Commissioners to Parliament, the Committee felt that this should be 'clearly defined and made complete', maintaining that the desired result would best be attained through a responsible Minister of Education. When it came to the inspection of grammar schools, the Committee found itself in two minds. On the one hand, it approved of the appointment of additional Assistant Commissioners who would act as inspectors of schemes when framed; on the other, it felt that the authority of the managers might be impaired by a periodical government inspection and that the natural development of schemes in accordance with local requirements might be checked. Apparently, an *administrative* inspection conducted by *lawyers* was desirable, whereas an *educational* inspection carried out by *HMIs* was not.

As far as this last recommendation was concerned, the committee had, in fact, been overtaken by events, for in 1887, after some months of negotiation, the Charity Commissioners obtained parliamentary sanction for a Bill amending the Charitable Trusts Acts. Under this new legislation, the Commission was authorized to appoint Assistant Commissioners as Inspectors; in this capacity they would, through the wider powers they now enjoyed, be better able to secure the efficient working of schemes. An amendment requiring that 'at least one in every three of the Assistant Commissioners to be appointed under this Act shall be selected from the working classes' was defeated. The social argument that, without this proviso, the poor would continue to be 'robbed' under the sanction of the Charity Commission, was answered by the legal argument that the Assistant Commissioners, to be able to fulfil their duties properly, ought to have 'some knowledge of the Mortmain Acts, the Statute of Limitations and other complicated pieces of legislation'. Members of the working classes, the Attorney-General surmised, would be unlikely to possess such erudition.

In 1887, too, an effort was made to improve the Commission's constitutional status. Thereafter, the unpaid Commissioner was required to be a member of the House of Commons holding no other office under the Crown. As such, he would be in a position to acquire, by attendance at the meetings of the Board, and otherwise, a general familiarity with its work, and would, in consequence, be able to represent it more effectively in Parliament. For a while after this development, relations between the Commission and the Legislature became less strained.

Following the Act of 1887 the Commissioners not unnaturally hoped that they would be afforded the services of additional Assistant Commissioners so that they might institute a systematic inspection of the schools for which they were, in some degree, responsible. But they waited in vain; and so, at the end of 1887, they acted on their own initiative by planning a pilot inspection of certain 'Schools and Educational Endowments appropriated by Schemes under the Endowed Schools Acts to secondary or higher Education, with the intention, if in the result it should appear desirable, to extend the process to other districts . . .'[1] A year later they were able to report that the partial inspection had been 'productive of results beneficial to the public service'. They proposed, therefore, to continue and extend it. They conceded that the inspection was more administrative than educational in character, as was perhaps inevitable considering they were obliged to employ their existing staff of Assistant Commissioners, who, being lawyers, were not as a rule fitted by training or experience for the educational inspection of secondary schools. This is not to suggest that educational aspects were totally neglected, for the Commission's reports indicate that attempts were made to assess such matters as the character and suitability of the curriculum.

Over the next few years, the Commission's work, as a consequence

---

[1] *36th Report of the Charity Commissioners*, 1888, pp. 27–8. Although the Commissioners could probably not be accused of acting *ultra vires*, they admitted that their powers under the Endowed Schools Acts did not extend, and under the Charitable Trusts Acts were not specially adapted, to the supervision of schemes.

9

of several developments, grew in scope and complexity. In the first place, the new local authorities established by the 1888 Act began to claim some share in the administration of charities, a move supported by the Commissioners who were anxious to secure a representative element on the reconstituted boards of trustees. But, owing to the complexity of the councils' administrative hierarchies, the pursuit of such co-operation gave rise to formidable problems. Again, the Technical Instruction Act, 1889, and the 'Whisky money' windfall the following year, led numerous local authorities to apply to the Commission for schemes designed to revive many grammar schools that had decayed for want of endowment. This initiative, too, while being welcomed by the Commissioners, created further difficulties for them. Finally, the Welsh Intermediate Education Act of 1889, by transferring to education committees in Wales the power of initiating relevant schemes, added yet another thread to the already tangled skein of administrative relationships, for the Commissioners were compelled to follow one procedure in England and a totally different one in the Principality.

All these fresh commitments, together with the wish to expedite the making and re-making of schemes and to assess their application, led the Commissioners frequently to petition the Treasury for extra staff. But the senior department viewed the expansion of the Commission's empire with some apprehension, especially as the latter's structure was 'somewhat top-heavy' and deviated markedly from the customary pyramidal arrangement found in other public service establishments. Receiving no satisfactory replies to its requests for information about the Commissioners' anticipated requirements, the Treasury eventually lost patience, and in 1893 appointed a departmental committee to inquire whether the work of the Commission was of such a character as to make it necessary 'that it should be administered by a Commission rather than be placed under the ordinary system of departmental organization', and if a Commission *were* considered desirable, what number of Commissioners would be necessary for the efficient discharge of the duties involved.

Proceeding at an extremely leisurely pace, the committee took two years to produce its Report, which recommended that the Department should continue to be administered by an independent Board and not be placed under a Minister of the Crown. The committee argued that direct political management was 'not applicable to the work of the Charity Commissioners, whose functions partake so largely of a legal and quasi-judicial character, and whose operations do not therefore lend themselves to the direction and control of a Parliamentary head to the same degree as those of an ordinary administrative department of State'.[1] And commenting specifically on the Commissioners' responsibilities under the Endowed Schools Acts, the committee considered that since their action was 'so minutely regulated by Act of Parliament . . . it [was] difficult to see what control a responsible Minister could exercise'.[2]

Turning to the possible requirements of the Department 'if a policy were hereafter adopted of extending some description of State organization to the Secondary Education of the country', the Committee declined to contemplate the contingency of such a system being entrusted to the Commission. This, it was argued, 'would involve either the creation of that Commission as an independent educational authority, without parliamentary responsibility (a most undesirable and scarcely practicable course), or the placing of the Department under the control of a Minister of Education'.[3] The latter alternative

would not only be open to all the disadvantages attending the union of judicial and administrative functions in the same authority, but would be a distinct reversal of the policy, deliberately adopted by Parliament, of having schemes for endowed schools prepared by an independent authority from which the influence of the Executive Government is entirely excluded, the Executive Government only taking the responsibility involved from the point of view of public policy in the approval or rejection of schemes submitted by this independent body.[4]

However unimpeachably logical and historically accurate these observations may have been, they were scarcely very helpful, and it was left to a second committee that was simultaneously investigating the Commission to offer constructive proposals as to its future development.

The demand for yet another inquiry had stemmed from the belief held by many Members of Parliament that, despite the more positive role recently assigned to the Fourth Commissioner, the relations between the Commission and the Legislature remained

[1] *PP* 1895, LXXIV, 3.   [2] *Ibid.* 4.
[3] *Ibid.* 5.   [4] *Ibid.*

defective. Accordingly, in April 1894, a Commons select committee was appointed 'to inquire whether it is desirable to take measures to bring the action of the Charity Commission more directly under the control of Parliament, and to give it more effectual means of dealing with the business which will come before it'.

Since it was the endowed schools side of the Commission's work that had proved most controversial, not surprisingly the committee closely examined the connexion between the Commission and the Education Department. Notwithstanding the improvement effected by Acland's Joint-Departmental Committee, the methods of procedure between the two departments were found to be 'cumbrous, unsatisfactory and not conducive to adequate Ministerial control and responsibility'. This lack of co-operation derived both from limitations imposed by statute and from the Education Department's disinclination to be too closely identified with the Commission's controversial activities.[1]

In discussing the Commission's acknowledged unpopularity, the committee judged that it arose largely from that body's constitutional status. In short, the Charity Commission's position had become 'somewhat analogous to that of the old Poor Law Commission, which it was found necessary to dissolve in 1847, and replace under a Minister'. A similar solution in the case of the Charity Commission presented itself as an obvious way out of the dilemma, and the committee made an unequivocal recommendation to that effect. If a change in the Commission's constitutional position were contemplated, then 'one single Minister should be responsible to Parliament both for Charitable Trusts and for the work under the Endowed Schools Act . . . provided always that necessary safeguards are secured for the rights, benefits and privileges of the poorer classes in the trusts and endowments dealt with by the Charity Commission'.[2] The Committee also entertained no doubts as to whom that minister should be: 'To the position and functions of the new Minister of Education recommended by previous Committees of your House should be added the control of endowments. Such a Minister would be

---

[1] See, for example, the evidence of both Acland and Kekewich to the select committee (qq. 3046, 3519); and the *Report of the Committee of Council on Education*, 1893-4, p. 7.
[2] *Report from the Select Committee on the Charity Commission*, 1894, p. vi.

really, as well as technically, responsible for the schemes which he presented to Parliament.'[1] There was, admittedly, one awkward obstacle to surmount, namely, the transfer of that part of the Commission's work which might be deemed to be of a judicial or quasi-judicial character.[2] But the Committee thought that, provided the Education Department employed the services of competent legal advisers, the transfer would present no insuperable difficulties. In conclusion, the committee stressed the urgency of the matter, arguing that the problems to which the existing state of affairs gave rise 'must grow and become more acute'.

This appeal for speedy action, and indeed most of the other suggestions put forward by the committee, were echoed by the Bryce Commissioners who, simultaneously, were considering how best to provide a national system of secondary education. Now, so far as the endowed schools were concerned, the Charity Commission was the closest approximation to a Department of Secondary Education that the nation possessed, not only because it 'acted as the guardian of their funds, and issued and revised schemes for their better government', but also because it attempted a measure of inspection as a means of ascertaining how far those schemes were being observed. As a central authority for secondary education it had to be judged as much on estimates of its future prospects as on the merits of its past performance.

There was, undoubtedly, much to praise in the Commission's record. Under the three Endowed Schools Acts 'schemes had been framed and approved . . . for no less than 902 endowments in England . . . leaving only 546 endowments . . . known to be subject to the . . . Acts, which have not felt the reforming hand of the Commissioners'. By these schemes, 'great improvements have without doubt been effected, both in the constitution of the governing bodies and in the educational work and character of the grammar schools'. But when this debt had been acknowledged,

---

[1] *Ibid.*

[2] The claim that serious difficulties were bound to arise if and when ministers came to deal with the legal side of the Charity Commission's work, was a favourite argument of those who opposed the transfer of secondary schools from the Commission to a Ministry of Education. It seems to have escaped their notice that the Vice-President had for some twenty-five years exercised legal functions in connexion with schemes for *elementary* endowments, and that the 1870 Act had provided the Committee of Council with considerable quasi-judicial powers to enable it to discharge its responsibilities towards the neglected districts.

most of what could be said in the Commission's favour had been said. Indeed, simply by transposing the words 'no less than' and 'only' in the progress report just quoted, the extent of its short-comings rather than its success could be demonstrated. There was still a long way to go before all the endowed schools would have been reformed, and it was calculated that, at the rate of advance maintained over the previous twenty-five years, it would require about another nine years to make schemes for the remaining endowments.[1] Yet it was unlikely that that tempo could be sustained, mainly because the Commissioners' time was being largely and increasingly occupied in making amending schemes. Moreover, the Commissioners had chosen, or been obliged, to assume additional responsibilities of late; and both these factors, combined with Treasury refusal to sanction a bigger office establishment, suggested that the completion of their original undertaking should be thought of in terms not of the near, but of the remote, future.

On the matter of inspection there was the same pattern of high endeavour and limited achievement. While the Commission was to be congratulated on voluntarily assuming supervisory responsibilities which were producing beneficial results, its influence in this respect was limited because the inspections its officers were able to conduct were administrative rather than educational in form.

Deficiencies in the Commission's performance could be matched by defects in its relationship to other central authorities for education. So far as the Charitable Trusts Acts were concerned, it had no organic connexion whatever with any minister or government department. Admittedly, in exercising their jurisdiction under the Endowed Schools Acts, the Commissioners were brought into contact with the Committee of Council, but the contact was slight, incomplete and sporadic.[2] In any event, this jurisdiction was only of a temporary nature, the statutes themselves and the Commissioners appointed under them being subject

---

[1] By comparison with the Court of Chancery, the Charity Commission's machinery operated with almost indecent haste. Nevertheless, a scheme under the Endowed Schools Acts, however non-contentious, was hardly ever passed under a year, and sometimes took several years to get through.

[2] The contact was improved when Acland instituted an advisory committee to facilitate inter-departmental consultation. According to D. R. Fearon, the Secretary to the Charity Commission, the conferences dispelled ignorance, and remedied 'some defects caused by our previous lack of co-operation'.

to yearly renewal. Furthermore, mainly because those Commissioners looked only to endowments and not to 'Secondary Education as a whole', their actions had been 'necessarily too piecemeal and too divorced from the educational policy of the period to accomplish all that was expected and desired'.

But these many disadvantages, which clearly detracted from the Charity Commission's ability to perform its function as the nation's central authority for secondary education, faded into insignificance beside the realization that endowments by themselves could not possibly provide an adequate *system* of secondary education. Henry Brougham had pioneered the notion that charities, if properly administered, could supply a large part of England's educational needs, and reformers following his lead continued to indulge in wishful thinking of this kind. In fact, the Schools Inquiry Commission had based its Report upon a delusion. But by 1895 such an assumption was manifestly untenable. For one thing, although the Bryce Commissioners were not prepared to prescribe a definite percentage of the adolescent age-group which ought to receive secondary schooling, the underlying tone of their Report indicates that, because they thought less in terms of social class and more in terms of national requirements, their sights were set higher than those of their predecessors. Yet educational charities were unable to meet even the existing demand for secondary education, and the almost spectacular maldistribution of endowments which so disturbed the Taunton Commission, had, thirty years later, by reason of population growth and movement, worsened rather than improved.

Clearly, then, the provision of a sufficient number of good secondary schools to meet current and anticipated requirements formed an immediate priority, and the Bryce Commissioners addressed themselves to the problem of how and by whom this want should be supplied. They pointed out that large powers were already shared among the various separate agencies which dealt with particular aspects of such education, and it was not so much the extension of these powers as the correlating of the bodies which exercised them, that was urgently required. The first need was for more unity at the centre, and they therefore urged the creation of a central authority 'not in order to control, but rather to supervise the Secondary Education of this country, not to over-ride or supersede local action, but to endeavour to bring about among the various agencies which provide that education, a harmony and co-operation which are now wanting'.[1] This central authority 'ought to consist of a Department of the Executive Government, presided over by a Minister responsible to Parliament, who would obviously be the same Minister as the one to whom the charge of elementary education is entrusted'.[2] Where the relationship of the Charity Commission to this Department was concerned, the Bryce Commissioners were faced by several choices, each of which had its attractions and drawbacks. In the end they recommended, as the least objectionable solution, that 'the work now done by the Charity Commissioners, so far as regards educational endowments, be transferred to, or placed under the direction of, the proposed Central Office, but without prejudice to any existing right of appeal to the courts of law from the decisions of the Charity Commissioners'.[3]

There still remained the problem of how the new central authority should be organized. At this point, the Bryce Commissioners faltered, declining to recommend a clean-sweep of the existing agencies and the substitution for them of a structure more logical and symmetrical, on the ground that by doing so they might 'retard the accomplishment of the necessary reforms'. As matters turned out, they may have learnt to regret their faint-heartedness.

By way of compensation, perhaps, the Commissioners' next proposal was both far-sighted and revolutionary. They expressed the conviction that the central authority ought to be an *educational* authority in the highest sense, that is one that comprehended not merely the legislative and administrative aspects of education, but also its practical application in the schools. Given this premise, the question arose as to how the responsible minister of state might 'be best informed and aided in making education itself, as distinguished from the machinery needed to its organised existence, more satisfactory and efficient, without having his authority in any way restricted or his responsibility lessened'.[4] The Commissioners' solution was the establishment of an Educational Council which would consist of persons with a special knowledge of educational problems who could advise the minister on 'judicial' and professional matters, and to whose custody a register of

[1] *Report of the Royal Commission on Secondary Education* [C. 7862], vol. 1, p. 257.
[2] *Ibid.*   [3] *Ibid.* p. 260.   [4] *Ibid.* p. 107.

teachers might be committed. Such a Council, it was hoped, would serve to liberalize the central administration, and would also enable the government to exert some influence over the independent sector which until then had remained largely isolated.

Finally, when they came to the topic of inspection, the Commissioners were cautious, though not unimaginative. Unwilling to place too much power in the hands of the central authority, impressed by the creditable achievements of certain local authority inspectorates, and subjected to heavy pressure from the powerful professional associations representing the grammar and public schools, they recommended that inspectors of secondary schools should be appointed by the local authorities and approved by the Central Office, the latter also having power to make general regulations as to inspection. They fully acknowledged that it would not be easy to secure the services of men possessing the necessary scholarship and experience, but this did not prevent them from making an almost sacrilegious attack upon the cult of the amateur: 'Inspection supervises the teacher at his work, and the inspector, therefore, should understand how to do the work at least as well as the teacher does'.[1]

After the publication of the Bryce Report in 1895, it could only be a question of time before the Charity Commission was relieved of its control over, and responsibilities for, educational endowments. This was made apparent when, over the next few years, the Commission's establishment was allowed to contract, although the requirements of the Endowed Schools Department called for a larger rather than a smaller staff.[2] By January 1900 the number of senior officials in this Department had dwindled to a mere half-dozen. Later that same year the first of the Orders in Council transferring certain powers of the Charity Commission to the Board of Education came into operation.

How had the Commission used these powers which Parliament had conferred upon it? To what extent had its trusteeship been beneficial or detrimental to educational development? On the credit side, there stood several substantial achievements. It had removed many long-standing impediments and abuses, reorganized – even democratized – governing bodies, diminished denominational restrictions, and framed new schemes thereby adapting the schools to meet contemporary needs. In its contribution

[1] *Ibid.* pp. 164–5.   [2] See note p. 281.

to one particular aspect – the advancement of secondary education for girls – the Commission could, and did, take legitimate pride. Whereas in 1868 there were only about fourteen endowed secondary schools for girls, in 1897 there were eighty-six, containing more than 14,000 pupils, and another twelve mixed grammar schools provided places for several hundred more girls.

The Commission, then, had done much to justify the faith that such men as Henry Brougham, Lord John Russell and W. E. Forster had placed in it as an instrument for reforming obsolete or useless trusts and dishonestly or inefficiently administered endowments, and putting them to better use. That the Commissioners had not done more was due to no want of effort or enthusiasm on their part. The responsibility for most of their failings lay squarely with successive Parliaments that tied their hands, with a niggardly Treasury that withheld essential funds, and with vested interests that resisted the new brooms they wielded.

But to say that the Commission justified the faith of its founders is not necessarily to suggest that it realized their expectations. The criticism could be levelled that although it had done much to improve the schools, it had been able to do little or nothing to maintain that improvement. Up to a point this censure is unfair, for the Commissioners were well aware of this weakness in their constitution and sought persistently to obtain a remedy; and in the end, rather than allow the defect to continue, they had deliberately stretched the law.

Yet there remained one serious charge which could not be answered merely by transferring the blame to other individuals or institutions. It was that the Commission, while creating an organized system of secondary schooling for the benefit of the middle class, destroyed the traditional entitlement of the poor to some form of post-primary education. In Brian Simon's words: 'This system was established at the expense of the working class, who were edged out of grammar schools where a free education had been available – whatever may have been its quality – and left only elementary schools provided and administered by voluntary bodies or small private schools of little value'.[1] This is to assert that the Commission, in the pursuit of policies of questionable probity, sacrificed precisely those children most qualified to receive its protection and support, and least able to defend their

[1] B. Simon, *Studies in the History of Education, 1780–1870*, 1960, pp. 335–6.

own rights and interests. It is to suggest that, having rectified one set of wrongs by securing the better management of endowments, the Commissioners committed another set themselves by flagrantly misapplying those same endowments. There is much evidence – to be found, for example, in the reports of the various select committees cited, in the histories of the schools concerned, and in the local newspapers of the period – to support these allegations.[1] Erring on the sides of caution and generosity, one might safely endorse the circumspect judgment delivered in the latest and most authoritative study of the Charity and Endowed Schools Commissions:

The Commissioners' vigorous rejection of gratuitous secondary training, their reliance on competitive scholarships (many of them drawn from funds left for the benefit of the poor), and their tendency to upgrade endowments to the secondary level, these policies, rightly or not, gave color to the suspicion that the education of the middle classes was being furthered at the expense of the poor.[2]

Certainly this suspicion was an important source of the Commissioners' increasing unpopularity, but it was not the only one. They also provoked mistrust and hostility because of their dubious constitutional position for, not through any fault of theirs, they functioned under no responsible minister and their relationship with the Legislature was never satisfactory. For most of its existence, the Commission was unable to rely on being adequately represented in either House or on having its actions explained and defended. Not that the imperfections of its parliamentary connexion account for more than a part of the dislike it incurred. Much antipathy and resentment stemmed from its interference with time-honoured privileges and long-established abuses. At the same time, it must be conceded that the Commission was, in one respect, its own worst enemy. Functioning primarily as lawyers

[1] See, for example, the *Report of the Select Committee on the Endowed Schools Act (1869)*, 1887, particularly the interrogation of witnesses by Jesse Collings, former Secretary of the National Education League; M. Kay, *The History of Rivington and Blackrod Grammar School*, 1966, for an illustration of local resentment towards changes in the school brought about by the Endowed Schools Commission; and, typically, the columns of the *Walsall Free Press* for 9 and 23 March, 11 May 1872 and the *Walsall Observer and South Staffordshire Chronicle* for 3 May 1873, for attacks on the Commissioners' scheme for the town grammar school.
[2] D. Owen, *English Philanthropy, 1660–1960*, 1964, p. 268.

and making little or no attempt to interpret and, if necessary, vindicate their policies in non-legal terminology, the Commissioners failed miserably to win public understanding – much less sympathy or support – for the task they were deputed to perform.

For one reason or another, then, the Commission over the years engendered much the same hostility as had been incurred by another autonomous administrative body – the Poor Law Commission; and for much the same reasons it was bound, in the long run, to experience a like fate and pass into the hands of a responsible minister of the crown.

Nevertheless, this account of its work should end, not with a catalogue of its shortcomings and mistakes, but with a word of approbation for the benefits it conferred. In the words of one historian: 'The Grammar Schools were suffering from a good many restrictions when the State began to intervene, and it is not difficult to show that the action of the State, from the first day of intervention onwards, has been much more that of a liberator than a tyrant'.[1] The record of the Charity and Endowed Schools Commissions – the agencies through which the state chose to act – testifies, whatever else it does, to the accuracy of this assessment.

[1] W. O. Lester Smith, *To Whom do the Schools Belong?* 1946, p. 209.

13

THE ESTABLISHMENT OF THE BOARD OF EDUCATION

The secondary schools are administered by gentlemen for gentlemen, the elementary schools by men for men, but the technical schools by cads for cads.[1]

Looking back on the event that forms the subject of this chapter, the 1950 Report of the Ministry of Education comments: 'Those whose memory goes back to the turn of the century will recall many dramatic events in the history of the Board, but its inception will not be one. On the contrary, the Board of Education Act, 1899, was something of an anti-climax'. As will become apparent, the author of this statement had every justification for making it.

In August 1895, the position was this: the Bryce Commission had just reported, and its recommendations for the establishment of central and local authorities were due to be considered by Lord Salisbury's third administration. In the interests of the church schools, the Cabinet decided to implement, at least initially, only those proposals relating to local administration. At the end of the following March, Gorst introduced his ill-starred Education Bill. Several members remarked unfavourably on the omission from it of any reference to a reconstituted central authority, but Sir John brusquely brushed them aside, asserting that as there was a perfectly good central authority already – the Committee of Council – reform in this direction was unnecessary and improvement scarcely possible.

But influential elements in the educational world were not prepared to accept so negative an attitude. With Gorst's Bill abandoned, and the government under heavy pressure, the Cabinet was forced to modify its policy of masterly inactivity, especially as back-benchers were becoming impatient, even to the extent of producing a private member's Bill of their own.

Eventually, at the beginning of 1898, the government decided

[1] Anon. Quoted in G. A. N. Lowndes, *The Silent Social Revolution*, 1937, p. 61.

to take a bite at the other side of the cherry by giving serious consideration to the remaining half of the Bryce recommendations. On 26 January the Duke of Devonshire prepared, for submission to the Cabinet, a memorandum on educational administration. In this document he expressed the belief that, even if the 1896 Bill had been enacted, the resulting local authorities would have experienced great difficulty in reorganizing secondary school provision in the absence of guidance from the centre, guidance which the centre was in no position to supply. From this it followed that 'a central authority has become an almost indispensable preliminary to the establishment of satisfactory local authorities'.[1]

As to the form this new body should take, the Duke pronounced in favour of a gradual rather than a radical change. His proposal was simply 'to take power to create a central authority to which might be transferred by Order in Council all the duties and powers of the Education Department, the Science and Art Department, and such of the powers of the Charity Commissioners as relate to education'.[2] He further recommended that there should be a minister of Cabinet rank exercising immediate responsibility for the direction to be given to secondary as well as elementary education, and having the assistance of a Parliamentary Secretary drawn from whichever chamber did not supply the minister. Acting under these political heads would be a permanent secretary and two under-secretaries, one for elementary, the other for secondary education. An Educational Council on the lines suggested by the Bryce Commission should also be constituted.

These proposals proving acceptable in principle, a draft Education Bill embodying them was drawn up. It provided for, *inter alia*, the appointment of a Secretary for Education who would be charged with the superintendence of matters relating to education in England and Wales,[3] and the creation of a consultative committee for the purpose of advising and aiding the minister in the performance of his duties. Less than a week later a second draft was prepared. The Secretaryship had disappeared; instead a Board of Education was to be established, consisting of a President

[1] PRO Ed. 24/8.   [2] *Ibid.*
[3] Mindful of the apprehension voiced by several witnesses appearing before the Bryce Commission, the government declined to place the Board in *control* of education. Its functions amounted to a compromise between those suggested by Russell and those approved by Lansdowne some sixty years previously. (See p. 20.)

and certain Cabinet ministers.[1] The proposed Board differed, in fact, very little from the existing Committee of Council which by this time had become virtually meaningless. The change seems to have been the work of Sir Courtenay Ilbert, Assistant Parliamentary Counsel, who, commenting on the original draft, ingenuously observed that 'the disadvantage of a single Secretary as compared with a Board, is that there is no one to act for him in case of illness. The principal Secretaries of State can act for each other'. Kekewich, however, entertained no doubts as to the real motive behind the adoption of the Board plan: 'Tradition and precedent . . . prescribed that a Board was the cheaper kind of organisation, as the salary of the President of a Board was, according to convention only £2000 per annum, while that of a Secretary had to be fixed independently of tradition'.[2] And so, whether owing to constitutional niceties or penny-pinching frugality, the 'Secretary' idea was dropped, and the Committee of Council was given a new and unexpected lease, hardly of life, but of a kind of ghostly existence. The new 'ministry'[3] was to follow the established pattern set by the Board of Trade, the Local Government Board and the Board of Agriculture, the last of these apparently forming the model on which the new Board was to be fashioned.

Although the draft Bill was extremely brief, it proved no easy matter to reach a form of words acceptable to all the parties concerned; indeed, no fewer than fourteen different drafts were printed and circulated before agreement was reached. The main difficulties were presented by the Charity Commissioners who fought a long rearguard action against the transfer of their powers to the new Board. After considerable discussion, Ilbert pointed out that there was no need to incorporate any precise division of responsibilities between the Commission and the Board, since this could be settled, after the Bill became law, by means of Orders in Council. By the time the officials had finished their work, the Bill, hardly bold or imaginative even in its original form, had become a pathetically inadequate measure, and it received a deservedly cool reception on being brought before Parliament in August 1898. In fairness one must add that its introduction at the close of the

[1] *Ibid.* 3 March 1898. Following this second draft the title of the Bill was changed from the 'Education Act' to the 'Board of Education Act'.

[2] Kekewich, *Education Department*, p. 108.

[3] To employ modern terminology; strictly speaking, the first 'Ministry' in British history was that of Munitions created in 1915.

session was a mere formality, the intention being to familiarize people with the concept of a central education department, and to invite discussion and comment upon it.

Public reaction was mixed. While there was little unstinted praise, there was also little outright condemnation. The general feeling was that it was better than nothing, but not by so very much, and that it would be acceptable only on the understanding that it constituted simply the first instalment in an extensive programme. Unexpectedly, perhaps, some of the severest strictures emanated from *The Times*: 'The shorn and attenuated measure which is all that the present Government offer indicates a desire to do as little as they can . . .'[1] Surprisingly, too, the least qualified approval came from the grammar and public schools, a phenomenon that might legitimately, if uncharitably, be ascribed to the fact that the Bill was agreeably innocuous. It afforded them such benefits as might be derived from an association with a department of state, without their being obliged to surrender any of the fundamental liberties they enjoyed, though they confessed to some uneasiness over the clause dealing with inspection.

In general, criticism of the Bill was directed at one or more of several features. There was widespread disapproval of the intention to surround the minister with the redundant paraphernalia of a non-existent Board, and an equally widespread agreement that the minister should be of Cabinet rank and unambiguously a member of the Commons.

Some dissatisfaction was expressed at the almost total absence of any indication as to how the new Department would be organized, the *Manchester Guardian* complaining that the measure was 'another instance of the recent tendency to entrust details of legislation to Government departments without specifying even the general lines on which such action should take place'.[2] Moreover, the little that was known of the future internal arrangements of the Department was discouraging, if not ominous. Commenting on the Lord President's introductory speech, the same newspaper observed: 'We may be mistaken, but this somewhat obscure statement seems to point to a Board with three departments under it rather than to one central authority.'[3] Similarly, doubts were voiced over the proposals affecting the Charity Commission,

[1] *The Times*, 26 December 1898.
[2] *Manchester Guardian*, 5 August 1898.   [3] *Ibid.* 3 August 1898.

whose existing judicial and financial control over the endowed schools promised to be diminished or circumscribed hardly at all. So far as the Consultative Committee was concerned, there were two main criticisms. It was felt, in the first place, that, in order to protect the interests of secondary and technical schools, the creation of the Committee should be mandatory on the government, and not at its discretion as laid down in the Bill; in the second, that the role assigned to the Committee was too restricted, for it was denied permission to tender advice for which it was not asked.

On the whole, then, the 1898 Bill was greeted with extremely subdued applause; and, considering how long the nation had had to wait for legislation on the subject, and how expectations had been raised by the Bryce Report, educationists could be forgiven for dismissing the measure as 'a miserable little piece of departmental machinery'.[1] Indeed, some MPs were so disenchanted by the government's proposals that in May 1899 they tabled a Bill of their own, providing for, among other things, the appointment of a Secretary for Education.

But by that time the government had already re-introduced the 1898 Bill in a slightly amended form. The changes were, however, of a relatively minor character and did little more than marginally improve the measure. Most important were those affecting the Charity Commission. Where the earlier Bill had interfered only to a very limited extent with the Commission's jurisdiction, the later one, while making but a single definite commitment, at least permitted the transfer by Order in Council to the Board of Education of such of the Commission's powers as appeared to relate to education.[2]

A second material alteration concerned secondary school inspection. Examination by the state was discarded and compulsory inspection abandoned, alternatives to inspection by HMIs were offered, and a charge for inspection was to be made. Explaining the amendments, Devonshire informed his fellow peers that the original Bill would actually – and mistakenly – have given the Board authority to inspect all the *public* schools, except Eton and

---

[1] Lyulph Stanley, Chairman of the London School Board, reported in *The Times*, 16 February 1899.

[2] The only power that would immediately be transferred from Commission to Board was that of the inspection of those schools which were being conducted under schemes framed by the Endowed Schools Commissioners.

Winchester. Inquiries had revealed that the schools generally were prepared to accept inspection in principle, but only on certain conditions; these the re-drafted section attempted to meet.

On the question of the political control of the projected Department, the government, in spite of almost universal protest, made no concessions. It merely added a clause stipulating that the then Vice-President should be a member of the Board until his retirement or promotion, when the office he held would be abolished. As a result, Sir John Gorst 'remained for some years as Vice-President of the Committee of Council on Education, which had no President and no members, and which in fact no longer existed . . .'[1] This same sub-section also placed Gorst in a unique and unprecedented position, since he was the one and only member of the administration having a *statutory* right to the post he occupied. In consequence, nothing short of an Act of Parliament or a change of government could remove Sir John if he chose to stay in office.

On 14 March, 1899 the Duke of Devonshire rose to commend the revised Board of Education Bill to his fellow peers. They found it almost as unsatisfactory as the earlier version, and for much the same reasons. The intention to create a phantom Board, providing imaginary colleagues for a single responsible minister, came under heavy attack. Lord Kimberley could not imagine that it was at all probable that the ministers involved would ever meet, adding sarcastically that he thought it was undesirable that they ever should. Replying, the Duke expressed sympathy with the objections, to which he confessed he had no ready answer, as he was unable 'to recollect the reasons which weighed in favour of a Board rather than a secretariat'. In any case, he added, 'It is perfectly well understood that there will be no Board at all'. Subsequently, Gorst, taxed on the same point, argued that, as his superior could not remember why one constitutional form was chosen in preference to another, it was unreasonable to expect him (the Vice-President) to supply the explanation.[2]

While this feature of the Bill met mainly with derision, a second

---

[1] Kekewich, *Education Department*, p. 109.

[2] According to one authority, ten years previously Salisbury's second administration had opposed the creation of a 'Ministry' of Education on the ground that this would be 'an undesirable innovation in official phraseology'. W. J. M. MacKenzie and J. W. Grove, *Central Administration in Britain*, 1957, p. 175.

caused considerable alarm. Members complained that they were being asked to approve a measure the consequences of which they could not possibly foresee. James Bryce remarked that it was not very easy to criticize a blank cheque, while another member asserted: 'Not a single individual in the House can tell what he is legislating about'.

Two fears prompted observations such as these. The first arose from the exceptionally permissive character of the Bill: there was no guarantee that urgently-needed reforms would necessarily follow its enactment. The second stemmed from its vagueness. It provided no indication whatever as to the form the future organization of the Department would take: whether, for example, it would consist of three branches, one each for elementary, technical and secondary education, or whether it would comprise only two, technical and secondary being amalgamated. The latter arrangement was strongly opposed by supporters of the endowed schools who were apprehensive lest a combined branch be merely the old (and despised) Science and Art Department in a different guise. Representatives from the grammar schools and universities pressed for an assurance on this matter to be written into the Bill, or, failing that, for a pledge from the government that there would definitely be a tripartite division of the Department. These same institutions were also troubled by the lack of precision in the clause dealing with the Consultative Committee, the formation of which seemed to them to furnish an indispensable safeguard for the maintenance of their independence. Viscount Cranborne, for example, complained that the House had not been told how the Committee was to be appointed, or whom it was to represent, or what powers it was to be given, or at what date it would begin to function.[1]

To all these objections the replies were the same. They amounted to saying that the government could not permit its hands to be tied as tightly as some critics seemed to suggest that they should be, that the interests of education would best be served if the future Department were given freedom to develop along pragmatic rather than pre-determined lines, and, specifically, that the question of the Department's structure was one for the

---

[1] Because of careless drafting, the Bill stipulated that the Committee was to consist in part of 'persons representing Universities and bodies interested in education'. In the Act the word 'other' was inserted before 'bodies'.

civil service, not Parliament, to resolve. However, these arguments failed to satisfy the grammar schools which threatened to revolt unless they received a categorical assurance on the issue of the Board's internal organization. Hurried consultations took place, at the conclusion of which Gorst announced that secondary education would be entrusted to neither of the long-established departments, but to a third official 'whose responsibility to the principal secretary will be distinct from and equal to that of the two existing assistant secretaries'.[1]

Finally, several adverse comments were aimed at those provisions affecting the Charity Commission. There were some who deplored the government's timidity: 'The Bill . . .' Bryce remarked, 'looks the difficulty boldly in the face, and then passes by'; but there were others who considered that the Board might be arrogating to itself powers of a quasi-judicial character which a political department ought not to possess. As there seemed, on the face of it, to be some substance in this argument (it had, after all, supplied the reason for not placing educational charities under the Education Department in the first instance), Devonshire asked Parliamentary Counsel to investigate its basis. Ilbert drew up a memorandum in which he explained that the functions of the Charity Commissioners were not really judicial, but administrative. The notion that they were of a legal kind probably derived from the fact that the Commissioners had inherited certain administrative powers which were formerly exercised by the Lord Chancellor and afterwards by the Court of Chancery. Indeed, the Act should improve the unsatisfactory constitutional position in which the Commissioners found themselves, for while they were, perhaps, less amenable to immediate political influence, they were also less exposed to public criticism. Ilbert felt that any misuse of power by an administrative department was subject to much readier correction if that department was directly represented in Parliament by a responsible minister, who could be questioned as to his own actions and those of his subordinates.

In the end, the Bill emerged basically unchanged and slightly improved from its passage through the parliamentary machine. One can scarcely pretend that its progress was particularly dignified, since on two occasions the House of Commons was in danger of being counted out, and since it was, according to rumour, des-

---

[1] *Hansard*, 4th ser., LXXIV, col. 1006.

tined to be dropped owing to lack of time. Thanks to some energetic lobbying by teachers and by MPs especially interested in education, A. J. Balfour, the Leader of the Commons, was prevailed upon to provide facilities for the remaining stages to be taken before the prorogation. On 9 August the measure received the royal assent, but its operative date was delayed until 1 April 1900, so that the reconstruction and absorption of the Science and Art Department could take place in the interim.

Because the Act was chiefly a statute with potential, that is to say it opened up possibilities much more than it afforded immediate benefits, judgment on it ought, to some extent, to be suspended. But not entirely, for the range of possibilities was itself limited by the measure's very terms. In this respect it suffered from two principal defects. First, it relegated the President of the Board to the second rank of ministers who, because they were novices or second-raters, could safely be offered the lower paid posts. Secondly, it failed to deal with education comprehensively. Section 1, Subsection 1 stated unequivocally: 'There shall be established a Board of Education charged with the superintendence of matters relating to education in England and Wales'. This was hardly accurate; there were numerous matters relating to education in England and Wales with the superintendence of which the Board was not charged. Indeed, even after the 1899 legislation, no fewer than seven different Cabinet ministers had some responsibility for, or control over, various educational institutions throughout the country; and they rarely made any effort to consult together.

Nevertheless, if the Act neither enhanced the status of education as a function of government, nor gave a sufficiently broad interpretation to the term 'education', at least it cleared the way for an improvement in the central administration of the service. As *The Times* remarked: 'It provides the raw material out of which some future Ministry more alive to the national importance of [education], and less timid and cautious in dealing with it, may frame a really efficient organization'.[1]

Initially, however, there was little indication that the Act was going to produce the transformation for which it was presumably designed. In July 1899 a departmental committee was appointed to advise on the reorganization of the Board. Its membership, com-

[1] *The Times*, 6 September 1900.

posed entirely of civil servants, was vigorously attacked in the Press on the ground that the internal arrangement of the new Department was a matter of national interest, not merely one of official concern, still less one of individual, private convenience. As it happened, the dismay, in one sense, proved unwarranted. The Duke of Devonshire, having *directed* the Walpole Committee to submit proposals for a tripartite division of the Board, proceeded to reject them. He decided, instead, on a bipartite division, thereby breaking his pledge to the grammar schools. In another sense, however, the worst fears of many were confirmed, for, as *The Times* complained, the arrangements amounted to 'little more than a reshuffling of the officials in possession at the Education and Science and Art Departments . . . framed with the tenderest regard for the existing machinery and for those who work it'.[1] The *Manchester Guardian* joined in the protest: 'The truth is that the newly constituted Board of Education is a sham. No genuine reorganization or remanning has taken place at all . . .'[2] Neither was any move made to amalgamate the Whitehall and South Kensington inspectorates, and to restructure the combined corps, although Gorst pressed persistently for early action on this matter.

At this stage, then, the prospects of the new Department, and hence in some measure of English education, looked anything but bright. But the fiasco of the Devonshire deployment marked, as it were, the darkest hour before the dawn.

In July 1900 the Draft Order in Council establishing the Consultative Committee was laid upon the table of the House of Commons, and the publication of its membership indicated that it would speak, when permitted to do so, with an authoritative and independent voice.

Next, contrary to expectations, the Board rapidly proceeded to assume all the powers of the Charity Commissioners to which the 1899 Act entitled it. First to be transferred, in 1901, was the authority to frame schemes under the Charitable Trusts and Endowed Schools Acts; and a year later the Commissioners relinquished virtually all their residual jurisdiction over trusts held solely for educational purposes.

Finally, in 1902–3, both the political chiefs and the permanent head of the Department vacated their respective offices. It was,

[1] *Ibid.* 28 June 1900.   [2] *Manchester Guardian*, 22 December 1900.

perhaps, expecting too much to suppose that a major reorganization of the Board could be effected while Devonshire, Gorst and
Kekewich remained, at any rate technically, in control. One
observer described the trio, as at April 1902, in these terms:

The Duke of Devonshire . . . failing through inertia and stupidity to
grasp any complicated detail half-an-hour after he has listened to the
clearest exposition of it, preoccupied with Newmarket, and in bed till
12 o'clock; Kekewich trying to outstay this Government and quite
superannuated in authority; Gorst cynical and careless having given up
even the semblance of any interest in the office; the Cabinet absorbed
in other affairs and impatient and bored with the whole question of
education.[1]

Clearly, few reforms were likely to materialize until these office-
holders had been replaced.

Salisbury's resignation from the premiership was the prelude
to change. Balfour, his successor, appointed the Marquess of
Londonderry as the new President of the Board of Education.[2]
At the same time, Sir John Gorst, doubtless without regret after
his humiliating experiences over the 1902 Act, retired from the
government, consigning the office of Vice-President of the Committee of Council to oblivion in the process. In October, Londonderry asked Kekewich to resign on the ground that the Board
needed as Permanent Secretary someone who could be relied upon
to administer that same Act in accordance with the government's
wishes. Robert Morant was appointed in his stead.

By 1910 Morant had remodelled the central administrative
apparatus – both the headquarters staff and the inspectorate – into
an efficient and co-ordinated machine designed to give shape and
purpose to the nation's educational system.[3] At long last the
primary purposes of the Board of Education Act had been
achieved.

---

[1] B. Webb, *Our Partnership*, 1948, p. 239. The source of the information is
given as Morant.

[2] Though not exclusively. Even at this stage, education was still not considered important enough to merit a minister's undivided attention. Londonderry held the office of Lord Privy Seal in addition to that of President. History
looked like repeating itself when, two years later, Londonderry, while retaining
his educational responsibilities, became Lord President of the Council.

[3] For two recent assessments of the way Morant reorganized the Board, see
Armytage, 'J. F. D. Donnelly', and E. J. R. Eaglesham, 'The centenary of Sir
Robert Morant', *British Journal of Educational Studies*, vol. xii, Nov. 1963, p. 16.

14

RETROSPECT

English education has suffered all along from two radical defects. It has been directed by people who knew nothing about it, and it has been the subject of permissive legislation from beginning to end.

– Manchester Guardian, 28 June 1899.

In 1899 England took a hesitant and long overdue step towards the establishment of a national system of education. Even then the legislation was distinctly half-hearted, as if the country was still not convinced that such a system was socially and educationally desirable, only that it was administratively and economically necessary.

The causes of England's backwardness in this respect relative to other civilized nations have been stated too often to need elaboration. Sir James Graham's epigram, 'Religion, the keystone of education, is, in this country, the bar to its progress', lays the reponsibility squarely, if not fairly, on sectarian rivalry and assertiveness. And there is much truth in the argument that no government, Whig or Tory, could devise a method of creating a national system which would not have mortally offended either the Anglicans, or the Noncomformists, or both. In G. M. Young's words, 'The dissenters would not stand the parson in a State school. The Established Church would not stand anyone else'.

But while religious differences played a part in retarding, as well as promoting, educational development, they were by no means alone in so doing. In the first place, there was throughout the nineteenth century, as George Bernard Shaw has observed, 'an obstinate prejudice against the organization of a competent bureaucracy'. The belief that state or official control generated inefficiency and corruption died hard; indeed the Commons and the civil service had to be reformed before this conviction lost most of its force. Nevertheless, the replacement of a traditional authority based on birth or wealth by a rational-legal authority exercised largely through public officials was essential to the emergence of a modern industrial democracy. But, because those who wielded the power, fiercely – and expectedly – resisted its transfer to others, the new departments of state were slow to develop; and because Parliament was jealous of its rights, and strong in its support of local autonomy, private enterprise and voluntary effort, the functions of those departments were often capriciously circumscribed and their efforts too frequently misdirected; and because they were created piecemeal, and their growth was almost entirely unsystematic, they rarely constituted models of administrative organization.

Political attitudes, too, affected progress. By and large, it may be said that periods of advance occurred when Whigs and Liberals were in power, while periods of stagnation or regression coincided with Tory and Conservative governments, though there were exceptions to this general rule. To Richard Cobden the reason was obvious. 'The Tories, whatever they may say to the contrary, are opposed to the enlightenment of the people. They are naturally so from an instinct of self-preservation.' And if this explanation be thought too facile, it is not unfair to assert that the primary aims of nineteenth century Conservative administrations were to preserve traditional institutions and to maintain the *status quo*. Unfortunately, the indiscriminate pursuit of these objectives frequently entailed the entrenchment of privilege and the perpetuation of injustice.

Yet even the Whigs and Liberals often showed little enthusiasm for educational reform, so that progress, when it did take place, tended to be halting and leisurely. According to Matthew Arnold, one did not have to look far for the cause. He asserted that the average British government, being aristocratic, did not move in the matter of popular education while it could avoid moving. As it happened, noblemen held a virtual monopoly of the position of Lord President, the nominal Minister of Education, during the Victorian era.[1] The creation of the Vice-Presidency might have redeemed the situation, and occasionally its incumbent did effect improvements, but too often the resultant division of executive responsibility led to confusion, if not dissension, and hence to a weakening of ministerial authority. As C. P. Scott observed, 'The one has knowledge and no responsibility; the other has responsibility and no knowledge'. Again, because the Education

[1] See note, pp. 281–2.

Department lacked prestige, it was generally disposed of to politicians of little standing and less ability.[1]

For these and other reasons – for example, the chronic instability of mid-century administrations – effective control of the Department passed into the hands of the permanent officials, particularly the Secretary.[2] Now, where the latter was genuinely interested in and knowledgeable about the education of children, the outcome was likely to be beneficial. Kay-Shuttleworth's occupancy illustrates the point. Where, as was more likely to happen, he was primarily concerned with the mechanics of administration, the result, in the absence of compensatory factors, was liable to be quite the opposite. This is most clearly demonstrated by Ralph Lingen, whose tenure of office was marked by three important developments.

The first was a disinclination to accept, far less seek, fresh responsibilities for the education of various classes of 'exceptional' children. To quote Arnold again, the very last thing the Department desired was 'to invade the provinces of education which are now independent of it'. In consequence, the fragmentation of educational services for the young persisted long after it need have done, and even at the present time the responsibility for certain categories of children lies not with the Department of Education but with other government offices and local officers under their statutory control. Again, a valuable connexion – through the emerging examination system – might have been established between the Committee of Council and the secondary schools, had Lingen responded to, instead of rejecting, their overtures.

A second feature of Lingen's reign was the deliberate policy of insulating the Whitehall officials from any direct contact with educational practitioners, whether teachers or inspectors. Professional advice was seldom invited, and, when it was offered, it was generally ignored. Policy decisions were made by the political heads, or more frequently, it would appear, by the senior civil servants, in both instances without reference to expert opinion. Moreover, the exercise of patronage – strongly supported by Lingen – ensured that the highest administrative posts would be filled by those whose ignorance of, indeed contempt for, elementary education was matched only by their lack of interest in it. Herein lies the basis for Sir Fred Clarke's assertion that 'the mass of the

[1] See note, p. 282.   [2] See note, p. 282.

English people have never yet evolved genuine schools of their own. Schools have always been provided for them from above, in a form and with a content of studies that suited the ruling interests'.[1] Such a situation largely accounts for the alarm displayed in certain quarters when the school boards, through their higher grade schools, showed signs of breaking out of their allotted native reserve. Conversely, the method of recruitment employed operated as a kind of mutual protection society for certain privileged educational establishments. In the late Professor Dover Wilson's words: 'The real and abiding safeguard of the institutions for higher education [i.e. the public schools and universities] against undue interference by the central authority is the fact that the Board of Education is . . . staffed and will always be staffed to some extent by the loyal sons of these ancient bodies'.[2]

The third characteristic of the period 1849–69 was the increasing unpopularity of the Education Department among those affected by its policies. So far as the teachers were concerned, their disenchantment sprang from the introduction of the Revised Code for which Lingen was only partly responsible; but the Permanent Secretary could be criticized for his cavalier treatment of the professional educators and for his insensitive application of the regulations. At all events, the narrowness of the Department's outlook and the illiberal character of its policies damaged its reputation to such a degree that, on the one hand, the politicians declined to place secondary education under a central authority of which it would form a part, and, on the other, the public schools refused to have anything to do with it. Though this is not to deny that the basic reason why the educational system developed upon lines of social class was to be found in the distinctive social structure of Victorian England.

Still another obstacle to the growth of a national system of education – as distinct from one providing mere rudimentary instruction – lay in the absence of any apparatus of local government within which local education authorities could operate. In this deficiency lie the roots of the Dual System, for when the state made the first grants-in-aid of education, it had virtually no alternative but to transmit them to the religious societies for distribution. And from this deficiency stemmed payment by results, for

[1] F. Clarke, *Education and Social Change*, 1940, p. 30.
[2] J. Dover Wilson (ed.), *The Schools of England*, 1928, p. 16.

the Department, faced by the grave threat of an administrative breakdown, adopted, as much in desperation as from conviction, the scheme which would at the very least relieve the pressure on the central office. In turn it was this pressure which helped to convince Lingen that the Department could not be expected to assume responsibilities beyond those it was obliged in duty to discharge. Finally, the lack of any units of local government that could be utilized for educational purposes inexorably led to an excessive, if unsolicited, concentration of power at the centre. The unhealthiness of this tendency was recognized, and attempts to reverse it were made long before 1870 when the process of decentralization began in earnest. By that date, however, the secondary schools and their champions had taken fright at the prospect of being controlled by Whitehall officials whose methods were as inflexible as their aims were limited.

While these several observations for the most part serve but to confirm those of other students of nineteenth-century educational history, one stubbornly-held belief concerning this period can be discounted. That is the supposition that the English educational system was, in some mysterious way, predestined to develop along the lines that it did, that its divisions and anomalies were not only natural but inevitable. Instead, the pattern that emerged can be explained more easily by attributing it either to a series of unfortunate accidents or to human frailty, than by regarding it as the work of Providence or as a necessary product of the age.

This argument is most strikingly illustrated in the case of the Science and Art Department. Throughout its existence, the central authority for technical education remained to all intents and purposes quite independent of that responsible for elementary education. Yet if some unknown official had not, in all innocence of the outcome, stipulated in precise terms who were to be the recipients of the government grant for art instruction when it was first voted, then in 1841 the embryonic Department would have been transferred to the Committee of Council. Again, but for Prince Albert's whim, and the readiness of the government to gratify it, the Department in 1857 would most likely have been moved not to distant South Kensington but to the vicinity of the Whitehall office, and the union provided for in the preceding year might well have become a reality. Lastly, had Francis Sandford, when he was Secretary of both departments, used his immense power and prestige to integrate their operations, the subsequent separation need never have occurred.

Similar factors were at work in the case of secondary education. The exclusiveness of the public schools owed its origins, at least in part, to a curious mischance. In 1818, when Brougham was seeking the appointment of a Parliamentary Commission to inquire into the management of educational charities, the ostensible reason why Eton, Winchester and Westminster were exempted from the provisions of the Bill was that these establishments had already been investigated by the select committee set up earlier on Brougham's initiative. Institutions, like citizens, should not, the argument went, be placed in double-jeopardy. But for this circumstance, presumably none of the schools could justifiably have claimed immunity, and consequently there would have been no precedent on which the other three endowed schools could legitimately have based their request for the same privileged treatment.

Later, in 1853, when it was decided to entrust the central administration of educational charities to a permanent body, a select committee of the House of Lords amended the Bill placing this duty in the hands of the Committee of Council, vesting it instead in a quite separate commission. The irony of this decision was that their Lordships' judgment was founded on a misconception. They contended that the authority which was responsible for the administration of endowments would be compelled to discharge certain judicial functions (in as much as these matters were so deeply embedded in Chancery law) and they felt that such jurisdiction ought not to be exercised by a department having a political head. Nearly fifty years afterwards it was discovered that this argument, which seemed tolerably convincing at the time, was in fact quite fallacious.

How different, too, would have been the course of English education had the Bill of 1868 passed into law. This measure would have raised the status, unified the administration and promoted the development of education at a particularly crucial stage in its history. Yet the primary cause of its abandonment was not the intervention of those forces that were usually responsible for retarding educational growth, but rather the coincidental and fortuitous resignations from the leadership of both great parties of two statesmen who strongly favoured the reform, and their replacement by two others who were sternly opposed to it.

Speculations of this kind may be sterile; nevertheless it is worthy of note that the emerging pattern of education in this country has been shaped to a considerable extent by bad luck and poor judgment, not simply by religious pride and prejudice, political and philosophical ideas, social and economic pressures, and administrative convenience – the factors which are generally held to have been its main determinants.

The rise of a central authority for English education had been a slow, tortuous, makeshift, muddled, unplanned, disjointed and ignoble process. By its very nature the form that authority assumed was bound to be a reflection of the social structure and educational philosophy of the age in which it evolved. But then, in the course of time, the authority itself helped to reinforce that structure and perpetuate that philosophy. Unconsciously at first, and later, perhaps, with deliberate intent, the architects of the English educational system proceeded to construct it along the lines of the Platonic model described in *The Republic*. The children of gold, silver and iron were given the education deemed appropriate to their supposed abilities and the state's requirements. This separate development found expression not only in the schools but in the institutions of central government, and the officials in control, whether through self-interest or inflexibility of thought, or what might be termed a kind of 'classical conditioning', found acute difficulty in breaking the existing mould and recasting the administrative machinery in a form more in accord with changed conditions; so that long after the Board of Education Act and the reconstruction which followed it, the hierarchial structure of the nation's schools continued to survive. Herein lay one of the principal legacies that administrators and politicians of the Victorian era bequeathed to their successors; for the three-fold division of the central authority which characterized the latter half of the nineteenth century supplied the blue print, if not the rationale, for the tripartite division of secondary education which characterized the greater part of the twentieth.

APPENDICES

A. NOTE ON THE COMMITTEE OF COUNCIL ON EDUCATION

An analysis of the composition of successive Committees of Council reveals a marked fluctuation in its numbers and little regularity in its membership. Consisting at the outset of four ministers, it grew in size until as many as ten were appointed. Subsequently these numbers fell to nine, and ultimately to eight.

No more predictable was its personnel. At one time or another the holders of seventeen different posts were to be found on the Committee. The only permanent member was the Lord President who, as *ex officio* chairman of all the committees of the Privy Council, was automatically chairman of the Committee on Education. The Chancellor of the Exchequer and the Home Secretary were invariably appointed; but even in these, apparently straightforward, cases there was confusion. This arose from the manner in which the appointments were announced. Some members were named without their offices being mentioned; sometimes offices were specified with no reference to their holders; occasionally both were listed. This lack of uniformity gave rise in 1861 to a faintly Gilbertian situation. Before a select committee some four years later, Lingen explained:

Sir Cornewall Lewis [the Home Secretary] had been appointed a member of the Committee, not *ex officio*, but by name; and after his decease, it was not observed for some little time that the appointment had been by name, and not *ex officio*. Sir George Grey attended several Committees as Home Secretary, he being not strictly entitled to do so otherwise than in his character as a Privy Councillor; but as soon as Lord Granville's [the Lord President] attention was called to the fact, an Order in Council was passed, and the Home Secretary is now made a Member of the Committee *ex officio*.[1]

But apart from the regular appointment of the three ministers mentioned above, there was a complete absence of consistency. The Prime Minister was often, though not always, a member. Generally included were the Secretary for War and the First Lord of the Admiralty, doubtless because military and naval schools came under their respective control. Some ministers were appointed not because of their office,

---
[1] *Report of the Select Committee on Education*, 1865, q. 57.

but on account of their experience of, and interest in, education; for example, Lord Russell, Foreign Secretary in 1859, Lord Granville, Colonial Secretary in 1868, and W. E. Forster, Chief Secretary for Ireland in 1880, clearly merited their place. However, it is difficult to account for the presence of the Secretary for India (the Duke of Argyll) in 1868. Cabinet status was not a condition of membership. Another odd feature was that attendance at a meeting was not always confined to the stipulated membership. Apparently, at least in the early period, any minister, or even ex-minister, who was interested, could take part in its deliberations. Thus at the meeting which appointed the first inspectors, seven Privy Councillors were present: the four nominated ministers, plus Labouchere (President of the Board of Trade), Spring-Rice (who had just resigned as Chancellor of the Exchequer), and Sir George Grey (Judge-Advocate-General). Conversely, at a later date, most of the nominated members rarely put in an appearance at meetings, if they attended at all.

The amoeba-like characteristics of the Committee baffled politicians and exasperated educationists. In view of the religious passions generated by the educational question, the government may have been wise not to define the Committee's terms of reference too closely. But there was a serious side to what might otherwise be regarded as a comic opera situation. Lack of firm, adequate and consistent political control meant that the management of state-aided education came to reside more and more with the permanent officials, and especially with the Secretaries. In the course of time, only the most determined of ministers could prevail against these powerful men, the majority of whom were interested primarily in administrative efficiency rather than educational advance.

B. NOTE ON THE WORK OF THE EDUCATION DEPARTMENT AS SUMMARIZED IN THE REPORT OF THE DEPARTMENTAL COMMITTEE OF 1896

Official number of section	Business	Present number of staff
0	Auditors	6
1	Accounts and payments	17
2	Act Record	19
3	Annual Grant Record	41
4	Calculation and verification	14
5	Correspondence and registration	55
6	Diaries and endowed schools	4
7	Examinations	28
8	Fee Grants, Training College Grants, etc.	16

C. TABLE SHOWING THE STAFF OF THE SCIENCE AND ART DEPARTMENT ON THE EVE OF MAJOR-GENERAL SIR J. F. D. DONNELLY'S RETIREMENT[1]

1 Secretary
1 Assistant Secretary
1 Chief Clerk
1 Private Secretary to the Secretary
6 Clerks of the Higher Division
1 Superintendent of Registry
37 Second Division Clerks
56 Assistant Clerks
1 Clerk in charge of Accounts
1 Assistant to same
1 Storekeeper
1 Deputy-Storekeeper
2 Stores Clerks
3 Warehousemen
1 Housekeeper
1 Medical Officer

Science Division

1 Director
1 Assistant Director
1 Official Examiner
2 Assistant Examiners
1 Science Examination Clerk

Art Division

1 Director
1 Assistant Director
1 Official Examiner
1 Assistant Examiner
1 Art Examination Clerk

Inspection

1 Chief Senior Inspector
3 Senior Inspectors
11 Inspectors
9 Junior Inspectors
1 Occasional Inspector for Science
3 Occasional Inspectors for Art

[1] 'History of the Department of Science and Art of the Committee of Council on Education'. *Calendar, History and General Summary of the Regulations of the Department of Science and Art.* 1899. p. iv. N.B. In view of the impending reorganization of the Department not all the offices were filled at that time.

10+

D. TABLE SHOWING THE NUMBER OF STAFF EMPLOYED IN
THE CLERICAL SECTIONS OF THE SCIENCE AND ART DEPART-
MENT AS IN JULY 1899[1]

	Normally employed	Occasionally employed	Total
1. Secretarial	9	–	9
2. Registry	22	–	22
3. Postal	4	–	4
4. Typewriting	15	–	15
5. General stores	25 Clerical	23	48
	45 Manual	29	74
6. Accounts	14	–	14
7. Committee	19	6	25
8. Science claims	15	–	15
9. Science correspondence	6	–	6
10. Science results	22	30	52
11. Schools of science	3	–	3
12. Technical instruction	4	–	4
13. Art	35	21	56
Inspectors' Division	1	–	1
Royal College of Science	4	–	4
Museum	15	–	15
	213 Clerical	80	293
	45 Manual	29	74
	258	109	367

[1] PRO Ed. 24/62. Office management and the conduct of business cannot have been much easier at South Kensington than they were in Whitehall. Papers placed before the Walpole Committee showed that office accommodation in 1899 was distributed among several different buildings; *viz*: 'Main building, East Iron building, West Iron building, Old Naval School premises; iron buildings, opposite Southern Galleries, Imperial Institute Road; other out-buildings and space'. *Ibid.*

E. NOTE ON THE INTERNAL STRUCTURE OF THE OFFICE OF THE CHARITY COMMISSION AS ORGANIZED IN 1894[1]

Designation of Department	Work of same	Staff (where given)
A Department	Legal and administrative	Chief Commissioner 1 Assistant Commissioner 1 Principal Clerk 4 Clerks
B Department	Legal and administrative	Second Commissioner 1 Assistant Commissioner 1 Principal Clerk 5 Clerks
C Department	Legal and administrative	Third Commissioner 1 Assistant Commissioner 1 Principal Clerk 5 Clerks
D Department	Drafting (of schemes and orders)	1 Assistant Commissioner 4 Clerks
E Department	Administration of Endowed Schools Acts	2 Commissioners 5 Assistant Commissioners 1 Secretary 1 Assistant Secretary 2 Clerks
G Department	Statistics and Accounts of Trustees of Charities	
O Department	Official Trustees of Charitable Funds	
R Department	Registration of letters and documents	
Secretary's Department		
W Department	New and unrecorded charities	

[1] *PP* 1894, XI, qq. 1827–62 (Fearon).

N.B. While E Department dealt exclusively with educational endowments the converse was not the case. In other words, Departments A, B, and C also took part in this aspect of the Commission's work.

F. LIST OF LORD PRESIDENTS OF THE COUNCIL

(from 1835 to the date of the first appointment of a President of the Board of Education)

Marquess of Lansdowne	18.4.35
Lord Wharncliffe	3.9.41
Duke of Buccleuch and Queensberry	21.1.46
Marquess of Lansdowne	6.7.46
Earl of Lonsdale	27.2.52
Earl Granville	28.12.52
Lord John Russell	12.6.54

Earl Granville	8.2.55
Marquess of Salisbury	26.2.58
Earl Granville	18.6.59
Duke of Buckingham and Chandos	6.7.66
Duke of Marlborough	8.3.67
Earl de Grey and Ripon	9.12.68
Henry A. Bruce (cr. Lord Aberdare)	9.8.73
Duke of Richmond and Gordon	21.2.74
Earl Spencer	28.4.80
Lord Carlingford	19.3.83
Viscount Cranbrook	24.6.85
Earl Spencer	6.2.86
Viscount Cranbrook	3.8.86
Earl of Kimberley	18.8.92
Earl of Rosebery	10.3.94
Duke of Devonshire	29.6.95

G. LIST OF VICE-PRESIDENTS OF THE COMMITTEE OF COUNCIL ON EDUCATION

William F. Cowper	2.2.57
C. B. Adderley	6.4.58
Robert Lowe	6.7.59
Henry A. Bruce	26.4.64
Thomas L. Corry	26.7.66
Lord Robert Montagu	19.3.67
William E. Forster	9.12.68
Viscount Sandon	2.3.74
Lord George Hamilton	4.4.78
Anthony J. Mundella	3.5.80
Hon. Edward Stanhope	24.6.85
Sir Henry T. Holland	17.9.85
Sir Lyon Playfair	6.2.86
Sir Henry T. Holland	3.8.86
Sir William Hart Dyke	25.1.87
Arthur H. D. Acland	18.8.92
Sir John E. Gorst	4.7.95

H. LIST OF SECRETARIES OF THE EDUCATION DEPARTMENT (1839–99)

James Phillips Kay (Kay-Shuttleworth)	26.8.39
Ralph Robert Wheeler Lingen	8.1.50
Francis Richard Sandford*	1.2.70
Patrick Cumin†	15.5.84
George William Kekewich	21.1.90

* Appointed also as Secretary to the Scotch Committee on Education on 16.1.73, and as Secretary of the Science and Art Department in April 1874.

† Appointed Secretary for both English and Scotch Committees; in August 1885 Henry Craik was appointed Secretary of the Scotch Committee.

SELECT BIBLIOGRAPHY

The bibliography is arranged according to the following classification:

A. OFFICIAL PAPERS

1. *Acts of Parliament*

42 Geo. III, c. 73. Health and Morals of Apprentices Act, 1802.
52 Geo. III, c. 102. Charitable Donations Registration Act, 1812.
58 Geo. III, c. 91. Charities Inquiry Act, 1818.
59 Geo. III, c. 81. Charitable Foundations Act, 1819.
2 & 3 Will. IV, c. 45. Reform Act, 1832.

3 & 4 Will. IV, c. 96. Appropriation Act, 1833.
3 & 4 Will. IV, c. 103. Factory Act, 1833.
4 & 5 Will. IV, c. 76. Poor Law Amendment Act, 1834.
3 & 4 Vict. c. 77. Grammar Schools Act, 1840.
16 & 17 Vict. c. 137. Charitable Trusts Act, 1853.
18 & 19 Vict. c. 124. Charitable Trusts Amendment Act, 1855.
19 & 20 Vict. c. 116. Vice-President of the Committee of Council on Education Act, 1856.
22 Vict. c. 26. Superannuation Act, 1859.
23 & 24 Vict. c. 136. Charitable Trusts Act, 1860.
25 & 26 Vict. c. 112. Charitable Trusts Act, 1862.
29 & 30 Vict. c. 39. Exchequer and Audit Departments Act, 1866.
30 & 31 Vict. c. 102. Representation of the People Act, 1867.
31 & 32 Vict. c. 32. Endowed Schools Act, 1868.
31 & 32 Vict. c. 118. Public Schools Act, 1868.
32 & 33 Vict. c. 56. Endowed Schools Act, 1869.
33 & 34 Vict. c. 75. Elementary Education Act, 1870.
35 & 36 Vict. c. 62. Education (Scotland) Act, 1872.
36 & 37 Vict. c. 67. Agricultural Children Act, 1873.
36 & 37 Vict. c. 87. Endowed Schools Act, 1873.
37 & 38 Vict. c. 87. Endowed Schools Act, 1874.
39 & 40 Vict. c. 79. Elementary Education Act, 1876.
43 & 44 Vict. c. 23. Elementary Education Act, 1880.
46 & 47 Vict. c. 36. City of London Parochial Charities Act, 1883.
50 & 51 Vict. c. 49. Charitable Trusts Act, 1887.
51 & 52 Vict. c. 41. Local Government Act, 1888.
52 & 53 Vict. c. 30. Board of Agriculture Act, 1889.
52 & 53 Vict. c. 40. Welsh Intermediate Education Act, 1889.
52 & 53 Vict. c. 76. Technical Instruction Act, 1889.
53 & 54 Vict. c. 60. Local Taxation (Customs and Excise) Act, 1890.
54 & 55 Vict. c. 56. Elementary Education Act, 1891.
56 & 57 Vict. c. 42. Elementary Education (Blind and Deaf Children) Act, 1893.
60 Vict. c. 5. Voluntary Schools Act, 1897.
62 & 63 Vict. c. 33. Board of Education Act, 1899.

2. *Parliamentary Debates*

Throughout the period, but in particular for the years 1818, 1833–9, 1841, 1853, 1855–6, 1858, 1862–5, 1867–70, 1874, 1881, 1883, 1887, 1896, 1898–9.

3. *Reports of Royal Commissions*

Report of the Commissioners of Inquiry into the operation of the Poor Law, 1834.

First Report of the Royal Commission on Municipal Corporations, 1835.
Final Report of the Commissioners for Inquiring concerning charities, 1837.
Reports of the Royal Commission for Inquiring into those Cases which were investigated, and reported upon, by the Charity Commissioners, but not certified to the Attorney-General, 1850–1.
Report of the Commissioners appointed to inquire into the State of Popular Education in England, 1861.
Report of Her Majesty's Commissioners appointed to inquire into the revenues and management of certain colleges and schools and the studies pursued and instruction given therein, 1864.
Report of the Schools Inquiry Commission, 1868.
Reports of the Royal Commission on Scientific Instruction and the Advancement of Science, 1872–5.
Reports of the Civil Service Inquiry Commission, 1875.
Report of the Royal Commission on the London Parochial Charities, 1880.
Second Report of the Royal Commission on Technical Instruction, 1884.
Final Report of the Royal Commission on the Depression of Trade and Industry, 1886.
Second Report of the Royal Commission appointed to inquire into the Civil Establishments of the different offices of State at home and abroad, 1888.
Reports of the Royal Commission appointed to inquire into the working of the Elementary Education Acts, England and Wales, 1886–8.
Report of the Royal Commission on Secondary Education, 1895.
Report of the Royal Commission on the Civil Service, 1912.

4. *Reports of Select Committees*

First Report from the Select Committee on the Education of the Lower Orders in the Metropolis, 1816.
Third Report from the Select Committee on the Education of the Lower Orders, 1818.
Report from the Select Committee on the State of Education, 1834–5.
Report from the Select Committee on Public Charities, 1835.
Report from the Select Committee on Arts and Manufactures, 1835–6.
Report from the Select Committee on the Education of the Poorer Classes in England and Wales, 1838.
Report from the Select Committee on the School of Design, 1849.
Report from the Select Committee on Civil Service Appointments, 1860.
Report from the Select Committee on the Schools of Art, 1864.
Report from the Select Committee on Education (Inspectors' Reports), 1864.
Report from the Select Committee on Education, 1865–6.
Report from the Select Committee on Scientific Instruction, 1868.
Third Report from the Select Committee on Civil Services Expenditure, 1873.

Report from the Select Committee on the Endowed Schools Act (1869), 1873.
Report from the Select Committee on Education, Science and Art (Administration), 1884.
Report from the Select Committee on the Charitable Trusts Acts, 1884.
Report from the Select Committee on the Endowed Schools Acts, 1886–7.
Report from the Select Committee on the Charity Commission, 1894.
Report from the Select Committee on the Museums of the Science and Art Department, 1898.

5. Reports of Official Committees

Report of a Committee of Inquiry into the Department of Practical Science and Art, 1853.
Report on the organization of the permanent Civil Service, 1854.
Report of a Committee of Inquiry into the Privy Council Office, 1854.
Report of the Departmental Committee appointed by the Treasury to inquire into the Department of the Charity Commission, 1895.
Report of the Committee appointed to inquire into the distribution of Science and Art grants, 1897.
Report of a Departmental Committee on Educational Endowments, 1911.

6. Other Reports

Reports of the Commissioners of Inquiry into the State of Education in Wales, 1847.
Report of the Endowed Schools Commissioners to the Committee of Council on Education, 1872.
The Education of the Adolescent. Report of the Consultative Committee of the Board of Education, 1926.
Secondary Education. Report of the Consultative Committee of the Board of Education, 1938.

7. Annual Reports

Board of Education. *Annual Reports, 1899–1900, 1900–01, 1902–03, 1913–14, 1922–23, 1926.*
Charity Commissioners. *Annual Reports, 1854–99.*
Committee of Council on Education. *Annual Reports, 1858–99.*
Committee of Council on Education. *Minutes, 1839–57.*
Department of Practical Art. *Annual Report, 1853.*
Department of Science and Art. *Annual Reports, 1854–99.*
Ministry of Education. *Annual Report, 1950.*

8. Other Parliamentary Papers

Census of Great Britain, 1851. Education, England and Wales, Report (1854).

Civil Service Estimates.
Papers on Education, presented to Parliament by Her Majesty's command. 1839.
Papers on the Reorganization of the Civil Service, 1854–5.
Papers relating to the Resignation of the Director of Special Inquiries and Reports. 1903.
Parliamentary Papers, 1837–8, XXXVIII.

B. BOOKS

1. General histories

Briggs, A. *The Age of Improvement,* Longmans, 1959.
Briggs, A. *Victorian People,* Penguin, 1965.
Burn, W. L. *The Age of Equipoise,* Unwin, 1964.
Clark, G. Kitson. *The Making of Victorian England,* Methuen, 1962.
Clark, G. Kitson. *An Expanding Society. Britain 1830–1900,* Cambridge University Press, 1967.
Cole, G. D. H. and Postgate, R. W. *The Common People, 1746–1946,* Methuen, 1961.
Davis, H. W. C. *The Age of Grey and Peel,* Oxford Univ. Press, 1929.
Ensor, R. C. K. *England 1870–1914,* Oxford Univ. Press, 1936.
Halévy, E. *A History of the English People in the Nineteenth Century,* 5 vols., Benn, 1949–52.
Hammond, J. L. and B. *The Age of the Chartists, 1832–1854,* Longmans, 1930.
Marriott, J. A. R. *England Since Waterloo,* Methuen, 1954.
Thomson, D. *England in the Nineteenth Century, 1815–1914,* Penguin, 1950.
Trevelyan, G. M. *British History in the Nineteenth Century and After,* Longmans, 1937.
Woodward, E. L. *The Age of Reform,* Oxford Univ. Press, 1938.
Young, G. M. (ed.), *Early Victorian England, 1830–1865,* Oxford Univ. Press, 1934.

2. Social and economic histories

Ashworth, W. *An Economic History of England, 1870–1939,* Methuen, 1960.
Bruce, M. *The Coming of the Welfare State,* Batsford, 1961.
Checkland, S. G. *The Rise of Industrial Society in England, 1815–1885,* Longmans, 1964.
Cohen, E. W. *English Social Services: Methods and Growth,* Allen and Unwin, 1949.
Fay, C. R. *Great Britain from Adam Smith to the Present Day – an economic and social survey,* Longmans, 1928.
Gray, B. Kirkman. *A History of English Philanthropy,* P. S. King, 1905.

Knowles, L. C. A. *The Industrial and Commercial Revolutions in Great Britain during the Nineteenth Century*, Routledge, 1947.

Owen, D. *English Philanthropy, 1660–1960*, Oxford Univ. Press, 1964.

Perkin, H. *The Origins of Modern English Society, 1780–1880*, Routledge, 1969.

Roberts, D. *Victorian Origins of the British Welfare State*, New Haven, Yale Univ. Press, 1960.

Trevelyan, G. M. *English Social History*, Longmans, 1946.

Various, *Ideas and Beliefs of the Victorians*, Sylvan Press, 1949.

Williams, R. *The Long Revolution*, Chatto and Windus, 1961.

Williams, T. G. *The Main Currents of Social and Industrial Change since 1870*, Pitman, 1935.

3. Political and constitutional histories

Anson, W. R. *The Law and Custom of the Constitution*, Oxford Univ. Press (vol. I, *Parliament*, ed. Gwyer, M., 1922; vol. II, *The Crown*, ed. Keith, A. B., 1935).

Bagehot, W. *The English Constitution*, C. A. Watts, 1964.

Barker, E. *Political Thought in England, 1848 to 1914*, Oxford Univ. Press, 1928.

Dicey, A. V. *Law and Opinion in England*, Macmillan, 1914.

Emden, C. S. *The People and the Constitution*, Oxford Univ. Press, 1956.

Hanham, H. J. *The Nineteenth Century Constitution*, Cambridge Univ. Press, 1969.

Holdsworth, W. *A History of English Law* (vol. XIII, 1964; vol. XIV, 1965), Methuen.

Jennings, W. I. *Cabinet Government*, Cambridge Univ. Press, 1936.

Keir, D. L. *The Constitutional History of Modern Britain, 1485–1937*, Black, 1945.

Keith, A. B. *The Constitution of England from Queen Victoria to George VI*, 2 vols., Macmillan, 1940.

Laski, H. J. *Political Thought in England, Locke to Bentham*, Williams and Norgate, 1920.

Lowell, A. Lawrence. *The Government of England*, 2 vols., Macmillan, 1921.

Maccoby, S. *English Radicalism, 1786–1832*, Allen and Unwin, 1955.

Maccoby, S. *English Radicalism, 1832–1852*, Allen and Unwin, 1935.

McDowell, R. B. *British Conservatism, 1832–1914*, Faber, 1959.

Maitland, F. W. *The Constitutional History of England*, Cambridge Univ. Press, 1908.

May, T. Erskine. *The Constitutional History of England since the accession of George III, 1760–1860*, 2 vols. (vol. III, *1860–1911*, by Holland, F.), Longmans, 1912.

Smellie, K. B. *A Hundred Years of English Government*, Duckworth, 1950.

Taswell-Langmead, T. P. *English Constitutional History*, edited and revised by Plucknett, T. F. T., Sweet and Maxwell, 1960.

4. *Administrative histories*

Beer, S. H. *Treasury Control*, Oxford Univ. Press, 1957.

Campbell, G. A. *The Civil Service in Britain*, Penguin, 1955.

Cohen, E. W. *The Growth of the British Civil Service, 1780–1939*, Allen and Unwin, 1941.

Craig, J. H. M. *A History of Red Tape: An account of the origin and development of the Civil Service*, Macdonald and Evans, 1955.

Fry, G. K. *Statesmen in Disguise. The changing role of the administrative class of the British Home Civil Service 1853–1966*, Macmillan, 1969.

Kelsall, R. K. *Higher Civil Servants in Britain: From 1870 to the Present Day*, Routledge, 1955.

MacKenzie, W. J. M. and Grove, J. W. *Central Administration in Britain*, Longmans, 1957.

Martindale, H. *Women Servants of the State, 1870–1938*, Allen and Unwin, 1938.

Montgomery, R. J. *Examinations. An account of their evolution as administrative devices in England*, Longmans, 1965.

Moses, R. *The Civil Service of Great Britain*, Columbia Univ. Press, 1914.

Mustoe, N. E. *The Law and Organization of the British Civil Service*, Pitman, 1932.

Parris, H. *Constitutional Bureaucracy*, Allen and Unwin, 1969.

Redlich, J. and Hurst, F. W. *Local Government in England*, 2 vols., Macmillan, 1903.

Reid, G. T. *The Origin and Development of Public Administration in England*, Macdonald and Evans, 1913.

Richards, P. G. *Patronage in British Government*, Allen and Unwin, 1963.

Traill, H. D. *Central Government*, Macmillan, 1908.

Webb, S. *Grants in Aid*, Longmans, 1911.

Webb, S. and B. *English Local Government: Statutory Authorities for Special Purposes*, Longmans, 1922.

Wright, M. *Treasury Control of the Civil Service, 1854–1874*, Oxford Univ. Press, 1969.

5. *Histories of education*

a. *General*

Adamson, J. W. *English Education, 1789–1902*, Cambridge Univ. Press, 1930.

Armytage, W. H. G. *Four Hundred Years of English Education*, Cambridge Univ. Press, 1964.

Bagley, J. J. and A. J. *The State and Education in England and Wales, 1833–1968*, Macmillan, 1969.

Barnard, H. C. *A History of English Education from 1760*, Univ. London Press, 1961.

Bartley, G. T. C. *Schools for the People*, Bell and Daldy, 1871.

Baron, G. *Society, Schools and Progress in England*, Pergamon, 1965.

Boyd, W. *The History of Western Education*, Black, 1950.

Curtis, S. J. *Education in Britain since 1900*, Andrew Dakers, 1952.

Curtis, S. J. *History of Education in Great Britain*, Univ. Tutorial Press, 1950.

Curtis, S. J. and Boultwood, M. E. A. *An Introductory History of English Education since 1800*, Univ. Tutorial Press, 1960.

De Montmorency, J. E. G. *The Progress of Education in England*, Knight, 1904.

Dent, H. C. *1870–1970. Century of Growth in English Education*, Longmans, 1970.

Jarman, T. L. *Landmarks in the History of Education*, The Cresset Press, 1951.

Leese, J. *Personalities and Power in English Education*, Arnold, 1950.

Lowndes, G. A. N. *The Silent Social Revolution*, Oxford Univ. Press, 1937.

Morrish, I. *Education since 1800*, Allen and Unwin, 1970.

Musgrave, P. W. *Society and Education since 1800*, Methuen, 1968.

Roberts, R. D. (ed.) *Education in the Nineteenth Century*, Cambridge Univ. Press, 1901.

Seaborne, M. *Education*, Studio Vista, 1966.

Simon, B. *Studies in the History of Education, 1780–1870*, Lawrence and Wishart, 1960.

Simon, B. *Education and the Labour Movement, 1870–1920*, Lawrence and Wishart, 1965.

Smith, W. O. Lester. *Education in Great Britain*, Oxford Univ. Press, 1967.

Smith, W. O. Lester. *To whom do the schools belong?*, Oxford, Blackwell, 1946.

Wodehouse, H. *A Survey of the History of Education*, Arnold, 1929.

b. *Elementary education*

Adams, F. *History of the Elementary School Contest in England*, Chapman and Hall, 1882.

Birchenough, C. *History of Elementary Education*, Univ. Tutorial Press, 1938.

Blyth, W. A. L. *English Primary Education*, 2 vols., Routledge, 1965.

Corlett, J. *A Survey of the Financial Aspects of Elementary Education,* P. S. King, 1929.
Greenough, J. C. *The Evolution of the Elementary Schools of Great Britain,* New York, D. Appleton, 1903.
Holman, H. *English National Education: a sketch of the rise of public elementary schools in England,* Blackie, 1898.
Jennings, H. C. *The Political Theory of State-supported Elementary Education in England, 1750–1833,* Pennsylvania, Lancaster Press Inc., 1928.
Kay-Shuttleworth, J. *Four Periods of Public Education,* Longmans, 1862.
Prideaux, E. B. R. *A Survey of Elementary English Education,* Blackie, 1914.
Raymont, T. *A History of the Education of Young Children,* Longmans, 1937.
Rusk, R. R. *A History of Infant Education,* Univ. London Press, 1933.
Selleck, R. J. W. *The New Education, 1870–1914,* Pitman, 1968.
Smith, F. *A History of English Elementary Education, 1760–1902,* Univ. London Press, 1931.
Sturt, M. *The Education of the People,* Routledge, 1967.

c. *Technical education*

Abbott, A. *Education for Industry and Commerce in England,* Oxford Univ. Press, 1933.
Argles, M. *South Kensington to Robbins,* Longmans, 1964.
Armytage, W. H. G. *The Rise of the Technocrats,* Routledge, 1965.
Bell, Q. *The Schools of Design,* Routledge, 1963.
Cardwell, D. S. L. *The Organization of Science in England: a retrospect,* Heinemann, 1957.
Cotgrove, S. F. *Technical Education and Social Change,* Allen and Unwin, 1958.
Millis, C. T. *Technical Education,* Arnold, 1925.
Ware, F. *Educational Foundations of Trade and Industry,* Harper, 1901.

d. *Secondary education*

Acland, A. H. D. and Smith, H. L. (eds.) *Studies in Secondary Education,* Percival, 1892.
Archer, R. L. *Secondary Education in the Nineteenth Century,* Cambridge Univ. Press, 1921.
Bamford, T. W. *The Rise of the Public Schools,* Nelson, 1967.
Banks, O. *Parity and Prestige in English Secondary Education,* Routledge, 1955.
Carlisle, N. *A Concise Description of the Endowed Grammar Schools in England and Wales,* Baldwin, Cradock and Joy, 1818.

Dent, H. C. *Secondary Education for All, Origins and Development in England*, Routledge, 1949.

Griffith, G. *The Endowed Schools of England and Ireland, Their Past, Present and Future*, Whittaker, 1864.

Kazamias, A. M. *Politics, Society and Secondary Education in England*, Philadelphia, Univ. Pennsylvania Press, 1966.

Mack, E. C. *Public Schools and British Opinion 1760 to 1860*, Methuen, 1938.

Mack, E. C. *Public Schools and British Opinion since 1860*, Columbia Univ. Press, 1941.

e. *Inspection*

Ball, N. *Her Majesty's Inspectorate, 1839–1849*, Oliver and Boyd, 1963.

Boothroyd, H. E. *A History of the Inspectorate*, printed for private circulation by the Board of Education Inspectors' Association, 1923.

Edmonds, E. L. *The School Inspector*, Routledge, 1962.

(See also under Biographies and Autobiographies)

f. *Administration*

Armfelt, R. *The Structure of English Education*, Cohen and West, 1955.

Balfour, G. *Educational Administration*, Oxford Univ. Press, 1921.

Balfour, G. *Educational Systems of Great Britain and Ireland*, Oxford Univ. Press, 1903.

Craik, H. *The State and its Relation to Education*, Macmillan, 1914.

Eaglesham, E. J. R. *From School Board to Local Authority*, Routledge, 1956.

Eaglesham, E. J. R. *The Foundations of 20th Century Education in England*, Routledge, 1967.

Gosden, P. H. J. H. *The Development of Educational Administration in England and Wales*, Blackwell, 1966.

Owen, H. *Education Acts Manual* (ed. Barker, R.), Knight, 1936.

Richards, H. C. and Lyon, H. *Guide to the Education Acts*, Jordan, 1903.

Selby-Bigge, L. A. *The Board of Education*, Putnam, 1927.

Smith, W. O. Lester. *Government of Education*, Penguin, 1965.

Spalding, T. A. *The Work of the London School Board*, King, 1900.

g. *Biographies and autobiographies*

Allen, B. M. *Sir Robert Morant*, Macmillan, 1934.

Anon. *Patrick Cumin, Secretary of the Education Department. A Sketch*, Hugh Rees, n.d.

Armytage, W. H. G. *A. J. Mundella*, Benn, 1951.

Cole, H. *Fifty Years of Public Work*, 2 vols., Bell, 1884.

Fitzmaurice, Lord E. *The Life of Granville George Leveson Gower, 2nd Earl Granville, 1815–1891*, 2 vols., Longmans, 1905.

Fitzroy, A. W. *Memoirs*, Hutchinson, 1925.

Grier, L. *Achievement in Education: the work of Michael Ernest Sadler*, Constable, 1952.

Hamilton, Lord G. *Parliamentary Reminiscences and Reflections (1868 to 1885)*, Murray, 1916.

Holland, B. H. *The Life of Spencer Compton, 8th Duke of Devonshire*, 2 vols., Longmans, 1911.

Holmes, E. *In Quest of an Ideal*, Cobden-Sanderson, 1920.

Holmes, E. *What is and what might be*, Constable, 1911.

Judges, A. V. (ed.) *Pioneers of English Education*, Faber and Faber, 1952.

Kekewich, G. W. *The Education Department and After*, Constable, 1920.

Martin, A. P. *Life and Letters of the Rt. Hon. Robert Lowe, Viscount Sherbrooke*, 2 vols., Longmans, 1893.

New, C. W. *The Life of Henry Brougham to 1830*, Oxford Univ. Press, 1961.

Parker, C. S. *Life and Letters of Sir James Graham, 1792–1861*, 2 vols., Murray, 1907.

Parkin, G. R. *Life and Letters of Edward Thring*, Macmillan, 1910.

Pollard, H. M. *Pioneers of Popular Education*, Murray, 1956.

Reid, T. Wemyss. *Memoirs and Correspondence of Lyon Playfair*, Cassell, 1899.

Reid, T. Wemyss. *The Life of W. E. Forster*, 2 vols., Chapman, 1888.

Russell, John Earl. *Recollections and Suggestions, 1813–1873*, Longmans, 1875.

Sadleir, M. *Michael Ernest Sadler*, Constable, 1949.

Smith, F. *The Life and Work of Sir James Kay-Shuttleworth*, Murray, 1923.

Sneyd-Kynnersley, E. M. *HMI. Some passages in the life of one of HM Inspectors of Schools*, Macmillan, 1910.

Walpole, S. *Life of Lord John Russell*, 2 vols., Longmans, 1889.

Webb, B. *Our Partnership*, Longmans, 1948.

Wolf, L. *Life of Lord Ripon*, 2 vols., John Murray, 1921.

h. *The Religious Aspect*

Binns, H. B. *A Century of Education, 1808–1908*, Dent, 1908.

Brown, C. K. F. *The Church's part in Education, 1833–1941*, SPCK, 1942.

Burgess, H. J. *Enterprise in Education*, National Society and SPCK, 1958.

Cruikshank, M. *Church and State in English Education*, Macmillan, 1963.

Murphy, J. *The Religious Problem in English Education: the Crucial Experiment*, Liverpool Univ. Press, 1959.

i. *Miscellaneous*

Armytage, W. H. G. *The American Influence on English Education*, Routledge, 1967.

Armytage, W. H. G. *The French Influence on English Education*, Routledge, 1968.

Armytage, W. H. G. *The German Influence on English Education*, Routledge, 1969.

Armytage, W. H. G. *The Russian Influence on English Education*, Routledge, 1969.

Baron, G. *A Bibliographical Guide to the English Educational System*, Univ. London, The Athlone Press, 1965.

Christian, G. A. *English Education from within*, Wallace Gandy, 1922.

Clarke, F. *Education and Social Change*, The Sheldon Press, 1940.

Connell, W. F. *The Educational Thought and Influence of Matthew Arnold*, Routledge, 1950.

De Montmorency, J. E. G. *State Intervention in English Education*, Cambridge Univ. Press, 1902.

Dobbs, A. E. *Education and Social Movements, 1700–1850*, Longmans, 1919.

Donaldson, J. *Lectures on the History of Education in Prussia and England*, Black, 1874.

Evans, W. and Claridge, W. *James Hirst Hollowell and the Movement for civil control in Education*, Manchester, Northern Counties Education League, 1911.

Gosden, P. H. J. H. *Educational Administration in England and Wales: a bibliographical guide*, Univ. Leeds Institute of Education, 1967.

Hans, N. *Comparative Education*, Routledge, 1958.

Higson, C. W. J. *Sources for the History of Education*, The Library Association, 1967.

Kamm, J. *Hope Deferred. Girls' Education in English History*, Methuen, 1965.

Kelly, T. *A History of Adult Education in Great Britain*, Liverpool Univ. Press, 1962.

Maclure, J. S. *Educational Documents. England and Wales, 1816–1967*, Chapman and Hall, 1968.

Magnus, L. (ed.) *National Education, essays towards a constructive policy*, Murray, 1901.

Magnus, P. *Educational Aims and Efforts: 1880–1910*, Longmans, 1910.

Maltby, S. E. *Manchester and the Movement for National Elementary Education*, Manchester Univ. Press, 1918.
Norwood, C. *The English Tradition of Education*, John Murray, 1929.
Osborne, G. S. *Scottish and English Schools*, Longmans, 1966.
Peterson, A. D. C. *A Hundred Years of Education*, Duckworth, 1960.
Pritchard, D. G. *Education and the Handicapped, 1760–1960*, Routledge, 1963.
Rich, R. W. *The training of teachers in England and Wales during the nineteenth century*, Cambridge Univ. Press, 1933.
Silver, H. *The Concept of Popular Education*, MacGibbon and Kee, 1965.
Smith, W. O. Lester. *Education: an introductory survey*, Penguin, 1957.
Stanley, E. L. *Our National Education*, Nisbet, 1899.
Tropp, A. *The School Teachers: the growth of the teaching profession in England and Wales from 1800 to the present day*, Heinemann, 1957.
West, E. G. *Education and the State*, Institute of Economic Affairs, 1965.
Wilson, J. Dover (ed.) *The Schools of England*, Sidgwick and Jackson, 1928.

C. UNPUBLISHED PAPERS; THESES

Department of Education and Science Archives. Various Education Class Files; Letter books; Tracts on Education; Education Miscellanies.
Duke, C. The Department of Science and Art: Policies and Administration to 1864. Unpublished Ph.D. thesis of London University, 1966.
Hipwell, M. E. A survey of the work of the Science Division of the Science and Art Department, 1853–1899. Unpublished M.Ed. thesis of Nottingham University, 1963.
Leese, J. The history and character of educational inspection in England. Unpublished Ph.D. thesis of London University, 1934.
Public Record Office. Various Privy Council and Education Class Files.
Rust, W. Bonney. Educational Administration in England and Wales, 1870–1950. Unpublished Ph.D. thesis of London University, 1955.
Sibellas, L. The work of the Committee of Council on Education from 1839 to 1856. Unpublished M.Ed. thesis of Leeds University, 1955.
Whitehead, E. A critical and historical survey of the growth and nature of state control in English education from 1886 to 1926. Unpublished B.Litt. thesis of Oxford University, 1934.

D. ARTICLES AND PAMPHLETS

Anon. 'History of the Department of Science and Art of the Committee of Council on Education', *Calendar, History and General Summary of the Regulations of the Department of Science and Art*, 1883, pp. xxx–xlviii; 1899, pp. ix–xliii.

Argles, M. 'The Gentleman in Whitehall', *The Journal of Education*, vol. 89, no. 1050, January 1957, pp. 13–15.

Armytage, W. H. G. 'Francis Richard John Sandford, First Baron Sandford, 1824–1894', *Bulletin of the John Rylands Library*, vol. 31, 1948, pp. 110–19.

Armytage, W. H. G. 'J. F. D. Donnelly: Pioneer in vocational education', *The Vocational Aspect of Secondary and Further Education*, vol. II, May 1950, pp. 6–20.

Armytage, W. H. G. 'Patric Cumin, 1823–1890', *Bulletin of the John Rylands Library*, vol. 30, 1946–7, pp. 271–7.

Armytage, W. H. G. 'Some sources for the history of Technical Education in England', *British Journal of Educational Studies*, vol. V, no. 2, May 1957, pp. 159–65; vol. VI, no. 1, November 1957, pp. 64–73.

Armytage, W. H. G. 'The Centenary of "South Ken"', *British Journal of Educational Studies*, vol. V, no. 1, November 1956, p. 81.

Arnold, M. 'The Twice-Revised Code', *Fraser's Magazine*, March 1862.

Balls, F. E. 'The Endowed Schools Act 1869 and the Development of English Grammar Schools in the Nineteenth Century', *Durham Research Review*, vol. V, no. 19, September 1967, pp. 207–16; vol. V, no. 20, April 1968, pp. 219–29.

Bishop, A. S. 'Ralph Lingen, Secretary to the Education Department 1849–1870', *British Journal of Educational Studies*, vol. XVI, no. 2, June 1968, pp. 138–63.

Cavanagh, F. A. 'State intervention in English Education', *History*, vol. XXV, September 1940, pp. 143–56.

Chester, D. N. 'Robert Morant and Michael Sadler', *Public Administration*, vol. XXIX, 1950, pp. 110–12.

Dictionary of National Biography, articles on H. Cole; J. F. D. Donnelly; R. R. W. Lingen; H. J. Roby; F. R. Sandford.

Duke, C. 'Robert Lowe – A reappraisal', *British Journal of Educational Studies*, vol. XIV, no. 1, November 1965, pp. 19–35.

Eaglesham, E. J. R. 'The centenary of Sir Robert Morant', *British Journal of Educational Studies*, vol. XII, no. 1, November 1963, pp. 5–18.

Edmonds, E. L. 'Education and the early factory inspectors', *The Vocational Aspect of Secondary and Further Education*, vol. X, Autumn 1958, pp. 85–93.

Edmonds, E. L. 'Inspection of Schools', *The Vocational Aspect of Secondary and Further Education*, vol. VIII, Spring 1956, pp. 65–72.

Edmonds, E. L. 'The Science and Art Department: Inspection and/or Examination?' *The Vocational Aspect of Secondary and Further Education*, vol. IX, Autumn 1957, pp. 116–27.

Gosden, P. H. J. H. 'The Board of Education Act, 1899', *British Journal of Educational Studies*, vol. XI, no. 1, November 1962, pp. 44–60.

Kay-Shuttleworth, J. 'Memorandum on Popular Education', 1868, Education Miscellanies, vol. XI. (Archives of the Library of the Department of Education and Science).

Morris, N. 'State paternalism and laissez-faire in the 1860s', *Studies in the Government and Control of Education since 1860*, Methuen, 1970.

Sadler, M. E. and Edwards, J. W. 'Public Elementary Education in England and Wales, 1870–1895', *Special Reports on Educational Subjects 1896–97*, HMSO, 1897.

Sadler, M. E. and Edwards, J. W. 'Summary of Statistics, Regulations, &c of Elementary Education in England and Wales, 1833–1870', *Special Reports on Educational Subjects*, vol. 2, HMSO, 1898.

Webb, S. J. 'The Education Muddle and the way out – a constructive criticism of English educational machinery', Fabian Tract no. 106, 1901.

Willson, F. M. G. 'Ministries and Boards: Some Aspects of Administrative Development since 1832', *Public Administration*, vol. XXXIII, 1955, pp. 44–57.

E. JOURNALS AND NEWSPAPERS

The Edinburgh Review.
The Educational Guardian.
The Educational Record.
The Educational Times.
The Educator.
The Manchester Guardian, especially January 1898 to December 1900.
The Saturday Review.
The School and the Teacher.
The Schoolmaster, especially April 1898 to July 1899.
The Times, especially July 1898 to December 1900.

INDEX

Printed in the United Kingdom
by Lightning Source UK Ltd.
135258UK00001B/127/P